# Reading Minjung Theology in the Twenty-First Century

# Reading Minjung Theology in the Twenty-First Century

Selected Writings by Ahn Byung-Mu
and Modern Critical Responses

Edited by Yung Suk Kim
and Jin-Ho Kim

READING MINJUNG THEOLOGY IN THE TWENTY-FIRST CENTURY
Selected Writings by Ahn Byung-Mu and Modern Critical Responses

Copyright © 2013 Wipf and Stock Publishers. All rights reserved. Except for brief quotations in critical publications or reviews, no part of this book may be reproduced in any manner without prior written permission from the publisher. Write: Permissions, Wipf and Stock Publishers, 199 W. 8th Ave., Suite 3, Eugene, OR 97401.

Pickwick Publications
An Imprint of Wipf and Stock Publishers
199 W. 8th Ave., Suite 3
Eugene, OR 97401

www.wipfandstock.com

ISBN 13: 978-1-61097-817-0

*Cataloguing-in-Publication data:*

Reading minjung theology in the twenty-first century: selected writings by Ahn Byung-Mu and modern critical responses / edited by Yung Suk Kim and Jin-Ho Kim.

xvi + 254 pp. ; 23 cm. Includes bibliographical references.

ISBN 13: 978-1-61097-817-0

1. Ahn, Byung-Mu. 2. Minjung theology. I. Ahn, Byung-Mu. II. Kim, Yung Suk. III. Kim, Jin-Ho. IV. Title.

BT83.58 R20 2013

Quotations marked (NRSV) come from the New Revised Standard Version Bible, copyright 1989, Division of Christian Education of the National Council of the Churches of Christ in the United States of America. Used by permission. All rights reserved.

Manufactured in the U.S.A.

# Contents

*List of Contributors* | vii
*Acknowledgments* | xi

1 Introduction—*Yung Suk Kim* | 1

Part I Introduction to Ahn Byung-Mu's Minjung Theology

2 The Hermeneutics of Ahn Byung-Mu: Focusing on the Concepts of "Discovery of Internality" and "Otherness of Minjung"—*Jin-Ho Kim* | 13

Part II Selected Writings by Ahn Byung-Mu

3 The Transmitters of the Jesus-Event Tradition | 27

4 Jesus and Minjung in the Gospel of Mark | 49

5 Minjung Theology from the Perspective of the Gospel of Mark | 65

6 Minjok, Minjung, and Church | 91

Part III Critical Responses to Ahn Byung-Mu's Minjung Theology

7 Minjung, the Black Masses, and the Global Imperative—*Mitzi J. Smith* | 101

8 "The Inhabitants of the Earth" in Revelation—*Greg Carey* | 120

9 Ambivalence, Mimicry, and the *Ochlos* in the Gospel of Mark—*David Arthur Sánchez* | 134

10 The Freedom to Just Peace—*Fernando Enns* | 148

11 Minjung Theology and Global Peacemaking—*Keun-Joo Christine Pae* | 164

12 "If They Send Me to Hell, Jesus Will Rescue Me"—*Min-Ah Cho* | 184

13 *Ochlos* and Phenomenology of Wretchedness—*Jin-Ho Kim* | 200

14 "The Person Attacked by the Robbers is Christ"—*Yong-Yeon Hwang* | 215

*Bibliography* | 233

# Contributors

**Yung Suk Kim** is Assistant Professor of New Testament and Early Christianity at the School of Theology at Virginia Union University. He is the author of several books: *Christ's Body in Corinth* (2008), *A Theological Introduction to Paul's Letters* (2011), *Biblical Interpretation* (2013), and *A Transformative Reading of the Bible* (2013). His next book about John's Gospel is forthcoming: *Truth, Testimony, and Transformation* (2013). He received a Lilly Theological Scholar Grant for a project on the Fourth Gospel during 2011–12. He edited a volume on *1–2 Corinthians* (2013). Kim serves as the editor of the *Journal of Bible and Human Transformation*.

**Jin-Ho Kim** is Chief Researcher of the Christian Institute for the Third Era in Korea. He served as the minister of Hanbaik Church established by Ahn Byung-Mu, and as the chief editor of *Contemporary Criticism*. Among his numerous publications, his Korean publications include *Historiography of Jesus History: Jesus beyond Jesus* (2000), *Radical Liberalists: Unfamiliar Travels with the Fourth Gospel* (2009), and *Citizen K, On the Threshold of the Church* (2012). Kim closely followed and worked with Ahn Byung-Mu during 1980s and 1990s.

**Greg Carey** is Professor of New Testament at Lancaster Theological Seminary and Resident Scholar at the Evangelical Lutheran Church of the Holy Trinity in Lancaster, Pennsylvania. He is the author of *Sinners: Jesus and His Earliest Followers* (2009) and *Ultimate Things: An Introduction to Jewish and Christian Apocalyptic Literature* (2005). Carey serves as cochair of the Society of Biblical Literature's Rhetoric and the New Testament Section and of the Apocalyptic Literature Section for the Society's International Meeting.

*Contributors*

**Min-Ah Cho** is Assistant Professor of Theology and Spirituality at St. Catherine University in St. Paul, Minnesota. Her research interests include Christian spirituality, feminist theologies, postcolonial theories, and Asian and Asian–North American religion and culture. She is particularly interested in ways individual Christians reshape and reconstruct the influence of traditional church institutions in their cultural context. She contributed a chapter to *Women, Writing, Theology: Transforming a Tradition of Exclusion* (2011).

**Fernando Enns** is Professor of Theology and Ethics at the VU University Amsterdam (The Netherlands) and Director of the Institute for Peace Church Theology at the University of Hamburg (Germany). He is a member of the Central Committee of the World Council of Churches and initiated the "Decade to Overcome Violence—Churches seeking Reconciliation and Peace 2001–2010." He is also Vice-Chair of the Mennonite Church in Germany. His publications include *Ökumene und Frieden. Theologische Anstöße aus der Friedenskirche. Theologische Anstöße Bd. 4* (2012).

**Yong-Yeon Hwang** is a PhD student at the Graduate Theological Union and a researcher of the Christian Institute for the Third Era. He contributed to the book *In an Era of Minjung's Death, We Re-view Ahn Byung-Mu* with an essay titled "Chugŭn minjung ŭi sidae, An Pyŏng-Mu rŭl tasi ponda"). He published articles about minjung theology in Korea. His main research interest centers on reinterpreting minjung theology and analyzing Korean society from a postcolonial perspective.

**Keun-Joo Christine Pae** is Assistant Professor of Ethics at Denison University Department of Religion. She was coconvener of Asian/Asian American Ethics Group at the Society of Christian Ethics (2011–2013). Her research interests include US Third World feminist ethics with a focus on war and peace, Asian/Asian American ethics, and interfaith approaches to popular resistance. She is currently working on a book manuscript called *Sex and War: A Christian Feminist Ethic of War and Peace*.

**David A. Sánchez** is an Associate Professor of Early Christian Literature at Loyola Marymount University, Los Angeles. He is the author of *From Patmos to the Barrio: Subverting Imperial Myths* (2008) and multiple articles on the book of Revelation and Mexican American muralism. He is coeditor of the forthcoming Fortress Commentary on the New Testament. His current research interests include apocalyptic movements in both antiquity and modernity. He is the Book Review Editor of the Journal of the American Academy of Religion and the President of the Academy of Catholic Hispanic Theologians of the United States.

**Mitzi J. Smith** is Associate Professor of New Testament and Early Christian Studies at Ashland Theological Seminary, Detroit. She is the author of *The Literary Construction of the Other in the Acts of the Apostles* (2011). She wrote in *True to Our Native Land,* the *New Revised Women's Bible Commentary,* and WorkingPreacher.org/. She is currently co-editing a volume entitled *Teaching all Nations: Interrogating the Great Commission* (2014). Her interest is Luke–Acts, Womanist and African American biblical interpretation, ancient slavery, and literary readings of biblical texts. She is founder and president of Living in Full Empowerment Inc.

# Acknowledgments

ONE DAY, YOUNG-SOOK PARK, a pioneer of the women's-rights movement and the environmental-protection movement, called me in 2007. She was the wife of late Ahn Byung-Mu, my mentor, and wanted to set up a memorial foundation in her husband's honor. Among the many things we talked about on that day was to publish the works of Ahn Byung-Mu in English. I believe Ahn's most important scholarly contribution is his thoughts on *ochlos/minjung*—a most creative theory on *minjung* theories that proliferated during the mid-1970s in disciplines such as economics, history, literature, and sociology. Young-Sook Park accepted all my recommendations and asked me to contribute to global theology by publishing a book on the topic of *ochlos*/minjung theology in English. This book began with her passion for the love of the *minjung* and her husband. Since then, she has supported this project both spiritually and financially.

Because of this meeting, I was planning the project, looking for a coeditor who could work with me. But it was not easy to find a scholar in America for this particular task. As I was beginning to feel the pressure and anxiety about the project, Professor Yung Suk Kim was introduced to me. Having looked up his research and having talked with many persons about him, I realized that he was the right person for the job. With the thought that I could not delay the project any longer, I cautiously sent my first letter to him in early 2011. He responded positively, and the project started off. From that day on, we have exchanged hundreds of e-mails and SNS conversations to make sure about the quality and direction of the project.

I give special thanks to Professor Seung Ae Yang from Chicago Theological Seminary for her timely advice and comments at difficult times of the project. I also give heartfelt thanks to Jae Won Lee, a former professor at McCormick Theological Seminary, to Minah Cho, professor at St. Kate's College, and to Pastor Wonjin Jung, the General Secretary of Byung-Mu

*Acknowledgments*

Ahn Memorial Foundation for all their selfless support. I also want to recognize the many contributions of the members of Ahn Byung-Mu Foundation, including Pastor Seung-Ku Whang who led foundation for a long time; the Christian Institute for the Third Era, which paid the expenses for me to travel throughout the country for this project. I also give special thanks to Arnold Sang Woo Oh, a Doctor of Theology student at Duke University, for his hard work of translating Ahn's essays into English. It is my regret that I cannot include in these acknowledgments the names of all the people to whom I should express my deepest thanks.

*Jin-Ho Kim*

# 1

## Introduction

—Yung Suk Kim

As a way of introducing this volume, I would like to begin with how I got involved as a coeditor along with Jin-Ho Kim. All of a sudden, I received an e-mail from Jin-Ho Kim, one of the best and most well-known minjung theologians in Korea today, who invited me to coedit a volume on Ahn Byung-Mu's minjung theology for the English-speaking readers. I was excited about his invitation, but a bit hesitant because my primary field is not minjung theology but biblical studies and New Testament studies in particular. Without delay, however, I accepted his invitation for good reasons. First, I realized minjung theology is deeply embedded in my soul, and inarguably, it is the birthplace of my spiritual journey. I witnessed a tireless wave of protests and cries for freedom and justice in a society after several military coups from the 1960s to 1980s. During this time Korea went through turmoil and chaos, violence after violence, suffering after suffering, partly caused by the government's dictatorship and partly caused by the government-supported conglomerates' exploitation of the masses. A group of religious leaders, college students, and factory workers rose against the unjust rules of the notorious state power. Minjung theology came out of this struggle for justice and freedom. It did not begin at school or the church, but came out of the gravest concerns about oppressive powers—the despotic state and the greedy exploitive economic systems—and in solidarity with the oppressed. Shamefully, most of the Korean churches were silent about this struggle and sought their own peace, prosperity, and security. In times of absence of witness to God's justice, minjung theology has been a voice crying in the wilderness, awakening people from their sleep, showing support for and solidarity with the marginalized, challenging unsympathetic self-seeking churches, and rewriting an authentic theology from the bottom. I share the same concerns with minjung theology today—seeing, more or less, the recurrent issues of the suffering of the masses in Korea and elsewhere. Because I received this great prophetic tradition from Korea, I strongly felt a sense of responsibility for my people and minjung theology in this globalized world, and that I could play a certain role in liberation scholarship. As a Korean American biblical scholar, I find myself committed to transformation that includes personal, communal, social and political aspects of change.

Second, I loved the idea of minjung theology focused on the *ochlos* in the Gospel of Mark as shown by Ahn Byung-Mu. Though I have reservations about Ahn's methods (form criticism or redaction criticism) or about his distinction between Jesus' teaching and Paul's *kerygma* when he claims the agency or rumors of the minjung as a secure means to convey the core of the Jesus-event, I marvel at his critical contextual engagement with the text and his capturing of the importance of the *ochlos* in the Gospel of Mark—not so earnestly raised by scholars as he did. Furthermore, Ahn brought back and forth the *ochlos* in Mark to the context in Korea.

Third, Jin-Ho Kim's proposal about this volume struck a strong chord with me, as he wanted to focus on all aspects of "suffering" of the minjung (*ochlos*) in global context. For all these reasons, I took my editorial participation as a mandate. As this volume deals with minjung (or *ochlos*) and today's world, I hope this book will be discussed during the tenth Assembly of the World Council of Churches (WCC), which will be held in Busan, Korea, from October 30 to November 8, 2013, under the theme "God of life, lead us to justice and peace."

Let me describe how we divided the editorial work between him and me. Jin-Ho Kim was kind of like a think tank; he provided all the resources about Ahn's minjung theology and was responsible for Ahn's select writings included in this volume. As Ahn's "beloved disciple," he wrote a very important introductory article about Ahn's life and legacy, succinctly showing Ahn's theological genesis, development, and transformation. My primary responsibility was to identify and coordinate international scholars/contributors for this volume and to edit their works by communicating with them, including communicating with the publisher. That is why I write this introduction to the volume.

This edited volume brings Ahn Byung-Mu's minjung theology into dialogue with twenty-first-century readers. The centerpiece of his minjung theology is focused on *ochlos* understood as the divested, marginalized, powerless people. Selected writings by Ahn Byung-Mu show the progression of his *ochlos*–minjung theology: "Minjok, Minjung, and Church"; "Jesus and Minjung in the Gospel of Mark"; "Minjung Theology from the Perspective of the Gospel of Mark"; "The Transmitters of the Jesus-Event Tradition." This book also contains a collection of articles from international scholars, who evaluate and engage Ahn's *ochlos*/minjung theology in their own fields and formulate a critical reading of minjung in their choice of the topics.

This book has three parts: Part 1, "Introduction to Ahn Byung-Mu's Minjung Theology"; part 2, "Selected Writings by Ahn Byung-Mu"; and part 3, "Critical Responses to Ahn Byung-Mu's Minjung Theology." In Part 1, Jin-Ho Kim, coeditor of this volume, introduces Ahn Byung-Mu's minjung theology: "The Hermeneutics of Ahn Byung-Mu: Focusing on the Concepts of 'Discovery of Internality' and 'Otherness of Minjung.'" In this essay, Kim keeps track of the development of Ahn's minjung theology from its birth to maturity, from the concept of national minjung to that of the suffering global minjung, and from existential struggle to reflective struggle based on *otherness*. We learn from this article how deeply and authentically Ahn did theology, and hear what it means to do theology when people suffer. Though he could have lived a quiet and comfortable life in Korea after years of studying in Germany for a PhD, Ahn did not stay in silence at school or church. Ahn roots his theology in the minjung whom Jesus, another minjung, loves and supports unconditionally.

Part 2 includes selected writings by Ahn Byung-Mu: "The Transmitters of the Jesus-Event Tradition"; "Jesus and Minjung in the Gospel of Mark," "Minjung Theology from the Perspective of the Gospel of Mark," and "Minjok, Minjung, and Church." All of these were written at different times for different purposes. In the first article, Ahn explores his unique theory of the so-called transmitters of Jesus-event tradition, which he argues that it is *ochlos* or the minjung who transmitted the true story of Jesus-event. The second article talks about Jesus' work for the kingdom of God and particularly for the *ochlos* in the Gospel of Mark. For Ahn, minjung is the *ochlos*, and vice versa. The third article examines the entire Gospel of Mark in terms of the story of the minjung (*ochlos*). The last article deals with the concept of minjung, people of suffering and the marginalized in the history of Korea and distinguishes minjung from nation, which is close to the political concept of people. Through these select writings, we will get to understand in what context or why he wrote. Part 3 contains eight essays by our contributors.

## Reading Minjung Theology in the Twenty-First Century

Since this book aims at critically engaging Ahn's *ochlos*/minjung theology in the world today, we made a set of guiding questions for our contributors, which include the following: Who are the *ochlos* (minjung) today? How can we respond to the various aspects of suffering of the minjung? What can the minjung do? What is the role of community or society? In the following, articles in part 3 will be briefly introduced.

Mitzi J. Smith, in her essay, "Minjung, the Black Masses, and the Global Imperative: A Womanist Reading of Luke's Soteriological Hermeneutical Circle," compares the Korean minjung experience and minjung theology with the black experience in America and black theology; she explores how African Americans can be truly liberated and empowered for making a just community and society. In doing so, Smith reads the Gospel of Luke through the black woman's experience, as Ahn does from the perspective of *ochlos* in the Gospel of Mark. Her distinctive reading is characterized by what she calls "a soteriological hermeneutical circle," by which she means that "the salvation/deliverance of individuals is inextricably connected with the crowds" (104). While Ahn examines the *ochlos* mainly in relation to Jesus, Smith analyzes "the relationship between individuals and the crowds and between Jesus and individuals that Jesus encountered in or out of the crowds" (113). Methodologically, whereas Ahn employs redaction criticism in examining the *ochlos* in Mark, Smith uses a narrative approach to Luke to examine the *ochlos* in Luke. The resultant reading is somewhat different from Ahn's; that is, "the salvation, deliverance, or wholeness (Greek: *sotēria* or *hygiēs*) of individuals is inextricably connected with the minjung and the minjung benefit from the salvation or wholeness that individuals receive" (114). Smith's organic reading of the *ochlos* in Luke is a corrective to a traditional liberative hermeneutics, including minjung theology, that prioritizes the minjung (like the preferential option for the poor). Smith put it: "Luke's Jesus creates and maintains a connectedness, rhetorically and pragmatically, between individuals and the masses; the salvation or wholeness of individuals is inextricably connected with the minjung" (118). In the end, Smith hopes for a holistic, organic understanding of the *ochlos* who suffer economically, psychologically, medically, sexually, politically or religiously. Her charge rings louder than ever before: "We are called to take a stand with God in solidarity with the minjung in the struggle for justice, restoration, and wholeness. I am minjung. The minjung are God's children." (120).

Greg Carey, in his essay, "The Inhabitants of the Earth in Revelation: Ordinary People in Imperial Context," explores how the book of Revelation, the New Testament's only literary apocalypse, "characterizes ordinary people, 'the Inhabitants of the Earth,' amidst a conflict between 'the testimony of Jesus' and fidelity to Roman imperial religion (121). Writing from the context of "a divided and decaying American empire," Carey qualifies the notion of the minjung (the masses), defining it not as a homogenous category but as a mixed loyalty group—members of which even participate in persecuting the followers of the Lamb (saints). Interestingly, Carey's approach to Revelation is similar to David Sánchez's to the Gospel of Mark. Whereas in Ahn's study the minjung are the subject of their participation in the Jesus-event and the object of Jesus' love and support without conditions, Carey points out that the crowds ("the inhabitants of the earth" in Revelation) participate in the work of the beast because of pressures under Roman imperial rule and the need to survive and grow under the protection of the state power. Carey puts this succinctly: "In contexts marked by imperialism and domination, the minjung do not constitute a homogenous category. Rather, as the Apocalypse "reveals," oppressive dynamics divide ordinary people over against one another (124). Carey's reading of Revelation in light of minjung theology is very pertinent in the complex life contexts of America when the masses suffer and yet they are divided among themselves. It is significant to hear Carey's point that the masses or the inhabitants of the earth are not a category of unified people with the same purpose or spirit. The point is who can follow the difficult truth of God when the present life is a mess, and when most members of the masses are uncaring for one another. Given that the masses in Revelation are uncaring, Carey admits that the book, being difficult to read, hardly provides them with hope or with a blueprint for their salvation. Nonetheless, Carey helps us understand how difficult it is to be the "faithful" minjung who can follow the way of the Lamb in times of cruel and cajoling powers of the empire.

David Arthur Sánchez, in his article, "Mimicry, and the *Ochlos* in the Gospel of Mark: Assessing the Minjung Theology of Ahn Byung-Mu," reads Ahn Byung-Mu's minjung theology from the perspective of postcolonial criticism. On one hand, Sánchez appreciates Ahn's unique contributions to contemporary liberation theology in terms of his keen analysis and recontextualization of the *ochlos* in the Gospel of Mark. On the other hand, Sánchez supplements Ahn's reading of the *ochlos* through the lens of *mimicry* and *ambivalence*—terms frequently employed in postcolonial criticism. Whereas Ahn thinks that there are two different *ochlos*es (Galilean and Jerusalem) and struggles to understand a crowd in Jerusalem who turns against Jesus, Sánchez aptly reasons that the *ochlos* in Galilee and those in Jerusalem are not two different groups. That is, Galilean crowds are transformed into Jerusalem crowds, and now act like different persons in the heart of the imperial city Jerusalem, where power, people, and politics are mingled and renegotiated. Sánchez therefore warns that any theological discourse can hardly deny the volatile nature of the crowd, and that the task of theology is not to grant a status of one kind or another to people, but to constantly fight the ambivalent nature of "political" humanity that involves constant negotiations with power and politics.

Fernando Enns, in his article, "The Freedom to Just Peace: Revisiting minjung theology for a Current Ecumenical Discourse," deals with the usefulness of Ahn's *ochlos*/minjung theology in a German church context. Deeply committed to ecumenical global cooperation for peace and justice, Enns takes Ahn's remarkable insight on the idea of *ochlos* in the Gospel of Mark and applies the same concept of *ochlos* to the German situation and beyond. He solicits the global efforts for the *ochlos* who still need peace and justice in the kingdom of God. Enns also emphasizes the voice of the minjung; they are subjects of history and active participants in the freedom and justice movement. He also emphasizes the church must be the place of the marginalized in light of the gospel preached by Jesus, not merely advocating for them: Jesus dies as minjung for the minjung. In return, the minjung find solidarity with Jesus.

Enns hopes that *ochlos*/minjung theology can contribute to the change of political realities against all odds, as he says: "It has proven that the churches are in fact able to play a decisive role in the minjung struggle for freedom and democracy. One condition seems to be that the churches are minjung churches, as marginalized as the most powerless, yet ready to provide ecumenical spaces, embracing the struggle of the people" (163). He is clear on his point that the church must be of the marginalized, not the victorious. Enns goes on to explore more about the role of the church: "After political freedom is won, the challenge arises to use that freedom responsively: the freedom to build just and peaceful relationships across all borders. Together with Christians from around the globe we realize that this is a gift and a calling that needs to form the ecumenical communion" (164).

Keun-Joo Christine Pae, in her essay, "Minjung Theology and Global Peacemaking: From Galilee to the U.S. Military Camptown (*kijich'on*) in South Korea," explores what minjung theology can do for camptown women (the so-called Western princesses) around the US military bases in Korea and elsewhere. Pae points out the problem of "militarized American imperialism" along with an ideology of nationalism that fuels the agony of the vulnerable camptown women (181). According to Pae, "U.S. military camptowns are where this resentment is most visible, and often creates a violent conflict between American servicemen and local Koreans. At the same time, camptowns are the arbitrary borderlands between South Korea and the United States. These borderlands create the third space, or the hybridized space, where the oppressive structures are maintained by both US military imperialism and Korean nationalism" (178). Pae advocates for these vulnerable, most marginalized women and seeks global peace, not by militarism but through nonviolent resistance against all of these oppressive powers. Pae also points out that "Western princesses are the most oppressed because their experiences embody multiple forms of oppression, whether they are cultural, religious, physical, economic, political, or psychological, to name only a few" (179). Pae's analysis of gender relations and sociopolitical power relations is a timely topic because in emancipation discourse, gender ideology is often ignored. Therefore, her critique is worth hearing: "Ahn Byung Mu's minjung theology does an excellent job of historically analyzing and reconstructing the *ochlos,* but his minjung further needs a historical and contextual analysis aided by gender consciousness. The minjung must be considered as the multiple groups whose struggles for liberation also have multi-faces. Each group's experience of oppression needs a careful analysis with focus on how multiple groups' experiences of oppression intersect with each other. The lives of Western princesses can show this intersection" (180).

Min-Ah Cho in her essay, "'If They Send Me to Hell, Jesus Will Rescue Me': Minjung Theology and the *Iban* Movement," takes the issue of sexual minorities (the so-called LGBQT community) in Korea and explores how minjung theology and the *Iban* movement (understood as the sexual minorities' movement challenging antigay Christian fundamentalists) can help each other in the fight for freedom and justice for the marginalized. Drawing on Ahn Byung-Mu's language of "rumor" as a tool of the minjung's self-survival, adaptive, and reshaping strategy against the oppressors' rumor in the Gospel of Mark, Cho deftly applies the idea of rumor strategy to the *Iban* people in Korea. Examining "a discursive space created by rumors about *Ibans*," Cho suggests how false rumors "reveal the cracks and gaps hidden in fundamentalist rhetoric and thus enable us otherwise to create a counter-discourse" (188). Emphasizing the role of rumors that lead us "to see the process of deconstructing and reconstructing truth wherein multiple perspectives and experiences gather together and assimilate with one another," Cho reveals the dominant homophobic rumor in Korea, most of which comes from fundamentalist antigay rhetoric and the ideology of anti-Communism (190). Cho makes explicit how minjung theology can hear from the most marginalized *Iban* people and witness to their struggle for justice by helping them to create healthy rumors against all oppressive ideologies and theologies.

Jin-Ho Kim's essay, "*Ochlos* and the Phenomenology of Wretchedness," focuses on the concept of suffering in Ahn's minjung theology as it relates to the *ochlos*—the masses of powerless people in Korea and elsewhere. Kim's reading of the *ochlos* is more far fetched than Ahn's because, as Kim argues, there are more complex elements of suffering (in the way Kim prefers "wretchedness" to suffering) than usually thought conceivable. This is where Kim finds great value to Suh Nam Dong's *han* theology, which emphasizes ineffableness of suffering or *han*—a Korean term that means, according to Suh: a "sound of depression which appeals to the heavens, the sound of the nameless and the helpless" (205). Thus Kim says Ahn's minjung theology focused on the concept of *ochlos* can be best understood with Suh Nam Dong's *han*-based minjung theology, and vice versa, because the concept of *han* can be manifest in the struggle of the *ochlos* or the minjung. Kim's bidirectional reading of the minjung and *han* addresses both the most rock-bottom experiences of the victims in what he calls "wretchedness" and the importance of witnessing to their *han* without giving facile solutions or explaining away the most difficult, wretched experience. In all of this, Kim raises a cry for vulnerable participation in liberation without subsuming the minjung under *han*, or vice versa.

Yong-Yeon Hwang's essay, "The Person Attacked by the Robbers Is Christ: An Exploration of Subjectivity from the Perspective of Minjung Theology," deals with the history of minjung theology in Korea and explores what minjung can do as agents of transformation, and what minjung theologians can do in an ever evolving, complex society— seemingly a very different environment as compared with the 1960s and '70s. While deconstructing and reconstructing the concept of minjung in that context, Hwang suggests that the minjung be the agents of their transformation. One of his remarkable claims is that the minjung are powerless, and therefore they *can be* powerful. This is a paradoxical statement, but the telling point is the minjung cannot give in to the oppressive power, and because of their experience, they can be people of freedom and justice. Put differently, because the minjung suffer, they know what it means to suffer; that is, their suffering of *han* can be a channel of transformation for the minjung. Therefore, Hwang argues the task of the minjung theologian is not so much defining or leading the minjung as witnessing to their struggle and suffering, as Jin-Ho Kim similarly observes in his essay about phenomenology of suffering.

In closing, I remain confident and blessed by being a part of this important collaborative work, and I share a few of my joys and comments. First, though minjung theology is a local contextual theology in Korea, it still carries volumes of significant insights for doing theology in an ever changing global context today, especially when we face issues of suffering everywhere, be it different in nature or in scale.

Second, I am glad that the concept or agency of the minjung is re-qualified and deepened by our contributors. Two notable tracks of response are worth mentioning. One is that the minjung are not a monolithic group (Pae, Cho, Carey, Smith, and Kim), and the other is that the minjung are ambivalent in their attitude toward powers when pressured by the empire (Sánchez, Hwang, and Carey). What we learn from these responses is that the minjung are divergent and they are not united. In terms of the role of the minjung, Smith makes explicit that salvation of the masses does not happen by themselves or for themselves only, but occurs through the "soteriological hermeneutical circle." Smith's view is a fresh challenge to traditional liberation theology, since in her view salvation must be a whole-to-part relationship.

Third, I hope that this book will invite theologians across the board to engage minjung theology from their diverse experiences and perspectives. There will be more extensive, international, interdisciplinary discussions about the diverse aspects of suffering of the minjung at the local or global level. In those future endeavors, we may ask the following questions: How can we explain the process of liberation or transformation? How can we involve more interdisciplinary studies in addition to what have been brought in this volume, such as political theology, psychotheology, and neurosociology (intersections between neuroscience and social psychology) in explaining the process of transformation?

# PART I

Introduction to Ahn Byung-Mu's Minjung Theology

# 2

## The Hermeneutics of Ahn Byung-Mu:

## Focusing on the Concepts of "Discovery of Internality" and "Otherness of Minjung"

—JIN-HO KIM

### Ahn Byung-Mu's Hermeneutics: Its Potentials and Limitations

THE NUMBER OF AHN Byung-Mu's writings amounts up to 918, including papers, essays, colloquies, prefaces, book reviews, columns, and editor's postscripts. Besides his published works (twenty-eight books and six edited books), there are about five boxes of preaching manuscripts/notes, lecture outlines, research notes, and the like—most of which have not yet been published. The recordings of his lectures and sermons were scarcely collected, and the extant recordings have not been organized. Therefore, it is impossible to use these sources for Ahn Byung-Mu study. However, some of the articles published in periodicals would be very helpful for understanding his theological concerns: *A Voice from the Wilderness* (monthly from November 1951 to January 1956), *Existence* (published monthly from July 1969 until August 1980; 113 issues published, and stopped by the military junta), *Theological Thoughts* (seasonal, summer 1973), and *Sallim* (monthly from December 1988 until December 2002).

The most useful sources for Ahn Byung-Mu study are his twenty-eight books that contain his 918 articles. However, there are some difficulties in using these books as sources for Ahn Byung-Mu study because

## PART I: Introduction to Ahn Byung-Mu's Minjung Theology

there is no proper information about each article's historical context. Therefore, we have to examine the historical context of various writings in the books. In addition, Ahn's articles were often published in duplication, and sometimes under a changed title.[1]

In my opinion, such confusion can be explained in the following way. Ahn preached a sermon title "Minjung Preacher" at Galilee Church in May 1978; however, we cannot verify the existence of the transcript. When we consider the way of his preaching, we can guess that it would have been in the form of a short memo. Then, in the following year, this sermon was republished in the hundred-first issue of *Existence* (May 1975) under the title, "Transmitter and Interpreter," which is the first printed version of this sermon as far as we know. What happened next seems to add to the confusion. The article identical to "Transmitter and Interpreter," except for some editorial changes in the epilogue, was republished under the title "Minjung Preacher," in a book of Ahn Byung-Mu's collected articles, *In Front of History, Together With* Minjung (Hangil Press, 1986). It is noted at the end of the article that it is a transcript of his sermon preached at Galilee Church in May 1978. Afterwards, these two articles were circulated as if they were different.

Given the conditions of existing books, it is no small task to conduct critical research on Ahn's theology. I became aware of these issues when I was commissioned to write a book on Ahn by the Commemorative Committee in 2005. The best solution was to establish a clear classification system and to republish his complete works according to certain principles. But because of publishing cost, instead we planned to produce a complete index of his works. Since then, the Commemorative Committee employed a researcher for six months and published a noncommercial product on October 15, 2006, on the tenth anniversary of his death. This index is chronologically organized, and marks the duplicate publications or the same work with different titles. Although this

---

1. Ahn Byung-Mu's masterpiece, "The Transmitters of the Jesus-Event Tradition," was published six times in duplication. "A Biblical Illumination of the Reunification of North and South Korea" was published five times in duplication, and in the case of the last three times, the title was changed into "A Biblical Illumination of the National Reunification." On other occasions, "Minjung Preacher" and "Transmitter and Interpreter" are the same articles. It goes by the title of "Minjung Preacher" in *Life Saving Faith* (published by the commemorating works committee for the 1997 commemorating event), and "Transmitter and Interpreter" in *Theology for Reformation of Christianity*, published for the 1999 event. This issue was not settled even in the complete catalog of Ahn Byung-Mu's works recently published.

new work is not completely satisfactory, I believe the time has come for us to thoroughly study Ahn Byung-Mu's theology.

Though there have been many studies of Ahn, including dissertations at home and abroad, most of them have been limited to specific themes. Moreover, most of them have been advanced without textual criticism of Ahn's overall texts, selecting texts somewhat arbitrarily. No sufficient, thorough studies have been made on chosen themes from the perspective of Ahn's overall theological historical framework. In short, the studies of Ahn Byung-Mu hitherto have not touched on the main gist of his theology.

In light of this, a controversial work, *In the Era of Minjung's Death: Re-Reading Ahn Byung-Mu*,[2] coauthored by the five scholars including myself, does not seem to make sense since there is no established standard reading of Ahn Byung-Mu. However, benefit of rereading is to engage his theology today. To reread Ahn's theology effectively, we have to exercise textual criticism and need a much greater accumulation of studies on Ahn's work. As one of Ahn's students who walked with him closely, I have examined the entire body of his work, the habit of his writing, and the method of his thought to forge a framework for hermeneutics of Ahn Byung-Mu. This is a necessary work for me as someone who continues to research topics related to Ahn (my Teacher), and I hope this will be a helpful reference tool for those who interpret Ahn Byung-Mu's minjung theology.

## Overview of the Development of Ahn Byung-Mu's Theology

While the periodization of Ahn's theology has not been established, it is common to divide his theology into pre- and postminjung theology. This division reflects the transition of his thought from existentialism to minjung theology. We can also think of the three themes of his thought, as Myung Su Kim suggests: existentialism, minjung, and *sallim*. This division is based on Ahn's theological imagination of *sallim* ("saving life") since late 1980s as an occasion for doing theology. However, Kim also points out that the relation between these three themes is not a linear development of Ahn's thought but a more complicated interaction between them. This relation can be explained with the structure of concentric circles where the next theme is present in the previous theme.[3] For example, the thought about *sallim* was already present during the existential period. Therefore, in establishing a theory of periodization, we should consider the continuity of his theology.

2. Kim Jin-Ho et al., *In an Era of Minjung's Death*.
3. See Kim Myung-Su, "Ahn Byung-Mu."

PART I: Introduction to Ahn Byung-Mu's Minjung Theology

Here I will seek to divide the periods of Ahn's theology into four parts, using the titles of periodicals he produced: *A Voice from the Wilderness, Existence*, Minjung, and *Sallim*. These four terms are useful for reading the changes in his theology and the continuity of his thought. I will describe the relation of these terms. To understand the convergence and the divergence among the four terms representing Ahn's theological development, I will define the characteristic of non-expressed inner self-consciousness in his thoughts through two antithetical pairs: enlightenment-leaning versus internality, and internality versus otherness.

"Enlightenment-leaning" refers to Ahn's self-consciousness as a "modern intellectual." Since his first encounter with Christianity in the Gando area of Myungdong, he lived his life in continuous opposition to the nonmodern "shadow of savagery," such as colonialism, antidemocracy, and antilife-forces until his death in 1996. As a leading Christian intellectual, theologian, professor, and teacher, he saw his calling as awakening the masses. "Internality" means Ahn's self-consciousness as someone who are not assimilated into the "external world," namely, the space of the dominant discourse. For Ahn, "existentialism" was the intellectual "food" for his rebellious self-consciousness.

On the other hand, Ahn's Christian faith made him to be in continuous discord with the model of modern, enlightened subject, pursuing exploration of anti- and postmodern thoughts of otherness. The discovery of minjung led him to have a critical consciousness about otherness. In the following, I will explore Ahn's theological development, considering his tension about internal consciousness and external conditions.

## From *A Voice from the Wilderness* to *Existence*:
## The Shift or Extension of the Narrative of Internality

In *A Voice from the Wilderness*, first issued in November 1951, we encounter Ahn's first published articles. He believes that the basic structure of the world is evil.[4] In other words, he holds to a view that the self is not to be captive to the world, but that the self is to be liberated from the world. This existential self-consciousness is expressed in the period of *A Voice from the Wilderness*, which dignifies the narrative of internality[5] separated

---

4. Ahn, "The Meaning of Sufferings."

5. In modern society the mechanism of social integration of the masses is much more complex than usually thought, since it involves the external, physical and symbolic order of social structure. The term *internality* is generally used to represent the

from the evil structure of the world. Ahn's narrative of internality is linked with his external activities such as reorganizing the Society for One Faith, which was scattered due to the outbreak of the Korean War, and starting a community movement.[6] Ahn also imagines a new church movement, namely, the movement for a faith community as "life community." His article, "Lay Ministry: the Direction of Group Movement," published in *A Voice from the Wilderness*[7] is a kind of inaugural statement for the movement. In the article he discusses why there should be a life community. He states that the life community is the antithesis and alternative to the church, which has not provided the space of true life community.[8]

When he wrote this article towards the end of the Korean War, Korean people were returning to their daily lives. Ahn greatly realized that the suffering of the war also had to do with that of everyday life. After the war, many people were tormented by the memory of harming others and of being harmed. Physically and spiritually, their lives were not normal. In this context, an extensive religious market was formed to allay feelings of torment and provide an easy consumable product of individual salvation. Ahn observes that the church degenerated into a religious marketplace and that corrupt religious leaders were busy preaching about personal sins to secure their own power in the market. In this regard, his community movement was a solitary voice in the wilderness, raising a message of salvation to the injured in society.[9] In short, Ahn thinks that salvation has to do with finding personal enlightenment (internality) through which one is liberated from the world.[10]

Ahn's narrative of internality marks an important element of change in his theology. He begins sharing his concerns about suffering about people and denounces church leaders as religious prostitutes. He also realizes

---

very self that is not captivated by the external regulations of social structure.

6. In 1945 or 1946, Ahn organized an association of Christian students called One Faith with like-minded students at Seoul National University.

7. Ahn, "Lay Ministry."

8. Ibid., 554. This concern continued into Ahn Byung-Mu's later thought. For example, in the Hanbaik Church established by Ahn in 1987, he renamed the "dedication offering" the "offering materials" and suggested a common meal instead of Communion.

9. When Ahn Byung-Mu reorganized the Group of One Faith and conversed with members of the community movement, he dreamed to be a pastor and understood his own view of the pastorate as a faith confession responding to the voice of people's suffering. See "Theory of Pastorate."

10. Ahn, "Lay Ministry," 554.

## PART I: Introduction to Ahn Byung-Mu's Minjung Theology

the new problems of colonized internality—the desires of the Christian masses,[11] who are captive to the interests of those in ecclesial authority.

It seems that Ahn's unique and deconstructive point about "sin" appeared in this period. The main focus of his criticism on the Christian view of sin at this time was directed at the religious authorities. In many of his articles written during the period of *Existence*, sin was understood as the mediation between the colonized internal discourse and the external world.[12] That is to say, the conventional discourse had internalized the dominant narrative. Such technique of reproduction of the system aggravated the suffering of the masses. The internality of colonialism is disintegrated in Ahn's thought during this period. There are two kinds of internality: one that indulges in self-desire in the dominant system, and one that alienates persons from the external world. According to Ahn, Christians have to resist the conventional scheming of dominating others.[13]

Such a division of internality demands the subject's decision. In that sense, Ahn's approach to theology is existentialism through which he pursues enlightenment. However, Ahn, instead of consulting or discussing with his colleagues in school, takes the issue to the public square. Ahn expresses this as "the outside of the castle gate," which means the church-centric theology that has turned away from history and the self-enclosing net that safeguards the fortress of speculative theology. He opens his mind to the currents of history, moving beyond "the castle."[14]

However, there was another reason for him going to the public square. Ahn was increasingly involved in the early Christian resistance movement against dictatorship in the early 1970s. The movement of young pastors devoted to the poor in the slum quarters, as known as "urban ministry in the cities" seemed to strengthen his interest in this movement. Interestingly, in an article written in 1971, "The Ethics of the Remnants,"[15] Ahn emphasizes that the ethical decision of a person who has to resist the dominant discourse of internality should bear witness to the suffering of the masses, who have mouths but cannot speak. In short, the theological concern about the masses at bottom of society takes the center stage in his theological reflection.

---

11. Ahn, "The Image of Korean Christians." This article was reprinted in "Sparks" with the changed title of "The Image of Christians."
12. Ahn, "What Is Sin?"
13. Ahn, "In What Sense Are You Christian?"
14. Ahn, "To the Outside the Castle Gate."
15. In *Existence* 26.

Thus far I have discussed Ahn's theological journey with a focus on themes of wilderness experience and struggle of existence. Whereas in the period of *A Voice from the Wilderness* he emphasizes the strategy of separating the self from the world, in the period of *Existence* he comes out to the public square and talks to the masses directly.

## The Discovery of Minjung: The Shock of Otherness

Ahn recounts the Jeon Tae-Il Event of 1972 (Jeon set fire on himself to protest the unjust labor practices) as a paradigm shift in his own theological thought.[16] According to his memory, it was in 1972 that he had written for the first time an article dealing with minjung as a theological theme called "Jesus and Minjung."[17] In fact, the first article that dealt with minjung as a central theological theme was "Minjung, Nation, and Church."[18] In this article, Ahn focuses on the term *ochlos* in the Gospel of Mark, which indicates the masses following Jesus in Mark. "Jesus and *Ochlos*," published in 1979,[19] and not "Jesus and Minjung," is the first article that critically explores the theory of *ochlos*. In other words, the Jeon Tae-Il Event was the watershed experience about the minjung, and Ahn begins to develop a theology about the minjung. Ahn's "minjung theory" began with the article of "Minjok, Minjung, and Church." Here he interprets minjung as *ochlos* and presents the framework of his theory about minjung. Ahn Byung-Mu's theory of *ochlos* is indebted to Takawa Kenzo,[20] and he argues that *ochlos* appears only in the Gospel of Mark and that it can be characterized as a group that is class conscious. In Tagawa's theory, *ochlos* in the Gospel of Mark refers to lower-class people, such as the sick, tax collectors, prostitutes, and the poor. However, whereas Tagawa interprets *ochlos* as limited to those marginalized in the Gospel of Mark, Ahn insists that the *ochlos* are also the general masses that followed Jesus.

Four years after the publication of this article, Ahn published "Jesus and *Ochlos*" in 1979, where he undertook the full development of the theory about *ochlos*, using the sociological category of the term—the loss

---

16. Ahn, *Talking about* minjung *theology*, 257.
17. Ibid., 25
18. Incidentally, Suh Nam-Dong's first theological work focused on minjung was published in the same issue of *Christian Ideology* (April 1975). These two works by Ahn Byung-Mu and Suh Nam-Dong were the beginning of minjung theology.
19. Ahn, "Jesus and *Ochlos*," 3–18.
20. Genzo Tagawa, *The Gospel of Mark and Liberation of the People.*

# PART I: Introduction to Ahn Byung-Mu's Minjung Theology

of belonging. But why the *ochlos* in Mark followed Jesus remains to be resolved. Gerd Theissen provided a breakthrough for Ahn. Among the three categories of inference (analytic inference, constructive inference, and analogical inference), analytic inference helped him most in his creative interpretation. He pays attention to the peculiarity of oral transmission distinct from literary transmission. While the former presupposes the congruence between the transmitted contents and the life of the transmitter, Theissen believes that presupposition of oral transmission is an important clue for analytic inference. This opens a huge possibility for the historical reimagination about the Jesus story and event. That is, Jesus' radical and strange sayings could be transmitted by wandering itinerants who could live out such sayings of Jesus. However, the limitation of Theissen's research is that it is based on literary material rather than oral material. Using Theissen's hypothesis about oral transmission, Ahn, however, considers the Gospel of Mark as a source of the oral transmission.

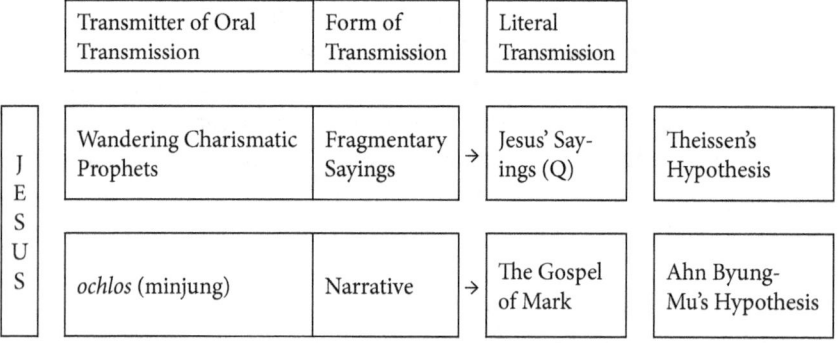

| | Transmitter of Oral Transmission | Form of Transmission | | Literal Transmission | |
|---|---|---|---|---|---|
| J E S U S | Wandering Charismatic Prophets | Fragmentary Sayings | → | Jesus' Sayings (Q) | Theissen's Hypothesis |
| | *ochlos* (minjung) | Narrative | → | The Gospel of Mark | Ahn Byung-Mu's Hypothesis |

Ahn's focus on the Gospel of Mark opens a new way of reading the story of Jesus, not focused on Jesus' sayings, but focused on the story of the *ochlos*. The two articles evince his efforts: "The Transmitter and Interpreter"[21] and "Christianity and Minjung Language."[22] In "The Subject of History in the Light of the Gospel of Mark,"[23] Ahn argues that separating the sayings of Jesus and the Gospel of Mark as we now have it is the oral transmission of the gospel stories. Moreover, at this time Ahn points

---

21. Ahn, "The Transmitter and Interpreter," 48–56.

22. Ahn, "Christianity and Minjung Language," 8–20. For more information about Ahn's articles, see Kim Jin-Ho, "Two kinds of Gospel."

23. This article was published originally with the title "Minjung Theology—Focusing on the Gospel of Mark" in *Theological Thoughts* 34 (Fall 1981).

out the central form of oral transmission is rumor.[24] Such a theory of *ochlos* opened up new vistas for new conceptualization of minjung.[25]

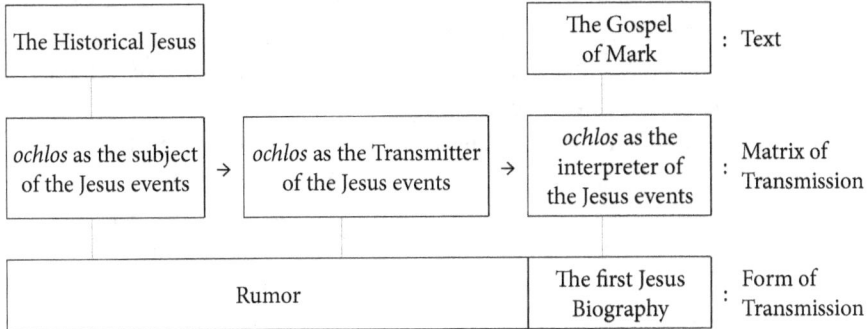

Most important, it is noteworthy that Ahn understands *ochlos* from the perspective of the deprived belongingness. They were pushed to the "outside." Now, while the "outside" is their dwelling place, they yearn for the "inside," being aware of their exclusion. This means that their experience of nonexistence defines their existence. Ahn's concept of *ochlos* takes the language of these people who are invisible yet expressive in their struggle. Such *ochlos*-centered imagination serves as an occasion for Ahn to cut himself off from the endless epistemological exploration of self-reflective subjectivity, which is the case for *A Voice from the Wilderness* and *Existence*. Formerly, Ahn's interpretation seemed to follow the traditional framework of theology in that the transformation of existence is possible through the encounter with the absolute otherness. Ahn made an existential reinterpretation of this soteriological framework of self-transcendence.

However, the discovery of *ochlos* served as the occasion to sever him from this kind of epistemological soteriology. Through the extraordinary experience of otherness, Ahn experienced a leap from wilderness to existence based on the radical otherness. Thus he describes the discovery of *ochlos* as an event of salvation. Jeon Tae-Il was a symbolic representative of this event. It was in this context that Jeon Tae-Il is identified with Jesus and that the theory of minjung messiah was brought forth. In addition, he states that the masses who are deprived of their own language are witnesses. Thus the witness of minjung theology is for those who suffer their loss of language due to dominant power in society and exposes such a mechanism of control.

24. Ahn, "The Matrix in Which the Jesus-Events Were Transmitted."
25. See Kim Jin-ho, "'The Death of Minjung and Re-reading Ahn Byung-Mu.'"

PART I: Introduction to Ahn Byung-Mu's Minjung Theology

Therefore, in Ahn's quest for the historical Jesus, he tries to overcome the subject/object dichotomy. Since Jesus did not utter monologue, but talked with the *ochlos*, Ahn thinks of the transmitter of the event or story about Jesus. The transmitters include specialized agents and the uneducated masses. The Gospel of Mark contains the oral narratives transmitted by these uneducated masses. Therefore, the Gospel of Mark needs to be focused on the study of politics in which the transmitting masses desire to realize their aims through Jesus' narratives rather than on Mark as an evangelist. In this regard, Ahn finds the masses in the Gospel of Mark have a role to play. That is, *ochlos* is not only the audience of the Gospel but the transmitters of the tradition. Furthermore, they are players of the original Jesus-event.

As we see here, Ahn believes that the *ochlos* are key players of the transmission process. Ahn also points out that the *ochlos* are those who are deprived of their language and yet transmit the salvific story about the Jesus-event. This is a healing event that enables the *ochlos* recover their language. The *ochlos* tell the story about Jesus and are healed from their wounds and memories of hurting. Jesus' story reflects their experience of marginality. Ahn understands this story of Jesus and the *ochlos* is the very story of Jeon Tae-Il. In other words, Jeon Tae-Il event is an embodiment of the Jesus-*ochlos* event in Korea. From this time on, Ahn's theological task is to work for the *ochlos* as a witness to the Jesus story.

In summary, Ahn's theory about *ochlos* emphasizes three things: 1) "event" as a theological concept of the minjung, 2) the overcoming of subject/object dichotomy, and 3) the theory of minjung messiah. In addition, the concept of salvation changes to include the experience of radical otherness—the discovery of minjung.

## Imagination for *Sallim*: Towards the Discourse of Reflective Otherness

In his article published in 1987,[26] recalling people being tortured and groaning in secret torture chambers, Ahn confesses, "I met minjung in these people." However, in July 1987, watching the huge funeral procession mourning the death of Lee Han-Yeol, he could not hide his excitement that some better future would emerge. His excitement did not last

---

26. Ahn, "Come and See." As far as we know, this article appeared first time in *Sallim* (Apr, 1992). Though we have no idea whether this article was a sermon or a manuscript for the media, it must have been written in the first half of 1987, immediately after the experience of the Kwon In-Sook event and Park Jong-Cheol event.

long because the mass uprising soon failed due to the state's suppression. All these experiences led him to reexamine the past events of 1987 and the minjung theory of the 1970s and 1980s. All his efforts and reflections resulted in producing the monthly periodical *Sallim* in December 1988.

*Sallim* means "living." At that time, Ahn often talked to the editorial staff of *Sallim*: "For example, explain the suffering of the minjung by the cup of coffee we drink everyday." In his editorial note, he says: *Sallim* is linked inexplicably with the expression of "getting over killing." In other words, *sallim* needs to understand what it means to kill. Through this idea of *sallim*, Ahn's theory of *ochlos* looks at the killing of the minjung deprived of their own language. However, his unique minjung theory was not completely free of the modern historical view that the so-called enlightened intellectuals are responsible for the civilization. However, Ahn understood democratization as a process of correction and as an alternative to overcoming the structure that makes the minjung be killed.[27]

Before the idea of *sallim*, Ahn's theory of *ochlos*, while emphasizing existence of otherness and the self alienated from the external world, did not pay attention to the conditions of political development and democratization. Because of this, it is easy to miss the suffering of the minjung in a society where dictatorship is transformed into democracy. Therefore, the theory of *ochlos* inevitably has to pursue a new kind of internality that deals with self and the external world together. In response, *sallim* appears as a minjung theological concept.

## Doing Theology in the Market of Suffering

Ahn introduced the idea of "alienated internality" into theological discourse in Korea. That is, Ahn's minjung theology begins with the discovery of the suffering of others. The theory of *ochlos* is an important framework for his critical discourse about the minjung. In addition, the concept of *sallim* is a mediation theory that strengthens the theory of the minjung in a postdemocratization society. With this idea of sallim, Ahn's focus on social suffering is significant because we should analyze the market system that causes suffering for people. In the global village today, Ahn's contribution to minjung theology still sheds light because we have to deal with the suffering of people.

---

27. Ahn, "Korean Democratization and the Responsibility of Intellectuals."

# PART II

Selected Writings by Ahn Byung-Mu

# 3

# The Transmitters of the Jesus-Event Tradition

—Ahn Byung-Mu

## Introduction

FORM CRITICISM CONCLUDES THAT the source of the Jesus tradition in the Synoptic Gospels is the community of Christians.¹ In spite of the fact that this community is an object of sociological analysis, there has not been any attempt to analyze it sociologically.² Therefore, the questions of the social location of the community, the function of it within society, and the relationship between the community and its members remains unanswered. Was the community (the church) the only body that exclusively collected all the passages of the Jesus Event? Was there a group that was a part of the community and yet opposed the powers that were more interested in the preservation of the institutionalized church rather than the Jesus-Event? Is it not possible that there was a group less concerned with the doctrines and dogmas of the church and remained affected by the impact of the Jesus Event? If so, what was the sociopolitical makeup of this group? And to what extent was this group socially and politically accepted? These questions are directly related to the questions of what methods the church used to sustain itself, the extent of freedom the community had to publicly bear witness to the JesusEvent, and how they transmitted the tradition of the Event.

Recently, Theissen, using form criticism, has made every effort to analyze the written form by employing the sociological method. He made

---

1. Dibelius, *Botschaft und Geschichte*, 293–358. Bultmann, "Die Erfoschung der synoptischen Evangelien," 1–41.
2. Dibelius, *Die Formgeschichte des Evangeliums*, 7.

a discovery in the process of his analysis: there was a group called the "wandering charismatics" (*Wandercharismatiker*), who carried the sayings of Jesus. According to Theissen, they were handing down "radical sayings of Jesus" (*Radikalismen*) in particular. This is to reappraise the traditional view that the radical sayings of Jesus were directly related to eschatology. To put it differently, the transmitters were not driven by eschatological convictions but by their social conditions to transmit the radical sayings of Jesus. The wanderers could hand down such radical sayings of Jesus because they had abandoned their possessions, families, homes, and all social and cultural roots and lived according to the extreme words of Jesus, who demanded they give up all possessions, authority, and even ethical regulations. What was uncovered in the process of Theissen's research was that while it is generally said that the Christian community (the church) was the mediator of the Jesus Event, there was another group who were deeply involved in the transmission of the tradition.[3] However, it is unclear in Theissen's research what the relationship is between the "wandering charismatics" and the church. Were these "workers" inside or outside the church? And if they belonged to the church, how bound to it were they? What were their positions inside of the church? Without addressing these issues, Theissen maintains that the apostles, including Peter, are a part of these workers. Theisssen, basing his assertion on the possibility that Peter and the few apostles who wandered around without their families and possessions away from their hometowns, too easily arrived at such a conclusion; however, he seemed to have overlooked the fact that Peter and other apostles were in positions of importance within the organized church, and the radical sayings contradicted the order of the church and the authority of its leaders. From what we know of the early church, it was not made up of people who abandoned their families, possessions, or hometowns.[4] From the knowledge we have, the early church's apostleship and hierarchy were established early.[5] In such a context, it is difficult to establish that "wandering charismatics" were the leaders of the institutionalized church. As when we argue that there are multiple traditions in the New Testament based on differences in the source documents,[6] so we can say that the source of the Jesus-Event Tradition is not one, but many.

---

3. Theissen, *Studien zur Soczologie des Urchirstentum*, 79–105.
4. See the book of Acts.
5. Bultmann, *Theologie des Neuen Testament*, 447–63.
6. Schmithals, *Jesus Christus*, 60; Marxsen, "Die urchristischen Kerygmata," 52.

## Ahn Byung-Mu—*The Transmitters of the Jesus-Event Tradition*

Form critics discover the *kerygma* in the New Testament. In fact, the foundation of the New Testament is the *kerygma*. However, it is incorrect to interpret the entirety of the New Testament kerygmatically. Especially if we understand the Jesus Event in the Synoptic Gospels through a kerygmatic lens, then it will result in the disregarding the historicity found in the Synoptics. This, therefore, justifies the calling off of the quest for the historical Jesus. Bultmann contended that the Synoptics are an enlarged *kerygma* and that to look for meaning behind the *kerygma* is unbelief.[7] Therefore, questions regarding the historical Jesus were truncated from the beginning. Fortifying Bultmann's argument, C. H. Dodd argued that the *kerygma* existed originally. Finding the framework of the *kerygma* in Paul's writings and the Acts of the Apostles, he attempted to identify the gospels with it.[8] Such perspectives are a result of the arbitrary decision to try to homogenize not only the content but also the transmitters of the New Testament traditions. Whether the *kerygma* in the New Testament was preached to believers within the church[9] or nonbelievers,[10] it was formulated by a community known as the church, which results in its public nature. The *kerygma* is the principle within the church and dogma towards the world. However, from the perspective of the Jesus Event, it is only secondary. This is because there was no *kerygma* in the beginning, only the Jesus Event. The transmission of the Jesus Event could have followed the form of the *kerygma*, however, eyewitnesses could also have transmitted it in the form of historical description. Generally, when people experience a particular event as witnesses, they can state or transfer the impact of the event or they can attest to the meaning rather than the facts of the event.

Generally, when we experience a certain event, we can describe the facts of the event or bear witness to its meaning. The testimony about the meaning of the event cannot be anything but subjective; therefore, it has, to a certain extent, an apologetic quality for the purpose of persuading an audience. The leaders of the community become responsible for this task. On the contrary, those who have experienced the event directly tell the story from their experience, which allows them to maintain historical

---

7. Bultmann, "Die Erforschung der synoptischen Evangelien," 32; and Bultmann, *Das Verhältnis*, 7.

8. Dodd, *The Apostolic Preaching and Its Development*, 36–56.

9. Bultmann, *Zwischen den Zeiten*, 9–43. See also "Didache of the New Testament," 349–51.

10. Dodd, *Apostolic Preaching and Its Development*, 7–35; Dibelius, *Botschaft und Geschichte*, 307.

objectivity. Although in the course of transmission testimony can be accompanied by interpretation, it is not for the purpose of persuasion, but motivated by existential reasons. Transmitters, in this way, are those who do not possess leadership conscience.

In the beginning, there was no *kerygma* but only the event. This event, of course is the Jesus Event. The *kerygma* focuses on the meaning of the death and resurrection of Jesus; however, prior to the *kerygma* are the events of crucifixion and resurrection of Jesus. Therefore, it is likely that the *kerygma* developed from this Jesus Event, and the reverse is improbable. There were certainly narratives and stories that were influenced by the *kerygma*; however, such narratives belong to a later period of redaction. The *kerygma* does not make up the entire content of the New Testament; it contains both the *kerygma* and accounts of the Jesus Event at the same time.

The topic of this paper is to differentiate between the two traditions. Between the *kerygma* tradition and the Jesus-Event tradition, I will focus on the latter, seeking to shed light on its social characteristic(s). For this task I will compare the contents of representative *kerygmata*, which were formed relatively early, and the transmitted accounts of the Jesus Event in narrative form in the synoptic gospels.

## The Character of the Kerygma

In order to shed light on the characteristics of the *kerygma*, we first need to analyze the earliest *kerygmata* formalized in the church.

### 1 Corinthians 15:3–8

This *kerygma*, which was formulated by the early community before Paul, is concerned with the death of Jesus and the resurrection of Christ. Some suggest that the original constitutes only verses 3–5, and the verses that follow were added later.[11] However, even if such a suggestion were true, since Paul did not redact the section, but rather the church before Paul, the discussion is irrelevant for our analysis. We can make the following observations about the *kerygma*.

First, it dehistoricizes the Jesus Event. The death of Jesus is a historical fact. However, this *kerygma* truncates the questions of "when, where,

---

11. Conzelmann, *Der erste Brief an die Korinther*, 293, 296; see also Jeremias, *The Eucharistic Words of Jesus*, 101.

why, and by whom." Although there are attempts by scholars to connect the Old Testament by employing the phrase "according to Scriptures" (*kata tas grapas*),[12] there are no verses, all the efforts notwithstanding, that directly mention the death and resurrection of Jesus. Expressions such as "according to Scriptures" or "for our sin" are results of evading the Jesus Event's accurate historical descriptions.

Second, what is remarkable is that, rather than searching for the truths about the Jesus Event, most of the energy was spent on the establishment of church leadership. For example, Cephas/Peter was designated as the first eyewitness and the name of James, Jesus' brother, was mentioned in the list of resurrection eyewitnesses, or a superficial concept of the twelve apostles as a collective entity, was used to influence the truth. We do not have any report that the resurrected Jesus first appeared to Cephas,[13] and while James exercised authority in the church in Jerusalem, we do not have any record of when he became a Christian. Rather, the only trait regarding Jesus' brothers handed down to us through the Gospels is their unfaithfulness. Furthermore, it is impossible that there were twelve apostles. If we follow Gospels' account, we have to conclude that there were eleven apostles (Matt 28:16). Besides this passage, Paul does not use the number twelve when referring to the apostles anywhere else. Therefore, the concept of the twelve apostles does not mean much more than a symbol of the authority of the church. Hence, the list and the order of resurrection eyewitnesses are not historical accounts.[14]

Third, the public nature of *kerygma* is evident. We must always consider the external factors that went into the formulation process of such a public document. If the resurrection cannot be separated from the suffering of the cross, then only when we elucidate the historical reality of the latter will the true nature of the resurrection be made clear. However, when the *kerygma* was promulgated there was not only the Roman Empire, that executed Jesus but also the Jewish authorities, who colluded with it. Undoubtedly, Christians in those days still held a grudge and rancor for the irrational execution of Jesus on the cross. Then, how was the *kerygma*

---

12. Barrett, *A Commentary on the First Epistle to the Corinthians*, 337. See also H. Conzelmann, *Der erste Brief an die Korinther*, 296–301.

13. In Luke 24:34, Cephas (Peter) is regarded as an eyewitness of the resurrection; however, this verse belongs to the work of a later redactor.

14. Bultmann says against Barth that if in any verse at all, only in this verse does Paul presuppose the resurrection of Jesus as a historical event. To assume that the resurrection is historical is one thing, but that the list and order of the eyewitnesses is historical is another. See Barth, *Die Auferstehung der Toten*, 74ff.

to be expressed within this context? It was possible only when the leadership of the church, in order to sustain the existence of the organized church, consciously deferred to powerful Rome and Judaism. Therefore, this *kerygma* is detached from both the truth and the emotions of the minjung who followed Jesus. It is a fact that becomes even clearer when we compare it to the passion history in the Gospels.

## Philippians 2:6–11

This pericope known as the Christ-hymn is generally accepted as an early *kerygma*.[15] This hymn is so metric that it can be divided into three stanzas.[16] Its content is also divided into three sections. The first stanza (2:6–7a) is concerned with preexistence, the second (2:7b–8) with incarnation, and the third (2:9–11) with the ascension. The fact that the expression takes on such a poetic form demonstrates that there was enough distance from the shock of the historical event as to be able to theorize it objectively. There are several suggestions concerning the *Sitz im Leben* of this hymn. However, the opinion of a Palestinian context of the hymn conflicts with the opinion of a Hellenistic context.[17] If we accept that there are differing opinions rising from regional differences, it further enforces the possibility that the hymn was changed. There are also varying opinions about where the hymn was sung. Lohmeyer believes that the context was the Eucharist (*Abendmahlsfeier*).[18] Jervell, on the other hand, argues that it was used in context of worship.[19] These two views concur in that they both agree that the context of this Christ confession is cult ritual and not historically situated.[20] This also shows that it was formulated in a stage that followed the trauma of the Jesus Event. Even when we examine the content, it is evident that this hymn obscures the historicity of the Event. Jesus' passion took place during his incarnation, which was between Christ's preexistence and resurrection. The questions about the nature of the incarnated life and passion, therefore,

---

15. Otfried, *Der Christushymnus Philipper 2:6–11*, 1.

16. Ibid., 206.

17. Deichgräber, *Gotteshymnus und Christushymnus*, 126ff. In contrast to Lohmeyer's suggestion that it might be from the Galilee of Palestine, Deichgräber contends that from the linguistic point of view that hymn came from an area influenced by Hellenism.

18. Lohmeyer, *Kyrios Jesus*, 65ff.

19. Jervell, *Imago Dei*, 206ff.

20. Lohmeyer, *Kyrios Jesus*, 133.

became relatively insignificant. Some contend that the last part of verse 8c, "death on the cross," was appended by Paul.[21] Hofius, on the other hand, has made every effort to prove the originality of this verse.[22] However, such a dispute is of little importance to us; rather, it should be noted that, in spite of the expression of "death on a cross," this hymn does not deal with the death of Jesus as a historical event or as an independent saving event that shocked Christians. Moreover, Hofius tries to prove the originality of the verse by arguing that there were also several God-hymns similar to the Christ-hymn, which would prove, if it were true, that the Christ-hymn was not related to the historical event. The death on the cross without historical inquiries, "by whom or why he was crucified," does not give us further insight into how "he became obedient to God . . . according to the Scriptures" in 1 Corinthians chapter 15. Hence there is little difference between this hymn and the hymns in 1 Tim 3:15 or Heb 12:2.

## Kerygmata in Acts

Dibelius points out prototypes of the *kerygma* in Acts 2:22ff, 3:13ff, 10:37ff, and 13:23ff.[23] Dodd, following Dibelius, adds 4:10ff to the list.[24] If we are to sum up Dibelius and Dodd's view of the *kerygma*, it can be summed up as follows: the death of Jesus and that God raised him from death. When we compare them with the Pauline *kerymata* it reveals some unique points.

First, there are some that cover Jesus' life very broadly. For example, they tell us that Jesus did "miracles, wonders and signs" (Acts 2:22), or he wandered around in Galilee, going from village to village, driving out demons (3:38). Acts 13:23 adds more specific information about Jesus' life —that Jesus was a descendant of David and that John preached the baptism and was crucified by the leaders of Jerusalem. In this context, we have to notice that the *kerygmata* in Acts reflect Aramaic factors that are found in Gospels.[25] Second, the *kerygmata* clearly indicate who is responsible for the crucifixion of Jesus. They exonerate Pilate and accuse the Jewish leaders. The Jews crucified Jesus (2:24, 3:14, 4:10, 10:39). Although Pilate tried

21. Ibid., 8, 44ff.
22. Hofius, *Der Christushymnus Philipper 2:6–11*, 3.
23. Bultmann also found the prototype of a Kerygma in Acts 2:22–24; 3:13–15; 10:37–41; 13:26–31. Bultmann, *Die Geschichte der synoptischen Tradition*, Göttingen, 396.
24. Dodd, *The Apostolic Preaching*, 22.
25. Ibid., 19.

to set him free, the Jews objected and released a murderer instead (3:13). Third, among these *kerygmata* the title Son of God was substituted for Son of David.[26] We cannot deny that among *kerygmata* found in Acts there are some prototypes. To mention the historical Jesus, however, is not for apocalyptic reasons,[27] but because Luke already knew Jesus' whereabouts and historical activities through Matthew. Luke added Jesus' whereabouts and acts to the early *kerygma*.[28] Accepting these presuppositions, we can agree with the argument that there is consistency between the *kerygmata* in Acts and the *kerygmata* of Paul.

We can also find several independent *kerygmata* handed down in the Pauline corpus.[29] However, there is little difference in the content between them and the aforementioned *kerygmata*. This means that Paul kept silent about the biographical elements or teachings on the historical Jesus except in Galatians 4:4. Therefore, his ambiguous statement, "we once knew Christ from a human point of view, we know him no longer in that way," (2 Cor. 5:16) should be interpreted in this context.[30]

On the basis of the character of the *kerygmata* examined above, we can say the following: the historical event of Jesus was made abstract by being proclaimed kerygmatically, connoting only its meaning instead of describing it as it happened.

What was the reason for this? Several possibilities can be proposed. First, the political and social situations were important factors. Because Jesus was a rebel within the Roman Empire, the church leadership tried to avoid conflict with the empire by abstracting Jesus' death, which affected the formation of the *kerygma*. Second, the leadership did not want to be identified with zealots who fought against the empire. Therefore, they did not want to assert the fact that Jesus died at the hands of the Romans and Jewish authorities. Third, the leadership tried to avoid the minjung's armed resistance by sublimating the minjung's hostility into spirituality. This is evinced by the fact that emphasis fell on God's providence rather than on holding anyone responsible for Jesus' death. Fourth, the leadership of the community wanted to be acknowledged by Judaism by interpreting the Jesus Event within Judaism, and at the same time they wanted to be

---

26. Ibid., 25.
27. Ibid., 31.
28. E. Haenchen, *Die Apostelgeschichte*, 152ff.
29. Rom 1:3ff, 6:3ff, 10:9; 1 Cor 11:23–26.

30. We cannot accept the suggestion that because of having already known the historical Jesus, Paul said so in forming his theology.

regarded as a sect of Judaism by the Roman authorities since Judaism was already an approved religion by Rome. As a result, these efforts to preserve the Christian community translated the historical events into the form of the *kerygma*. These factors not only resulted in the *kerygma* being silent about the Jesus Event, but also caused distortions of the event. Moreover, it did not represent the will of the majority of the community, and also contracted the facts of the event. We have arrived at a point where we now have to examine the Jesus Tradition as transmitted in the Gospels. As a means of outlining the task, we will start by analyzing the general character of the language of the minjung.

## The Character of the Language of Minjung

The most essential characteristic of the language of minjung is that it is a story. This language is radically different from that of proclamation or apologetic arguments. The Jesus Event, including the passion history which Mark handed down, consists of the stories and the special sources passed down by Matthew and Luke, and parts of the Q source. By studying socially the transmission process of the minjung narrative in the Synoptics we will gain new insight into the Jesus Event.

We should first examine the political situation following the Jesus Event. As already mentioned above, because the Jesus Event took place under political authority, the stories about the event must have been handed down privately. Thus, it would make sense that the method of transmission remained oral, not in written form, for some time. This method of transmission can be called rumor. Rumor, for the minjung of Jesus, is an effort to ascertain their position by correctly recognizing the historicity of that event. However, for the authorities, it can be regarded as a form of rebellious and riotous movement. On the whole, rumor has the following characteristics:

1. Rumor usually occurs when there is social and political persecution.[31] If some group's movement is banned or restricted by the authorities, or they are falsely accused, and if they are too small and weak to resist, then rumor arises to demonstrate and bear witness to the facts about their persecuted existence.

---

31. Lee Sang-Hee, "The Ecology of the Rumor," 216–17.

Part II: Selected Writings by Ahn Byung-Mu

2. Rumor develops through the efforts of a group to reveal the truth of certain event which is closely bound up with the fate of that group.[32] Rumor is largely circulated by two classes. First, rumor is employed when the oppressive class is at fault or carries out its unreasonable policies by deluding the oppressed. When the experience of the persecuted is distorted publicly, then rumor is created in a collective effort to reveal the truth. In the case of the latter (different from the former) they do not manipulate or distort the content of the historical facts; rather, they make every effort to make obvious the truths of the event.[33] Therefore, rumor takes the characteristics of bearing witness. Though there is, to some extent, a distance between rumor and historical facts, it can be a more exact interpretation that reveals the essence connoted in the historical event.

3. Rumor is not a public medium; instead, it is circulated in secret. Since the government or authorities cannot find a way to reasonably justify carrying out certain illegal policies, they cannot do anything but circulate rumors in secret without any public disclosure.[34] Under the weight of the mounting pressure of public opinion and being cut off from mass communication, the persecuted also circulate rumors in secret. In the latter case, they cannot but do so because they are not in the position to proclaim the truth of the event publicly, and if they proclaim it publicly, they would suffer persecution from the clash with authorities.[35] Carlyle said it well when he said that history is "the distillation of rumors."[36]

4. Rumor can be circulated by minjung within a certain group when the leaders of that group cannot or will not stand by the event, or when for particular reasons they make it obscure. There are various cases in which the leaders, though in the position of the persecuted, do such a thing. In almost every case it is primarily due to the persecution by the authorities. Owing to the persecution, the leaders of the group either keep silent, come to fold the consequences into the religious dimension, or sublimate the motif of the persecution and shift

32. Ibid., 134.
33. Ibid., 217–18.
34. Examples include the rumor saying that Christians were responsible for the fire after the great fire broke out in Rome, and the rumors circulated by the Japanese government when the earthquake happened in Gwan-Dong.
35. Lee, "The Ecology of the Rumor," 217.
36. Ralph and Rosnow, "Lives of a Rumor," 214.

the responsibility to evade clashes with the persecutors. Such actions are inevitable compromises[37] of leaders for the preservation of their group and themselves.

5. Rumor is triggered when the context of an event is correlated with an existential situation of a particular group. For example, there is a fundamental difference between how city dwellers and intellectuals talk about the Peasant Uprising, Jeong Bong-Jun, and the farmers who groan under oppressive conditions. The minjung experience joy and sadness of the past event by uncovering the existential hope rooted in the event through rumor. Therefore, rumor, by mingling its present concerns with the past, possesses the character of being an existential witness. We have thus far considered the theoretical dimensions of rumor. It is from this theoretical framework we will now examine the tradition of the Jesus Event in the Gospels.

The eyewitnesses of the Jesus Event could not but be politically persecuted. As long as Jesus was crucified as a political upstart against Rome, the political situation of the followers of Jesus was self-evident. The Jesus Event can be viewed as a political persecution resulting from collusion between the ruling authorities of Judah and Rome. In Acts, there are stories about the persecution of apostles, including one of Peter, for having publicly preached about Jesus, which reveals the true nature of the persecution. However, despite the certainty that minjung handed down the story of the Jesus Event, there is no record of direct persecution of them. This is an undeniable proof that they circulated the story of the Jesus Event by the means of rumor. Though many note that there is a long oral tradition, the questions about the political situation in which it was handed down are not asked. Supposing that the prototype of the tradition in the gospels has the character of rumor, I cannot but challenge the suggestion that, in the beginning, there was the *kerygma*, or the critical studies that would come to conclusions through the usage of the tools of form criticism. Dibelius mentioned briefly that after the Jesus Event, for at least several decades, the tradition could not have taken a concrete form.[38] This suggestion should be taken seriously. When rumors formed under persecution are written down, there is no room for aesthetic pursuits. Rumors that are formed under such conditions are not concerned with propagating ideologies or

---

37. As one example, we can indicate that the attitude of the leaders of the Dong-Hak Movement developed after the Peasants War.

38. Dibelius, *Die Formgeschichte des Evangelisiums*, 1.

philosophies, but are more concerned about the description of the event. Therefore, it is not incidental that compared with Matthew and Luke, most of Mark's stories consist of events, and the words of Jesus take on a secondary emphasis.

The Jesus Event was ignored or distorted. It is inexplicable that there is no record of the Jesus Event in the Jewish or Roman corpus. When there are many records of Pilate and messianic movements, why is there such a silence about the Jesus Event? However, the gospel depicts Jesus as deranged (Mark 3:21, 30), a greedy drunkard (Mark 2:16), the destroyer of the Jerusalem temple (Mark 15:30), and one possessing an ambition to become king (Mark 15:2, 9). It is probable that all these reflect a certain part of the forged rumor circulated by the persecutors. Taking it a step further, a rumor that regarded Jesus as a denunciator of the law or an unfaithful blasphemer of God, may have circulated as well. Therefore, under such circumstances, many could not obtain clear information regarding the crucifixion of Jesus. So we can conjecture without difficulty that one certain group, which had witnessed the works of the passion of Jesus and the empty grave, made efforts to disclose the truth of the Jesus Event. Such efforts could only take the form of rumor.

It is evident that under such an aforementioned situation, the minjung did not have any means or way of handing down the Jesus Event publicly. They felt the importance of communicating the truths of the Jesus Event because their fellow believers were struggling with ambiguities surrounding it.[39] The communication necessarily had to be in the form of rumor. Therefore, this rumor is fundamentally different from the preaching that claims Jesus as the Christ. Despite this, the image Mark paints of the apostles in his gospel, which portrays them not only as ignorant and unfaithful, but also as those who betrayed and ultimately abandoned Jesus,[40] is concrete proof of Mark's critical attitude toward the apostles' authority.

From early on, the Christian community, due to the influence of Judaism, took on an institutional form, which meant that the conferring of authority on the leaders of the church was essential to sustaining the order of the institutional church. The "twelve disciples" in this context is a symbolic concept denoting the authority of the apostles. This authority was supported by apostolic eyewitnesses to the resurrection, and we can see in 1 Corinthians 15 James the brother of Jesus exercising his

39. Allport and Postman, "The Basic Psychology of Rumor," 61–81.

40. Mark 6:49–52; 8:16–21; 9:32 (about the ignorance and misunderstanding of the disciples); Mark 4:40ff (their unbelief); Mark 14:43–46, 66–72 (betrayal and denial); Mark 14:50–52 (fleeing away).

authority on this basis. They were not only conscious of proclaiming the church's creed and position on its behalf, but also carried a sense of duty to preach their faith. As already indicated above, this appeared in the form of the *kerygma*. In the *kerygma*, historical realities such as inspiration and frustration, delight and rage, hopelessness and triumph, and the thoroughgoing failures are covered up, especially since the *kerygma* does not reflect the misery of the crucifixion of Jesus, the wretchedness of the event, and the questions of whom and why are obscured. Compared with the *kerygma*, the tradition of the Jesus Event in the Gospels discloses those facts covered up by the church leadership.

In spite of having experienced the euphoria of Jesus' resurrection, the minjung still had to endure persecution and live in darkness. The resurrection of Jesus did not mean the advent of the kingdom of God. The historical reality is that, like the situation surrounding the crucifixion, the situation after the resurrection was also mired in godless darkness.[41] We cannot know the exact historical situation. We know that persecution began early through Acts. We have reports that Christians, with the exception of its leadership, including apostles in Jerusalem, were exiled, and martyrs began to appear. However, by examining the political condition that deteriorated leading to the Jewish War in 66 CE, we can guess the conditions of existence for Christians. We can see their situation reflected in the passion story of Jesus handed down by them. Even during the time of peace in Galilee, Jesus from the beginning was depicted as if his antagonists threatened his life. This exposed the existential situation of the minjung and the similarity of their conditions gave them comfort and consolation. Therefore, the passion story of Jesus could be triggered as rumor.

Until now, I have argued that the story of the Jesus Event had the form of rumor, and the subject of the rumor was the minjung of Jesus. Hence, we have come to a point where we have to ask what the content of the story of the Jesus Event is. First, we will deal with the passion story.

## The Passion Story

The pioneers of form criticism, K. L. Schmidt and Dibelius, held to the view that the passion story, unlike other pericopes, maintained a fixed form.[42] Bultmann contends, against this position that the passion story,

41. Ahn Byung-Mu, "The Theology of Mark in the Passion History."

42. Schmidt, *Der Rahmen der Geschichte Jesu*, 303–5; Dibelius, *Die Formgeschichte des Evangelisiums*, 57.

like other pericopes, consists of several fragments in a collected form.[43] He sees that especially the passion predictions (Mark 8:31; 9:31; 10:33ff.) were the source of the passion story. This view argues that even in the passion story, the *kerygma* precedes the stories and they are supplemented and amplified on the basis of the *kerygma*. However, I cannot agree with such a view. Of course we can find out the "isolated *apophthegm*" in the passion story.[44] Nevertheless, this *apophthegm* does not destroy the organic unity of the passion story. Before depending on the written form and style entirely, we ought to ask a more essential question. The passion and the resurrection stories of Christ are the other side of the same coin. Therefore, the presupposition that the transmitters of the story would have handed down only a portion of the passion story is not convincing. So it is natural that the minjung who had experienced the bitter and shocking event handed down the entire passion story of Jesus. We do not contend, however, that the order of the events of the passion is historical. However, it is very evident that there was a complete passion tradition that had described the order of events leading up to the crucifixion.

We will now compare the characteristics of the passion story in the Synoptics in comparison with the speculative characteristics of the *kerygma*. First, it is said in the passion prediction that Jesus will suffer much and be handed over by the chief priest and the scribes.[45] On the contrary, in the passion story, Jesus was betrayed first by Judas, the disciples (including Judas) and by the Jewish authorities of Jerusalem, being crucified at the court of Pilate. The very executioner of Jesus is, of course, Pilate. This greatly differs from the abstract expression, "according to the Scriptures."

Second, in the passion story, the premise that Jesus will rise again in three days is not found anywhere. If there was such a premise, the disciples' betrayal, the prayer in Gethsemane (struggle), or the final cry from the cross cannot be explained.[46] The most decisive cause of Jesus' agony is not the abandonment by the Jewish or the Roman authorities, or by the disciples, but the abandonment by God.

---

43. Bultmann, *Geschichte der synoptischen*, 166ff; Marxsen, *Einleitung in das Neue Testaments*, 120.

44. Dibelius sees the story of the woman who anointed Jesus' head with oil (Luke 7:36–50) as a paradigma.

45. Considering the contents of the passion prediction (8:41ff, 9:31ff, 10:33ff), we can say that 10:33ff was affected by the passion event. There are not the concrete descriptions about the passion of Jesus in the passion prediction.

46. If the resurrection was presupposed, all these are nothing but a drama, and therefore the passion of Jesus cannot be the true passion.

Third, the subject of the *kerygma* is the apostles. However, according to the Synoptics, the apostles were ignorant of Jesus' passion (this is why Peter is called Satan, the apostles assumed the kingdom of God without the cross and struggled for their own positions on the road to Jerusalem) and were not regarded as eyewitnesses to the passion (they were asleep at Gethsemane, they were not in the place of the crucifixion, or they fled away, and so on). Instead, it was transmitted by the first eyewitnesses of the passion and the empty grave of Jesus. Jesus' appearance after the resurrection was not to a member of the apostles, but only to the women who were the symbolic minjung in those days.

Fourth, the list of the eyewitnesses to whom Jesus appeared after the resurrection in chapter 15 of 1 Corinthians is entirely different from the contents of the stories about the Jesus Event. Most important, women do not appear in the *kerygma* in 1 Corinthians. Further, in the passion story in the Synoptics, Peter does not appear as an eyewitness.[47] What is more, as we have already indicated, it is impossible on the basis of the Synoptics to regard Peter as an eyewitness of the resurrection at all. According to Mark, only the women are eyewitnesses of the empty tomb. There is no other reference to the empty grave, except in this Markan source.[48] This story about the empty grave is the most concrete proof supporting the historicity of the resurrection. By eliminating the historicity of this story, some come to the conclusion that the resurrection is the meaning of the cross.[49] Mark omits the story about the appearance after the resurrection by ending with 16:8.[50] However, Mark already presupposes that Jesus appeared to the disciples at Galilee. Even if this were the case, the women could not be excluded as eyewitnesses.[51]

Fifth, the passion story is not a transitional story, but an independent story which uncovers the hopelessness of the situation. The scene shows us the literal dark reality of being separated from God in which no supernatural possibility is to be expected, even less God's intercession. From the struggle at Gethsemane, the judgment process under Pilate, to the cry on the cross, one only finds miserable and hopeless depictions which one cannot find in

---

47. Luke 24 is an exception. Luke 24:34 may have been added later.

48. Cf. 1 Cor 15:4

49. Bultmann, *Theologie des Neuen Testaments*, 292–306.

50. Perhaps Mark ended the story with verse 8 intentionally. Dibelius, *Die Formgeschichte*, 190; Marxsen, *Mark the Evanglist*, 51–59; Bultmann, *Die Geschichte der Syroptischen Tradition*, 319.

51. We can see this possibility in the Gospel of Matthew in which the women are regarded as the first eyewitnesses of the resurrection (Matt 28:9ff.).

heroic epics or religious biographies. This is fundamentally different from the *kerygma*, which focuses on the resurrection or triumph, only describes the death of Jesus to give meaning to the resurrection, and corresponds more with the *Sitz im Leben* of the minjung who handed it down.

As already mentioned, the Christ hymn is close to the passion story. As the notion of preexistence, however, became the basis of the hymn, it became oppositional. We cannot find traces of the concept of pre-existence anywhere in the gospel of Mark, not to mention in the story of the passion.[52] The passion story of Jesus vividly depicts a lonely struggle of the powerless who are miserably defeated without any tools of resistance. Through transmitting the stories about the Jesus Event, the minjung were venting their bitterness about the way that the Jesus Event was condemned, because, in the face of the Jewish and Roman authorities colluding together to execute Jesus, the crowds who had followed Jesus, of course, and even the disciples, fled, leaving no one to defend the event. The cry on the cross, therefore, becomes joined to the cries of those who witnessed the injustice. The contents of such stories are fundamentally different from the passion of Jesus preached by the apostles in Acts.

## Acts of Jesus

### The Miracle Stories and Acts of Jesus

The reports of miraculous acts of Jesus occur twenty-nine times in the four gospels. The gospel of Mark, especially, focuses on the miracle stories rather than the words of Jesus. In form criticism, it has become the generally accepted view that each miracle story was handed down independently. However, I cannot agree with the view that the miracle stories have the preaching of the primitive community as its *Sitz im Leben* (Dibelius), or the view that the stories developed from an apologetic motivation of that community (Bultmann).

From the perspective of kerygmatic theology, the focus of the preaching of the primitive church was the death on the cross and the resurrection of Jesus. From this basis, the demands of faith have become an indispensable factor.[53] However, except for a portion of the miracle stories, this is not

---

52. Bultmann, *Die Geschichte der synoptischen Tradition*, 374.
53. Theissen sees these exceptions in Mark 2:5, Luke 5:8, and John 5:14. Theissen,

the case.⁵⁴ We can agree that a portion of the miracle stories are reflected in the resurrection; however, we cannot find in them even a hint about the suffering of Jesus. Not only that, there are only three stories in which faith is a prerequisite for a miracle.⁵⁵ Therefore, we cannot make miracle stories normative based on a few examples, nor can we assimilate all the miracle stories into the *kerygma*.⁵⁶ Miracle stories are not the main point of christology. The point of the miracle stories is not an ostentatious display of the identity of Christ, but the liberation of the ill, the hungry, the possessed, and others who are in oppressive conditions. As mentioned above, faith seen through such exceptions is very different from the Christ-*kerygma*. No matter from which perspective we examine it, the argument that the body of the miracle story is the *kerygma* is not valid.

Then who handed down these stories? About this question, we should first of all indicate the fact that the miraculous acts were transmitted in the style of a narrative. As we have already mentioned, the narrative is the most characteristic language of minjung. It is generally accepted that the miracle stories were readily accepted by the lower class and became the content of their faith. Theissen sees that in the early days the miracles had taken root among the minjung and it was not until about 3 CE when it spread among the upper class.⁵⁷

We can see reflected in these miracle stories, not only the economical motive of the poor and the social motive of the alienated, but also their political hope. We cannot deny that in the miracle stories the sorrows and hopes of the minjung who lived under wretched conditions far outweigh the intellectual curiosities, missionary concerns, and apologetical motivations of the church. Especially in Mark, there are many stories of exorcisms of the possessed. Many scholars have explained away this fact through a history of religions approach by connecting it with eschatological motifs, which means that they did not take into account social conditions. There is a close relationship between the demon-possessed (mentally ill) persons and the political situation. Some argue that political persecution by

---

"Synoptische Wundergeschichten im Lichte unseres Sprachverständnisses," 292.

54. According to Theissen, the resurrection of Jesus is reflected in the three stories (Luke 7:11–17, Mark 4:28–31; 14:22–26) among the miracle stories. Ibid., 293. See also Montefiore, *The Synoptic Gospels*, 1:43.

55. Mark 5:34; 9:23ff; 10:52.

56. Theissen, "Synoptische Wundergeschichten im Lichte unseres Sprachverständnisses," 292.

57. Ibid., 294.

a foreign nation is the cradle for producing demon-possessed persons.[58] Hence, to conceptualize the stories of Jesus by lifting them from their context and absolutizing the religious motifs such as eschatology, Christology or soteriology is to take the focus away from the relationship between Jesus and the suffering of the minjung. The miracle stories in the Synoptics, in contrast to the Gospel of John, are not overly concerned with the question of who Jesus is. Rather they focus on what he did for the minjung. What is most important for the suffering minjung is liberation from suffering. Therefore, the question about the identity of the liberator is possible only for those who have been liberated. Moreover, to speculate metaphysically about the liberator is the work of those who objectify the event.

Form critics are searching for a fixed form from documented stories of miracles; however, it is too much to try to unify the forms into a singular category.[59] The prototype of the oral tradition, which is a primitive form, does not rely on these forms; rather, it relies on the words of the witnesses. However, if we disdain this fact, then it would be a big mistake. If we do not ask historical questions when we analyze the miracle stories of Jesus and assume the premise that Jesus can do miracles, then it would be theologically prejudiced.

## Apophthegm and Acts of Jesus

Since Schmidt the combined contents of Jesus' words and acts have been called *apophthegm* by Bultmann and *paradigma* by Dibelius. Since then, Jesus' words were considered independent and original, and the context of the spoken words were considered only as a "frame" (Rahmen), which was edited by later redactors of the church. In form criticism, most scholars do not examine the historicity of the context: Jesus' acts. However, if we suppose that *apophthegms* were handed down by the minjung, then we cannot agree with such a view. Here are a few examples. If we were to separate the words, "the sabbath was made for humankind, and not humankind for the sabbath," from the *apophthegm* concerning picking the heads of the grain on the sabbath (Mark 2:23–28), then the sentence becomes very abstract. However, this story is related to the reality of hunger. By being related to hunger, this story makes clear the conduct of Jesus in opposition to the Jewish religion. It is the general view that this story is regarded as a debate about

---

58. Mühlmann, *Chilasmus und Nativismus*, 252.

59. Dibelius suggests that the miracle stories always end in the form of a chorus. Dibelius, *Die Formgeschichte*, 50.

the sabbath. The reason that the story is included in the Bible is to explain the church's opinion about Judaic law. Linking this story to hunger is very different from the *kerygma* of the church. What is more, even though this *apophthegm* is regarded as a debate discourse, the *Sitz im Leben* of it cannot be the preaching of the church. It is more probable to regard this *apophthegm* as a description of an historical account transmitted by the minjung.

This is the same with the debate about the washing of hands (Mark 7:1–19). This story represents the confrontation with the Pharisees who imposed the responsibility of purification rituals of the priestly class on the minjung. However, the group that was most directly affected by the purification codes was the minjung, who were controlled and labelled sinners by them. This code was for the wealthy, who were concerned about cleanliness but was an object of contempt for the poor and hungry minjung, who had to toil every day in order to eat, and yet they were still hungry. The acts and words of Jesus that liberated the minjung from the hated laws were transmitted as being precious to their survival.

Like the examples mentioned above, other *apophthegms* are also related to the acts of Jesus, who delved into the life-scene of the minjung: the ill, the hungry, the widows and the children. Their context was not directly concerned with the institutional problems of the church or with christological issues.[60] In the tradition of the Jesus Event in the Gospels, the relationship between Jesus and the minjung takes up the greatest portion, which is why the Gospels repeatedly mention that Jesus' activity was centered in Galilee, and the first followers all came from Galilee.[61] Research that only seeks to theologically understand the tension between Jerusalem and Galilee at the expense of their historical relationship can only come from the lack of historical understanding of the Jesus-Event tradition. Although in the Jesus Event, Galilee holds a decisive meaning and the people of Galilee were the central figures of Jesus' passion and the formation of the Jerusalem Church, Galilee is not mentioned anywhere except for the gospels.

Therefore, we have briefly covered the general tradition of Jesus' acts, and we have come to conclude that we cannot interpret it through the framework of the *kerygma*.

Furthermore, we cannot interpret it beginning from Jesus' passion and resurrection, which is the core of the *kerygma*. Starting with the

---

60. Other documents, including Paul's letters, do not mention the fact that Jesus focused on a special class of people in his ministry. Although Paul advocated for the poor and the weak in the church, he does not mention Jesus' acts.

61. Ahn, "Jesus and Minjung, in the Gospel of Mark," 11. See also, Ahn, "The Subject of History of the Gospel of Mark."

miracles, the fragmentary traditions which described Jesus' acts were gathered together by Mark. The fragments might have consisted of eyewitness accounts about historical events. Therefore these simple stories, which excluded theological motives, have preserved the historical facts about the acts of Jesus.

## Logion and Acts of Jesus

Only in the miracle stories and *apophthegms*, Jesus' words are not overlooked in relation to his actions. Theissen has already contended that the transmitters of the radical words of Jesus were wandering-charismatics (*Wandercahrismatiker*). Then, who had handed down the Q source? If we state the conclusion first, the transmitter of these words might be a new group of people who were different from the transmitters of the Christ *kerygma* or the Jesus Event *kerygma*. As evidence, we can suggest several unique characteristics.

First, the Q document has just one miracle story. Except for this, all others are records of independent short sayings by Jesus, which tells us that the transmitters of Q were more concerned with words rather than events. Second, in Q there is no passion story, which is the most decisive event in Mark. Third, consistent with the minjung tradition, the editor of Mark redacted to minimize Jesus' words in favor of emphasizing the events, which is very different from Q. And last, we can point to the fact that the words of Jesus have similar characteristics to wisdom literature.

Was it not the intellectual class that emphasized words over acts? The wisdom literature was transmitted by the intellectual class, who were influenced by Hellenism.[62] However, the parables, which are Jesus' most unique sayings, are different. As many people have pointed out, there are some parables in Q that were written to sustain the church's faith or to strengthen the structure of the church. However, there are many more parables that have no relationship to the church (Luke 15:17ff.) or have conflicting interests to the church (Luke 14:15–24). The parable of the Great Banquet (Luke 14:15–24), the parable of the Lost Things (Luke 15:17ff.), and the parable of the Mustard Seed (Mark 4:30ff.) have elements that cannot be interpreted only from the eschatological perspective. For example, the parable of the Great Banquet, which is not a story of the establishment, but one where the

---

62. Some even suggest this was a Q community. However, we cannot say that the community was formed in such a way. Hoffman, *Studien zur Theologie der Logienquelle*, 199ff.

poor, the disabled, and the blind become the heroes and heroines of the new kingdom, reflects the sorrows and desires of the minjung.

These parables, in contrast to Wisdom literature, appeal to the minjung as language that criticizes reality and yearns for a new world. The minjung who heard these parables could never forget them. However, we cannot conclude from this that the transmitter of these parables is the same minjung that transmitted the Jesus-Event Tradition.

## Conclusion

I have tried to demonstrate that the transmitter of the Jesus Event is the minjung, including women, as mentioned in Mark. It was Mark who first collected the minjung's tradition and documentation for the Gospel. It was a revolutionary decision under the circumstances of the early church, and thanks to it we can learn about the historical Jesus Event that was hidden under abstract *kerygmata*. Then did Mark transmit the minjung's tradition as it was? It is unlikely. Mark was a second-generation Christian who was already steeped in the Christ *kerygma*. The reason that he drew minjung tradition into the church was to revitalize the church by challenging the ossified church, which had become doctrinaire and institutionalized in the process of forming the *kerygma*. The events of the Jesus Event faded away or disappeared.

Mark—the person standing between the Christian kerygma and minjung tradition—compromised in some ways, in the course of formulating the document. Most distinctly, Mark obscures the party responsible for the death of Jesus. However, the fact that Jesus was a political criminal tells us clearly that Rome was responsible for Jesus' crucifixion. However, the description of Pilate, who crucified Jesus, is ambiguous. Pilate's role in the crucifixion of Jesus was made to look involuntary as a result of public opinion.[63] And, by inserting a sprinkling of kerygmatic elements, Mark made them inconsistent with the original tradition and made the tradition itself more obscure.

We have come to a conclusion that the transmitter of the Jesus Event was not one person but at least two and probably more. The transmitters of the Christ *kerygma* and the historical Jesus Event are clearly different.

---

63. See Mark 15:9, 12; 15:14ff. Besides, the reports in Matthew and Luke differ from that of Mark (cf. Matt 27:15ff and 27:24ff). In those days, it is said, Pilate's personality was very strong and arrogant, and his regime was established by corruption, violence, robbery, intimidation, and ruthlessness, and executed people without trial.

Schmithals recognized this fact and differentiated between the primitive church that has had its basis in the understanding of the Christ *kerygma*, and the community that had preserved the tradition of the Jesus Event. Marxen also acknowledged the difference between them and used the technical term "Jesus Kerygma" in explaining the Christ *kerygma*.[64]

I have tried to demonstrate that the transmitter of the Jesus-Event Tradition was not a sect or the church, which had preserved the Jesus Kerygma, but the minjung who were witnesses of the Jesus Event before becoming members of the church, and who could not hand down the tradition in an official capacity owing to their political situation and the situation of the church. Therefore the minjung transmitted it in the form of rumor.

---

64. Marxsen, "Die urchristichen Kerygmata," 52ff. Marxsen argues that the basic difference between the two *kerygmata* lie in the Christology and that only in soteriology are the two *kerygmata* able to be unified.

# 4

# Jesus and Minjung in the Gospel of Mark

—Ahn Byung-Mu

Scholars of the New Testament have focused a great deal on the audience of Jesus. However, scholars have not paid much attention to the social characteristics of the audience. To ask the questions of what and to whom he spoke is to reveal the historical nature of the audience. This task requires a close examination of the politics, culture, and economic situation of Jesus' audience. For a more comprehensive understanding we have to see what kind of social structure and position they belonged to. This essay will seek to examine the author's editorial process and Jesus' words.

## *Ochlos* in the Gospel of Mark

From the beginning, Mark is conscious of the audience that surrounds Jesus. Form critics only used the audience as a framework for unveiling the meaning of Jesus' words or the *kerygma* that Jesus is Christ, which resulted in the exclusion of the people and a failure to see an important aspect of the process.

The crowd is already mentioned in Mark 1:22. The author draws attention to them by using an abstract word like "people," or the third-person plural, "everyone"; however, the author does not reveal their identity (1:22, 30, 32, 33, 37, 44, 45; 2:2). Such a description draws the reader's attention to the social composition of the people. Eventually a concept that represents "many people" (*polloi*) appears: *ochlos* (2:4). In Mark, even without the indicative pronoun, this word is used thirty-six times.

## Part II: Selected Writings by Ahn Byung-Mu

There are reasons other than the frequent use of the word that draw our attention. First is the availability of *laos*, a far more common word that was used widely during that period. For example, this word is used a surprising two thousand times in the Septuagint. It is overwhelmingly applied to members of nations, and it is especially used to indicate Israelites as the people of God. Curiously, Mark, other than in a quotation (7:6) and in the words of chief priests and lawyers (14:2), does not use the word even once.

Without a doubt, Mark was the first to introduce *ochlos* in the New Testament. We can be certain of this because the word does not appear in documents written prior to Mark; in the Gospels and Acts, written after Mark, this word appears frequently, clearly indicating Mark's influence. It also appears three times in Revelation (7:9; 1:9; 1:6), which reflects persecutions of early Christians.

If we especially consider the fact that the word was not used in the Pauline epistles written before Mark, we must pay close attention to Mark's usage of the word. All of Paul's epistles were written more than ten years before Mark, between 50 and 60 CE. Paul's letters, which were written with a clear purpose of Gentile mission, focus on Christology and soteriology, and have a strong sense of apologetics. Paul made almost no references to the historical Jesus. What is more, he declared that he did not really want to know about the historical Jesus (2 Cor 5:16). In contrast, the Gospel of Mark was written either when the Jewish War had already begun or when Jerusalem had already fallen in 70 CE (I believe the latter), and the Jews were expelled en masse from the land of Judea. Unlike Paul, Mark concentrates on the transmission of the historic Jesus. It contains many materials that cannot be seen simply as badly formed *kerygma* (Bultmann). Mark, contrary to Paul, is not spreading ideological, abstracted Christology or soteriology, but he is using historically grounded, simple folk-like narratives.

In the above comparison, there are certain things to point out related to our subject matter. Not only was Mark in a different social location than Paul, not allowing him to accept the fully integrated kerygmatic theology, but it also appears that it was an intentional distancing on his part; such a position made Mark move towards a more historical Jesus. Under such a circumstance, the term *ochlos*, which Mark introduces, has a very important function demanded by Mark's situation. During Mark's time, the Jews, including Jewish Christians, were exiled from their homeland, and were wandering like sheep without a shepherd.

# The Characteristics of *Ochlos* in Mark

Typically, we would begin with the etymology of *ochlos*; however, here we will begin with finding the characteristics of *ochlos* as the word appears in the Gospel of Mark. This will minimize the subjective interpretation based on preconceptions of this term.

## The Characteristics of the *Ochlos*

The following is an examination of passages that use the word *ochlos*:

1. *Ochlos* refers to people who follow and gather everywhere Jesus goes (2:4; 13:3; 9:20, 32; 4:1; 5:21, 24, 31; 8:1; 10:1). In most cases, the reasons why they follow are not known. They form the background as well as the object of Jesus' activities.

2. These are people who were condemned by society, and were considered "sinners." Mark not only was the first to use the word *ochlos*, but also applies it to tax collectors and sinners. Mark criticizes the Pharisees' critique of Jesus' sharing the table with the *ochlos*, and unveils the injustice of socially ostracizing them.

3. There are occasions when they (the *ochlos*) are distinguished from the disciples (8:34; 9:14; 10:46); at times, Jesus only teaches the disciples in the absence of the *ochlos* (4:36; 6:46; 7:17). From this perspective, Jesus placed the disciples above the *ochlos*. However, what we have to comparatively keep in mind is that the disciples were often objects of Jesus' criticism (usually for being ignorant), while there is no account of the *ochlos* being rebuked. Matthew and Luke boldly deleted criticisms of the disciples or idealized them. This is an important point to remember when we assume that the disciples were the very symbols of the church.

4. The *ochlos* are contrasted with the ruling hierarchy from Jerusalem, who attack and criticize Jesus as the enemy. The *ochlos* took an anti-Jerusalem position and were clearly on the side of Jesus (2:4–6; 3:2–21; 4:1; 11:18, 27, 32). What is important to note about this is that they were the minjung from Galilee.

5. They stood in tension with the ruling class and were the object of consternation to the authorities. Therefore, the authorities tried to avoid arousing their anger (11:18, 32, 12:12; 15:8, 15). Accordingly, the only way to get the *ochlos* on their side was to bribe them. It is said that the

authorities paid *ochlos* money in order to mobilize them for the execution of Jesus. This demonstrates the strategies of the authorities and at the same time their potential, not inevitability, to be manipulated.

### Jesus' Attitude towards the *Ochlos*

Jesus had compassion on them the *ochlos* like a sheep without a shepherd (6:34). The expression "sheep without a shepherd" has its roots in the Old Testament. This expression has two traditions: the first is the tradition of criticizing the ruling authorities who have the responsibility of taking care of their people (e.g., Ezek 34:5), and the latter is of the crowds who were directionless due to their betrayal of YHWH; however, there is no example of the latter in the Gospels. In Moses' supplication for a successor, he prays "so that the congregation of the LORD may not be like sheep without a shepherd" (Num. 27:17). When we consider *ochlos* from this perspective, we can see that they were a hungry and leaderless crowd who followed Jesus; at the same time, they were an alienated class at the hands of the ruling authorities.

After the narration in 3:34, which says, "and looking at those who sat around him," Jesus declared that *the ochlos* were his mother and brothers (3:34). The editorial process names the "crowd" in 3:32 as the *ochlos*. This is to announce, on one hand, a break from the ties of blood kinship and, on the other hand, to declare that *ochlos* is the basis for a new community (family). This was a hard declaration to accept at that time. This is why in Matthew it is *mathetai* (disciples) instead of *ochlos*, and in Luke it is deleted.

Jesus always teaches the *ochlos* (2:13; 4:11–12; 7:4; 10:1; 11:18). Especially, 10:1 ("and, as was his custom, he again taught them") signals that Jesus always wanted to teach the *ochlos*. This corresponds to passages that indicate that the *ochlos* was enthralled with Jesus' teaching (13:18b). In Matthew and Luke, the above-mentioned verses have either been altered or eliminated. This is certainly to weaken the case that the *ochlos* were the main audience of Jesus' teaching. This was not because the *ochlos* were ignored, but points to the expansion of the authority of the apostles and the church.

### Synthesis

If we summarize the above argument, we come to the following conclusions:
1. There is no account where the *ochlos* are qualitatively evaluated. There is no attempt to evaluate the *ochlos* in terms of an established

religion, ethical standard, or even in terms of a new paradigm (3:35 is a later addition).

2. The *ochlos* always gather around Jesus and follow him. If Jesus was a wandering missionary (*wanderprediger*), they were a wandering band, *wander-ochlos*. In 8:2, we see that they followed Jesus without eating for three days. This fact demonstrates that they did not have recognized social positions nor were they economically established.

3. When we consider the fact that the *ochlos* are contrasted with the ruling class of the time, and that Jesus was criticized for his association with them, it is clear that *ochlos* were a marginalized class.

4. There is one last thing to note about Jesus' attitude towards them. That is, Jesus accepted and advocated them without condition and received them just as they were, promising them a new future (The kingdom of God). Such actions were unacceptable to the Jewish establishment, Pharisees, and Sadducees of course, but also to those who were anti-Jerusalem: the Essenes and the followers of John the Baptizer. This begs the question, who are the *ochlos*?

## Those Who Followed Jesus

There is a diversity of people who followed Jesus and those whom Jesus referenced; however, there is a commonality that emerges when we examine them through the lens of social stratification: they are the *ochlos*. Mark 2:13–17 presents the *ochlos* as the model of the new paradigm.

Mark 2:13–17 can be divided into two parts: verses 13–14, and verses 15–17. The center of the first section is Jesus' saying, "follow me" (14b), and the second section focuses on the joyful meal (15a). Both, from what we can tell, are sourced in independently transmitted material. The link between the two sections seems to be Mark's editorial work. When we separate section 1 and section 2 we cannot tell with certainty that Levi was a tax collector, and the meaning of the dinner becomes vague. However, when we combine the two, the dinner becomes a joyful feast celebrating the fact that they were called to be disciples. Luke narrates the story of Levi in order to emphasis this point. The disciples who were not mentioned in section 1 appear in section 2 in verse 15. However, what is interesting is the fact that Levi, who is the main character when we examine the entire narrative, does not have any role in section 2; rather, the Pharisees' debate about Jesus' sharing of a meal with sinners becomes the central issue. When we examine Mark's editorial process with such questions, we gain a key to unlocking it.

There are many opinions about the interpretation of this pericope; however, there is no debate about whether verses 13 and 15c were edited by Mark. In verse 13b, Mark called those who followed Jesus and listened to his teaching "the whole crowd" and in verse 15a he says that many tax collectors and sinners sat at the meal with Jesus and his disciples. By saying that people like this followed Jesus in verse 15c, it not only includes tax collectors and sinners as a part of the "crowd," it highlights that such categories of people are the overwhelming majority. In Mark, among many who follow Jesus are the *ochlos* (2:2—2:4). Among them, the overwhelming number is the sick and the hungry (6:34–35; 8:1ff.). It also includes widows, who appear more often in the Gospel of Luke (12:41 and others) [than in Mark]. It is important to reveal how they were treated within the system; however, if we examine a few examples, it should give us the entire picture of the social situation.

As seen above, tax collectors and sinners as included in Mark's category of the *ochlos* are found in the Q source (Matt 11:19; Luke 15:1). In Matthew, the categorization of prostitutes is also mentioned with "tax collectors and sinners" (Matt. 21:32); this category is also a part of the designation of "sinners." Therefore, clarification of the social characteristics of "sinners" and "tax collectors," while the latter being a category that marks a particular profession, will provide a good outline of the *ochlos*.

### Sinners (*hamartolos*)

No one can deny the fact that Jesus was intimate with "sinners." The question is, in what sense were they "sinners"? In the tradition of Judaism, a sinner signifies someone who is a criminal before God. More specifically, it designates people who cannot fulfill the divine laws. However, after the introduction of the Pharisees, the purity laws, which were previously limited to the priests, were applied to daily life in Israel.

J. Jeremias points out two ways that "sinners" were construed in Jewish society (*Zöllener und Sünder*). The first is the publicly recognized criminal (offender against the law), and the other is the worker who worked socially unacceptable jobs as defined in those days. He differentiates these two and says that the latter were socially despised as "sinners" because of an "immoral conduct of life" or a "dishonorable occupation." Being labelled a "sinner" was because the occupation violated the Sabbath, either directly or indirectly, and not because of the occupation itself. Due to the nature of their occupation, they could not rest on the Sabbath (boatmen, shepherds, and prostitutes), or were persons who were ill-smelling or handled things defined as impure (tanners, coppersmiths, and butchers, for example). They were alienated from the congregation, and were barred from worship. Jeremias, while drawing attention to these marginalized groups, overlooked the most important fact: some were considered sinners because they were sick or too poor to carry out the requirements of the law.

The belief that sickness was a consequence of sin was a dominant tradition, of course, in the Old Testament (see Psalms 73, Job, etc.). But even in the New Testament, such a belief had not dissipated (John 9:1ff.). In particular, the lepers, hemophiliacs, and mentally ill were regarded as either unclean according to the laws or condemned by God. They were not criminals; they were either motivated by their circumstances or perceived as criminals by the larger society. Poverty also brought the same results since poverty prevented them from keeping the Sabbath or the requirements of the purity laws.

They are different from believers in ecclesial law. They are nevertheless labelled sinners by the law that upheld the system. In the Synoptic Gospels, Pharisees and experts in the law are introduced as symbolic enemies of Jesus. They were the ones who defined the parameter of who the "sinners" were. As we have already noted, the Pharisees applied the label "sinner" broadly, especially to those who infringed on the laws of purity, which greatly expanded the sphere of the law. This resulted in the social marginalization of those in lowly professions, the poor, and the sick. Therefore, both those defined according to their occupation and those criminalized were alienated by the system. They were considered "sinners" because they broke the law or could not adapt to the system of the law. From this perspective, religious sin and social exclusion are two sides of the same coin. Women during that time, especially widows and girls, were also held in contempt by the larger society. However, as a part of the minjung who came in contact with Jesus, they become central figures in the narrative.

## Tax Collectors

Tax collectors are not included in the comprehensive category of "sinners," but are in a parallel category to them. The usage of "tax collectors" and "sinners" is not only seen in Mark but also in the Q source (Matt. 11:19) and in the special source of Luke (15:1).

In Mark, the tax collector is only mentioned in 13:7. Mark regarded tax collectors as a part of the *ochlos* and included them within the category of sinners. Mark also points out that many such persons were among the followers of Jesus.

If Mark regarded the tax collectors as a part of the minjung of Jesus, then the *ochlos* cannot be defined purely in nationalistic or economic terms. This is because the tax collectors were agents of the Roman Empire and cannot be regarded as a part of the class of the poor. Mark was not reluctant to describe Levi, the tax collector, as someone who could afford a larger dinner party. However, we cannot universalize the characteristics of all tax collectors because among them, too, were the rich and poor. There was a class that received contracts from the Roman Empire to collect taxes and then exploited the people. There were also a number of others who worked under these people as employees. Among the category of employees, there were many who worked only part time. All of them, however, were treated as tax collectors in the society and were alienated. They were marginalized in society and we can see this by the fact that they were identified with Gentiles (Matt. 5:46–48; cf. 6:7, 32; 10:5). Matthew 11:19, which is famous for using the Q source ("the Son of Man came eating and drinking, and they say, 'Look, a glutton and a drunkard, a friend of tax-collectors and sinners!'"), coincides with Mark's account. In such a religious and political context, the fact that Jesus embraced the tax collectors is very meaningful, considering that the anti-Roman movement was engaged in guerrilla warfare, which received much fanfare from the people of the nation. It was also a time when people rose up in rebellion against the census that was being carried out for the purpose of tax collection. They made Galilee their stronghold, and made resisting the census the rally cry for the resistance. Even in the rabbinic tradition, they grouped the tax collectors with murderers and thieves.

Why did Mark include the tax collectors in the category of *ochlos*? First we have to see that it is because this was the tradition of Jesus, who associated with them. The uniqueness of this tradition is that, regardless of the reason, he embraced the socially ostracized and discriminated classes. It is clear when we examine economic practices that the tax collectors were excluded not only from the sense of nationalism, but also by the religious authorities, landowners, and merchants. The tax collectors were denied the rights to make offerings to the poor, one of religious rituals of Judaism, and their testimony was not permitted in the court of law.

## Jesus' Attitude Towards the Tax Collectors and Sinners

Mark, in response to the criticism, "Why did Jesus eat with tax collectors and sinners?" answers, "Those who are well have no need of a physician, but those who are sick; I have come to call not the righteous but sinners" (16b-17). This links the aforementioned *logia* together to include the tax collectors in the category of sinners, and declare that Jesus came to call sinners.

Here, we have to pay attention to the word, *kalesai* ("to call"). Luke's concept [of this word] "to call" is very different than Mark's. While he draws attention to them by introducing numerous "tax collectors" and "sinners," he always qualifies them by calling them individually the "repenting sinner" (Luke 15:7, 10, cf. 18). Such qualification not only is not present in Mark, but the word *kalesai* is used to denote disciples (cf. 1:20; 21:7b).

This basic posture of Jesus can be also applied to other groups: the sick, fishermen, women, and children. While there are some differences between these groups and tax collectors, there is also something in common: they were marginalized and discriminated against. If we take into account the fact that the Zealots were also included with tax collectors (Mark 3:18), Jesus' posture towards minjung was not limited to the politically oppressed. We are able to see a unique aspect of Jesus through his actions towards the sick he healed.

## The Sick

In Judaism, sickness, like other misfortunes, was considered a form of punishment resulting from sin (see J. Schniewind and others). There is also a trace of this belief in the Gospels (cf. John 9:1; Luke 13:2; Mark 2:5, etc.). This idea became more dominant when the Pharisees, who enlarged the purity laws, came to power. As a result, lepers, the mentally ill, and hemophiliacs were particularly ostracized. The sick appear many times in the Gospels; in many cases it seems that their family and neighbors had already deserted them. The reason why the sick were socially alienated is generally because of poverty, and because they also violated the purity laws, they were religiously alienated as well. The belief that their misfortunes were a result of sin justified the community's exclusion of them.

There are some who view Jesus, on the basis of Mark 2:5b, from such a premise. However, this is wrong. This verse is talking about faith, but it is not talking about the faith of the patient, but the faith of those who carried him. There are two other cases like this (5:35; 9:23). However, we should not ignore that this faith has nothing to do with the belief about redemption, but simply indicates simple trust. If this text gives any weight to the concept of redemption, it is the notion of the advent of the kingdom of God, meaning liberation from the old system and the ideas that underpin it (J. Schniewind shares this interpretation, and John 9:2–3 clearly supports it).

From this perspective, we need to take note of the characteristics of the healing stories. There are two things I want to point out: the first is that most of them [the sick] left their homes and were alienated as wanderers, and the second is that Jesus, after healing them, sent them back to their homes. The story of the healing of the leper in chapter 2, which focuses on healing, is especially a prototype. The characteristics of the story are as follows. First, the subject of the healing was a leper, who was among the most alienated people by purity laws. Second, he was isolated from his own home and places where others lived. Third, Jesus ordered the healed leper to show himself to the priests to prove that he was cured, and to offer sacrifices, which were commanded by Moses. Jesus did this in order for the leper to return to the very people who alienated him. This means the restoration of the right of survival. Except for cases where the sick were children (5:3ff; 7:24ff.), and where healing stories have a different purpose (5:35ff; 7:24ff.), Jesus says, "Go back home!" or "Go!" (2:11; 5:19; 5:34; 8:26; 10:52). In 5:19, the cured man wanted to follow Jesus; this verse actually serves to emphasize Jesus' command to "go home." This is different from [the aforementioned notion of] "to call." We cannot help but understand this as liberation as the meaning of restoration to the society.

## "Sayings" in Mark

"I came not to call the righteous, but sinners" (2:17b). This logion suggests Jesus' basic concept of love. In this verse, we cannot easily pass over the words "not" and "but." This cannot be interpreted as "not only . . . but also." Jesus did not love generally and did not preach philanthropy, but his love was particular, and the subjects of his love were the oppressed, the persecuted, and the weak. This fact becomes clear when we examine the Q source found in Luke's parable of the Lost Sheep (15:2ff.), where the heart of the shepherd, who leaves the ninety-nine sheep to go after one lost sheep, is well demonstrated.

As aforementioned, Mark assumes that the "sinners" are the *ochlos*. So it is evident that Jesus came to the world for the *ochlos*. It is necessary to clarify whether sinners were defined by Jesus or by society. Luke, in using

Mark, adds the phrase "who repents," which makes them sinners in the perspective of Jesus. The King James Version follows Luke's opinion in adding the phrase in Mark. However, the condition of repentance is the opinion of Luke and not Mark (e.g., the parables of the lost in Luke 15). This logion shares the same attitude towards the *ochlos* with Jesus. We, therefore, need to add "so-called" before the word "sinner." For Jesus, those labeled "sinners" by the rulers were victims who were robbed and oppressed.

"There is nothing outside a person that by going in can defile, but the things that come out are what defile" (7:15). These are the words of Jesus about the purification laws. This logion reflects the situational language related to the verses 1, 2, 5, 14b, and 15. However, verses 6–14, which contain material unrelated to the original verse, make the meaning less clear. Verse 15 reveals Jesus' negative opinion about the laws of purification generalized within the Pharisaic system. As mentioned before, the purification laws resulted in the alienation of many people. These words of Jesus are a proclamation rejecting the entire regulatory system. People argued whether this revolutionary proclamation was a development within Judaism or fell outside of the pale of orthodoxy; however, people failed to ask why Jesus had to do it. The context of these words is the Pharisees and scholars of law from Jerusalem denouncing Jesus' disciples, who eatwith their unclean hands. Eating with unwashed hands violates the purity laws. In those days, in Jewish society, if someone violated the laws of purity, then that someone was branded as *'am ha'aretz* (J. Jeremias). Through Mark's edited clause (7:14a), he confirms that the audience [of Jesus] was the *ochlos*. Mark confirmed that by demolishing the purity laws, which were a heavy burden to the *ochlos*, it was a declaration of liberation from that system. This verse (2:27), "Then he said to them, 'The sabbath was made for humankind, and not humankind for the sabbath'" is like a proclamation that liberates the oppressed people from the sabbath law. The oppressed people, if we borrow an expression from Matthew, are the "weary and heavy burdened" (Matt 11:28).

## Mark 9:37 and 10:13–15

The content of these two logia is the respect for children. In 9:37 children, Jesus, and God are identified together. Mark 10:14–15 declare that the kingdom of God belongs to children. Judaism was the religion of adults. That is because there was a duty to know and to keep the law. In this understanding, children and women were treated contemptuously. There is a controversy over the meaning of the words "like children." In the context where the disciples were quarrelling over who is "higher" or who is "first," Mark makes the children the symbol of lowliness (9:37). Mark 10:14–15 are the same because these are the words Jesus speaks in response to the disciples' contempt for children. Luke adds a clause to Mark, "for the least among all of you is the greatest" (9:48). By adding this clause, he makes clear that the symbol of the socially disdained people is the children. In fact, the children stood in common with *mikroi* ("minority").

Bultmann considers Luke 17:1–2 to be the original source that reflects the attitude of Jesus, which was later Christianized, identifying "little ones" with *ton pisteuonton* ("believers"; Matt 18:6–7). Kümmel identifies the "little ones" with the "poor in spirit" of Matthew 5:3. However, "little ones" does not point to an attitude of humility, but social position. As participants in the kingdom of God, it is proper that they are linked to those described in Luke: the poor, the weeping, and the hungry. There are similarities between Jesus' words about children recorded in Mark and his attitude towards the crowd—the *ochlos*.

## The Linguistic Meaning of *Ochlos*

We have noted above that Mark was the one who introduced the term *ochlos* in the New Testament. Mark used the term to identify the followers of Jesus and those whom Jesus particularly loved. We now have to ask about the linguistic tradition of this word. By asking this question, the meaning of *ochlos* as Mark understood it will become clearer. In this thesis, we will summarize the characteristics of the *ochlos* with Kittel's *Dictionary of the New Testament* as the central tool for analysis.

### *Laos* and *Ochlos*

*The Pre–New Testament Period*

The word *laos* is introduced and its meaning enlarged by the Septuagint in Jewish society. The Hebrew *am* is translated as *laos* two thousand times in the Septuagint. The most common meaning of the word is the "national people" in today's parlance. This means they belonged to the community of a political regime. The expression "Pharaoh's *laos*" is an example of this. And this kind of usage can be found in Homer, Pindar, and Herodotus. The Septuagint reflects the meaning "ethnic group," and it applies especially to Israelites. When *am* indicates Israelites, it is translated into the Greek word *laos*; however, when it indicates non-Israelites, it is translated as *ethnos*. Especially when *am* is used for "God's people," it is translated as *laos*. Another characteristic usage of the Septuagint is that *laoi*, plural of *laos*, is used only 140 times, and it has the same meaning as *ochlos*. This fact is very important, considering that *laos* in the Septuagint has no characteristics of the lower class.

This kind of tradition is also transmitted in the rabbinic documents. In rabbinic documents, *laos* is sometimes used when indicating non-Israelites, but the added clause, "offended the law," differentiates them from the Israelites. In the epigraphic material from the Jewish diaspora, there are also many examples where Israel is designated with the simple word *laos*. Compared with this, *ochlos* is used only sixty times [in the Septuagint] (see H. Bietenhard). There is no usage of the word *ochlos* in the ancient Old Testament documents; but only in the documents from later periods we find its usage. *Ochlos* is the translation of Hebrew, *hamon*, which means minjung. The common meaning of all these usages is "the crowd."

In this usage, there is no meaning of "group" or "member of the group." For example, expressions such as "crowd of Israelites" (*ochlos laou*) or "crowd of foreigners" (*ochloi ethnou*) represent this quality vividly. This possessive case does not represent possession. After Pindar, the term *ochlos* appears in Greek documents referring to a confused and unorganized majority or to ordinary soldiers in a combat unit, rather than a unified and organized group.

What needs to be noted is that these anonymous people are contrasted with the ruling class, and when we consider that *ochlos* is used to indicate an ignorant and burdensome crowd, it suggests many things. The Septuagint accepts this Greek meaning in its general usage: "the mass." The meaning of the word changes with the adjective clauses used. It can mean "insurgents," "mercenaries," or simply "the majority," who have no uniqueness. Sometimes it can designate children or a crowd of women. It is no different in the rabbinic documents. Mark, on the other hand, calls Jesus' minjung the *ochlos*.

*Usages in the New Testament*

The two terms *laos* and *ochlos* are interchangeable in the Septuagint. *Laos* is used 141 times, and *ochlos* is used 174 times. In Luke alone, *laos* is used eighty-four times (H. Bietenhard), which means Luke uses this term intentionally. Then, if we focus on Luke's usage of *laos*, the meaning of the word will become more clear. Here, I will point out some unique features about Luke's usage. First, due to Mark's influence, Luke used *laos* more extensively than *ochlos*; however, the usage and the meanings are interchangeable. Second, Luke sometimes applied *laos* to the Israelites to distinguish them from other ethnic groups (Luke 19:47; 22:66; Acts 4:8; 23:5, etc.). This kind of usage of *laos* is the influence of the Septuagint. Related to this, it is worth noting that Jews who persecuted Christians are also called *ochlos* or *ochloi*. Third, in Luke, there are some examples where *laos* is contrasted with those in authority, which corresponds to Mark's usage of the term *ochlos*. However, examples such as priests or scribes of the people (*hoi archriereiskai Grammateis ton laou*) or elders of the people (*Hoi Presbuteroi tou laou*) regarded *laos* (the people) as the same group as the ruling class. Mark exclusively uses *ochlos* due to the nature of the followers of Jesus. One thing that is clear is that Mark's *ochlos* has nothing to do with the Jews or the ruling authorities.

### *Ochlos* and '*Am Ha'aretz*

'*Am ha'aretz* is not used throughout the Old Testament, but was only used in the beginning of the first century. Before the Israelites were taken into exile, this term designated the Jewish upper class, landowners, and aristocrats. However, the meaning of this word changed during the exilic period. Once the leading members of the society were taken into exile, the ownership of the land passed to the common people, including the Samaritans, who were left behind. They are known as '*am ha'aretz*. This term already took on a negative connotation (E. Würthwein) both in nationalistic and religious senses (R. Meyer). However, from the time of Ezra until the time of Jesus, it becomes a negative sociological term designating a class of people who were uneducated and ignorant of the law. This corresponds with the period when rabbinic Judaism was being established, which systematized the law and set up the social and religious system. If '*am ha'aretz* has come to be defined in such a way, then it refers to the despised, alienated, poor, and weak of Jesus' time. It shows that rabbinic Judaism excluded them. The Jews were banned from marrying a daughter of '*am ha'aretz*. It became tradition not to eat with '*am ha'aretz*. The prohibitions concerning the '*am ha'aretz* in the *Babylonian Peashim* is important in understanding the *ochlos*. The following are the prohibitions:

- *'Am ha'aretz* cannot be witnesses.
- Their witness is not credible.
- No secret is to be revealed to them.
- They cannot be supporters of orphans.
- They cannot be in charge of offerings to the poor.
- Jews are not permitted to travel with them.

As we have observed, *'am ha'aretz* is used for a socially despised group, making them closer to *ochlos* than to *laos*. Geographically, Galilee symbolizes the *'am ha'aretz*. Expressions such as "Galilee of the Gentiles" and "Galilee," or "Galilee, you hate the law!" need further examination. However, for our purposes, we will simply point out that Mark's intention of choosing the word *ochlos* was to show that *ochlos* were the victims of that society.

## Summary

Mark deliberately uses *ochlos* rather than *laos* to indicate class characteristics of *ochlos*. Mark did not use a fixed, but a flexible definition of *ochlos*, which prevents it from becoming idealized. *Ochlos* is not a group that is seeking to establish its power base, but is a group that seeks to find their own existential living space. It means that they cannot be externally defined since they possess a coherent internal value system. The Pharisees sought to mobilize the *ochlos* for an ideological deployment of the law. However, the *ochlos* resisted such gestures. In their struggles we are able to find a meaningful story line. Jesus did not seek out the *ochlos* to mobilize them for his own purposes; instead they approached Jesus according to their own needs. In this sense, Jesus was passive, and related to them from a standpoint of equals rather than seeking to be their ruler, rabbi, or leader. Mark's *ochlos* is not the proletariat, nor are they "the people" in a democratic or national sense of the term. In a word, what Jesus communicated to the *ochlos* is the advent of the kingdom of God. Mark's summary of Jesus' message—the advent of the kingdom of God (1:15)—is very meaningful. Apocalyptical declarations such as "the Kingdom of God is near" and "the kingdom of God is coming!" mark the end of the old and the beginning of the new age, which gives the *ochlos* a new path and a new hope. Mark's Jesus was confident of the advent of the new world. Therefore, his relationship with and actions towards the *ochlos* reflect this confidence.

Part II: Selected Writings by Ahn Byung-Mu

The minjung wait for the new world because they are presently suffering. Jesus fought alongside with the minjung for the advent of the Kingdom of God. In this sense, he is the Messiah. This is without a doubt one aspect of Mark's concept of the Messiah.

# 5

# Minjung Theology from the Perspective of the Gospel of Mark

—Ahn Byung-Mu

This essay is based on the analysis of *ochlos* in the Gospel of Mark.[1] It aim is to present the theological tendencies of Mark, the book of the minjung, from political, economic, and social perspectives. I will intentionally raise issues or insights stemming from the context of minjung theology in Korea. While orthodox biblical methodologies (form criticism and redaction criticism) will be employed, I will maintain some distance from them at the same time.

## *Sitz im Leben* of Mark

It was the contribution of form critics that emphasized the importance of *Sitz im Leben* of the tradition in the formation of the Bible. They held the premise that *Sitz im Leben* is the community and not the individual. However, they were not interested in political, economic, and cultural situations that decide the character of community, but pursued the transmittal process of "religious ideology" that made facts abstract. Dichotomizing, for example, mind and body, personal and social, is pure speculation and does not bring us closer to real life.

Religious scholars especially view religion in isolation from other aspects of life. For example, Culmann believes that the redemption history flows

---

1. Ahn, "Jesus and Minjung in the Gospel of Mark."

uninterrupted within general history. To believe, however, that it [the gospel] can maintain its original quality is a big mistake. If this is not the case, then how could they only be interested in the process of religious transmission?[2] The context of the editor of Mark, which may have been an individual or a community, was that of a people wandering around like a band of beggars because, not only were they stripped of their country by the Roman Empire, but they also had been expelled from their country, land, and home. Between 66 CE, when Israel's resistance to Rome took place, and 70 CE, when Israel collapsed with the fall of Jerusalem, the tragedy of Israel was at its uttermost. The Jews who rose up in Judea, Edom, Berea, and Galilee engaged in a bloody war. Romans suppressed them in the order of Galilee, Berea, and Jerusalem. A record of eighteen thousand people massacred shows the horror of those days. Jerusalem was burned to the ground from the fierce war, which lasted for five months, and the Jerusalem temple, which was the center of Judea, was completely destroyed. Not only the mainland but also the diasporic Jews rose up, which resulted in a purge of Jews everywhere. The Jews scattered, Jerusalem became a restricted area, Jupiter's statue was built in the place of the Jerusalem temple, and the name of Jerusalem was changed to *Aelia Capitolina*, which has its etymological roots in Jupiter and was dedicated to the god of the same name. Israel and Judea were named *Palestina*, after the enemy of Israel, Philistia. The context of Mark[3] is post–70 CE, after all these tragedies had occurred.[4] In Mark, people whom Jesus called "sheep without a shepherd" (6:34), those who followed Jesus for three days hungry, represent the situation of Israel, including Christians.

The context of Mark is very different from that of Paul. After Bultmann said the Gospel is an expanded *kerygma*, Marxen and his disciple Suhl stressed that Mark's theology is identical with Paul's.[5] However, I think the fundamental reflections about Christianity, which became *kerygma* under Paul, are also reflected in Mark. The past issue of "Jesus or Paul?" has a fault in that it ignores the historical context. However, this is the right

2. Theissen, "Wanderradikalismus: Literatur-soziologische."

3. I am confident that Mark was written after the fall of Jerusalem. I corrected my view about this as written in *The Introduction of New Testament*, Daehan Gidokgyo Seohui. J. Gnilka also argues that it was written between 70 and 73 after all these tragedies happened in 70 CE. See Gnilka, *Das Evangelium nach Markus*.

4. On the Jewish Wars, refer to the writings of F. Josephus; and Foerster, "The History of Inter-Testament Period"; Baek, "The History of Israel"; Kingdon, "Who Were the Zealots and their Leaders in AD 66?"; Kreissig, *Die sozialen Zusammenhänge*.

5. Marxsen, *Mark the Evangelist*, 85–92, 98–101; Suhl, *Die Funktion der altestamentliche Zitate*, 180.

time to revaluate these scholars' discoveries about the differences between Jesus portrayed in Paul's letters and Jesus portrayed in the Gospels. If we try to shed the ideological theology of Germany by merging the "socially traditioned"[6] Jesus narrative (*Erzählung*)—which can be seen from the choice of reference, language, and content in Mark, with Paul's Christology—this attempted merger demonstrates ignorance of the historical character of both Markan and Pauline thought. When we compare both, we should not forget for a moment the separation that resulted from the Jewish War.

Paul's writings appeared between 50 and 60 CE, far earlier than the Jewish War. Already in the Judean area (in Jerusalem) there was persecution, and many people left; but, as it was a limited scene among the diasporic Jews, it was not a big event. Paul was a Jewish intellectual who lived in a Hellenistic culture and was a citizen of the Roman Empire. Although he was a Jew, he was a Pharisee who was politically, economically, and culturally in a different situation from those in Palestine.

Instead of establishing his historical context, I want to summarize four tasks that he confronted. First, his task was to emancipate Christianity, which was rooted in the tradition of the Jews, from Judaism, but not to break off from it. Second, his task was to indigenize Christianity, which was different from the Hellenistic culture. Third, his task was to establish the church, which would organize with new social groups ideologically and institutionally. Fourth, his task was to decide the missionary strategy.

The fourth task set its sights first on cities, next on Rome, and last on Spain, thought to be the end of the earth (Rom 15:20, 23). This was the idea that tried to use the route of conquest Rome had already used. When Rome conquered a city, it absorbed all surrounding areas of that city. Paul developed his strategy of mission from this. It may have been the best option for Roman intellectuals. However, it changed the agrarian culture of the Jesus tradition.

When we see the Corinthian church, we can easily guess that the third task was not simple. One problem was the complex makeup of church membership. The church was located in a Hellenistic area, but its members were mostly Jews. This caused a serious problem because of the exclusiveness of the Jews. Members who were too different from one another socially and economically caused the other problem. When we examine the Corinthian church, most of the members of the new community were political, economic, and cultural bottom-feeders. Paul points this out when he writes,

---

6. I have learned the term "social tradition" (of minjung) from Kim Yong-bok. See Kim, "Social Tradition of Minjung and Theology."

"not many of you were wise, influential, and of noble birth." We can call them minjung: they were politically, economically, and culturally alienated persons. Paul called them "the foolish things," "the weak things," "the despised things," and called them collectively, "the things that are not." It means a nameless class. There were, however, a very few middle-class persons (1 Cor 1:26–29).[7] However, we can guess that the minority was the cause of trouble when we see that Paul tried to persuade this class of people to become God's people. Among the Corinthian church members, there were problems concerning blood relationships and social class, so people claimed to belong to Apollo, Peter, Paul, or Jesus rather than to belong together as a unified church. Such group dynamics disrupted community life, and what was worse was that the middle-class people despised those of the lower class (1 Cor 11:17–32). In this situation, the theological position of Paul was very clear. He made clear that standing with the weak was the will of God.[8] But his aim was a "church for all," and not a "church for minjung" (Rom 10:12). He tried to overcome the class problem through the concept of "the body of Christ" (1 Cor 12:12–20), and he argued that "there is neither Jew nor Greek, slave nor free, male nor female" (Gal 3:28) rendering the problem a dead issue historically. His position became even clearer in Philemon (v. 16), and when he wrote, "from now on, we regard no one from a worldly point of view" (2 Cor 5:16), which meant that he would not evaluate people by their status, power, or money, arguing for equity of people, but [by doing it] he made this issue a dead issue historically. In this context, he preached about reconciliation (especially in 2 Cor 5:18ff.).

For the second task, Paul instituted a gnostic view that was sweeping through the Greek culture, and developed Christology and soteriology in light of it. What we should be skeptical of is that gnosticism was the intellectual worldview of those days.[9] Gnosticism was a speculative and humanistic worldview. And instituting such language resulted in Christianity not being minjung-like. Although Paul borrowed the worldview (language) of gnosticism, he tried to overcome it on a different level.[10] But we cannot deny that he targeted Greco-Roman intellectuals in his mission first, seeing his introduction of Greek, and not Hebrew,[11] such as in the use of "freedom"

7. On the membership of the Corinthian church, see Theissen, "Die Straken und Schwachen in Korinth."

8. Ahn, "Chosen Minjung."

9. Theissen, "The Weak and the Strong," 48, 50ff.

10. On this issue, Bultmann thoroughly established the argument. See Bultmann, *The Theology of the New Testament*, especially the chapter on Paul.

11. Bultmann, *Theologie*, 211, 332.

(1 Cor 9:19; 10:29; 2 Cor 3:17; Gal 2:4; 5:1), "truth" (Rom 3:7; 15:8; 2 Cor 7:14; 12:6, which actually means "truth" or "help" in 2:5, 14; 5:7), or "reason" (*nous*). This was done in an effort to indigenize; however, Paul's choice replaced the uniqueness of Jesus with ambiguous Christology, because the life of Jesus was not acceptable to the elites of the Hellenistic area. To accomplish the first task, Paul challenged Judaic law and at the same time offered "belief" (*pistis*) as the chain to link up to tradition. Reinterpreting the primitive religious attitude of people like Abraham in Israel's history as "belief," Paul instituted the language of the elites, which incorporated the concept of "freedom." Since Paul's aim was to conquer the world with the Christian gospel, he needed the elite language of the world.

It is right to think that Marxen understood the gospel of Paul as an active contemporary power, claiming that we have to understand Mark in the same way. However, understanding the Gospel of Mark is not limited by certain events since it was the account of acts of Jesus.[12] This difference is huge—like the difference between concept and real life. We should not forget that Mark was written after the Jewish War. We cannot think that Mark rejected "Pauline theology" on purpose, or that he was Paul's rival. However, it is not too far fetched to consider Mark from the presupposition that Mark thought "Paul's Jesus" could not console or give strength in real-life situations. There is an opinion that the author of this gospel was John Mark, who had an intimate relationship with Paul, which would then be very important evidence.

Urgent issues for Mark can be summarized in the following:[13] First, Mark reevaluated the Jewish tradition. The Jewish tradition was a source of life for the Jews, which was not limited to politics, but also religion and culture. With Judaism's loss of sovereignty, Mark was in a position to reevaluate Israel, the law system of rabbinic Judaism (which was formed through the Pharisees), and the notion of Jerusalem as the symbol of Judaism and David's royal authority—negative perceptions of ritual religion.

Second, Mark asked these questions: How can I explain Christianity to Jewish Christians who are wandering in anxiety after losing their country? How will they hear the explanation that the cross and the resurrection is an apocalyptic event, and now is the time of salvation? How does

---

12. Marxsen, *Mark the Evangelist*, 83. He said, "For him Jesus is the subject and the object of the gospel" (99). But Mark actually said that his entire writing is the gospel. J. Gnika, 42. Haenchen, *Der Weg Jesu*, 39.

13. This is my supposition. I conclude this from the premise that the target of Mark was people who wander without a home, and my clue about that comes from the biases in Mark.

the resurrection explain the contemporary situation, which is forty years removed from the resurrection? Does the doctrine that you are already saved make sense to them? Can the Jesus of the past, or the Christ who is now the object of worship, be the source of their power, for they had asked for a Christ who was now present and with them?

The third issue was regarding Jesus, who had already become idealized within the church, the already institutionalized church that required authority. When Paul could say, "But even if we or an angel from heaven should proclaim to you a gospel contrary to what we proclaimed to you, let the one be accursed! As we have said before, so now I repeat, if anyone proclaims to you a gospel contrary to what you received, let that one be accursed," (Gal. 1:8–9), it already highlighted a situation in which the church was losing mobility. Arguing for the superior authority of the apostles and the Jerusalem church was meaningless because the Jerusalem church was already gone and the leadership had collapsed, and it blocked the way to the present Christ.

Fourth, minjung Christians were constantly under threat of death. They were facing death unrelated to the resurrection, without hope for rescue or transcendental experience. In this situation, how can the doctrine of the cross that sets people free from past sins be appealing? In such a context, can we speak of sin? What is the relationship between the cross and the threat of death? Such questions cannot be answered to satisfy intellectual desire, but to satisfy the desire to live. I want to study Mark from this premise as a means to find answers to this desire.

## The Basis of Minjung Theology in Mark

There are various theories about the theological basis of Mark.[14] Kümmel affirmed that 1:14–15 is the theological basis of Mark. Mark can be divided into many stages.[15] He said that 1:14–15 is the summary of Mark. The

---

14. See Kümmel, *Einleitung in das Neue Testament*, 46–53: Gnilka, *Das Evangelium nach Markus* 17–35.

15. For example, Kümmel divided Mark into five sections: 1) Jesus in Galilee, 2) journeys inside and out of Galilee, 3) the road leading to Jerusalem, 4) Jesus in Jerusalem, and 5) the passion and resurrection. Gnilka divided Mark into seven: 1) start; 2) minjung and Jesus; 3) lessons and miracles of Jesus; 4) journeys without direction; 5) pressing towards the cross; 6) events in Jerusalem, 7) passion, death, and the vacant tomb. If we compress events geographically, both have the order that starts with 1) the public life, moves to 2) minjung and Jesus in Galilee, and ends with 3) the passion and execution in Jerusalem.

so-called *kerygma* theologians already pointed out this fact, but they were only interested in verse 15 and saw it as the summary of Jesus' preaching;[16] however, they rarely tried to interpret the meaning of verse 15 with verse 14. Klostermann presupposes that verse 14 is edited by Mark, and pointed out that the core of Jesus' preaching is characterized by the framework of time and space; yet, as language of mission in the early church, it only has a secondary meaning. Through the John the Baptizer Event, the only new emphasis of Jesus' kingdom-of-God sermons was that it was the "eternal truth."[17] Also, Gnilka said that even if this verse is historically accurate, the meaning is not about historicity (*Historie*) but about salvation.[18] If we apply this to form criticism, it is the form of *paradigma*. In these verses, verse 14 is the context (form). We should reject interpretations that ignore verse 14 since it plays an indirect role in explaining the nature of verse 15.

## Post-imprisonment of John the Baptizer (verse 14a)[19]

This speaks of the political situation. The context is Jesus declaring the coming of the kingdom of God. The fact that Jesus preached this in Galilee, which was under the ruling authority of Antipas, who arrested John the Baptizer, means that Jesus tried to speak some other truths at a time when the kingdom of God was in retreat, and the untimely concept (the justice of God) had become dominant. Jesus going to Galilee in Mark is very different from Matthew's account. In Matthew's account, although Jesus' home was Bethlehem, he went to Egypt because of Herod's persecution, and afterwards went to Galilee because of the information that Archaleus, the son of Herod, was still dangerous. However, Mark, completely opposite from Matthew, reports that Jesus went into dangerous areas during a dangerous period. If we define minjung as people who are controlled in relation to those who have power,[20] Jesus is also minjung in Mark. Mark includes Jesus in the reality of John's imprisonment, foreshadowing Jesus' fate. We can see that the Greek word *paradothenai* is the same word used

---

16. Bultmann, *Die Geschichte der Synoptische Traditions*, 124, 134; Bornkamm, *Jesus von Nazareth*, 58.

17. Klostermann, *Das Markusevangelium*.

18. Gnilka, *Das Evangelium nach Markus*, 65. Klostermann also commented on this and asked the question: "Is this for salvation or historical retrospection?" He also agrees to the former.

19. The word *paradothenai*, which has been translated "caught," can be translated as "execution." Refer to Klostermann.

20. See Suh Nam-Dong, "The Theology of Minjung."

in Jesus' announcement of his passion (9:311; 16:33; 14:41). Mark uses many pages to explain the reason that Antipas imprisoned John the Baptizer and the process of his execution. Some argue that there is no political motive in this narrative. Perhaps Mark directly transmitted materials from John the Baptizer's group.[21] What is important, however, is that this tradition has been intentionally edited to link Antipas's words, "John, whom I beheaded, has been raised," spoken after he heard of Jesus' activities.[22] This put Jesus in the same historical context with John the Baptizer, who was executed because of his relationship with the ruler.

In Mark, John the Baptizer was executed because of his rebuke of Antipas for his immoral behavior. Josephus on the other hand, wrote that John was executed as a Roman political prisoner; he was a false prophet who had the power to deceive the minjung like a demon (*daimonion*). This report is not contradictory to Mark's. Criticizing any person in power is a political act, no matter the reason. Mark also points out that he had the power to influence the minjung (11:32). Moreover, one thing that we should note is that the new Q source recorded people saying that Jesus had an evil spirit (see Matt 11:18), and we understand, just like Josephus, it means that he instigated the minjung. Therefore, John the Baptizer was executed as a political prisoner.[23]

The context at the beginning of Jesus' public life is similar to the political and cultural context of Mark. The *Sitz im Leben* of Mark is a time when Israel was "executed" by Rome, like the situation of Jesus after John the Baptizer was executed. However, the reason that Jesus went to Galilee was not only to flee but also because it was his place of life—his home (Refer to 1:9).[24] Mark's minjung did not choose the path of suffering, but were condemned to it (*paradidomi*). For the Greek intellectual class, the deified, unhistorical Jesus might be preferable to the fleshly Jesus; however, for the Galilean minjung, the Jesus who was politically persecuted might feel more intimate. This thesis will be repeated in this paper.

---

21. Bultmann, *Die Geschichte der Synoptischen Tradition*, 328ff. Bultmann says there are other traces of John the Baptizer's group in the Greek area. Dibelius and Haenchen see it as an anecdote about Herod. See Haechen, *Der Weg Jesu*, 241.

22. We can see an example of this tradition in 8:28.

23. Wellhausen, *Israelitische und Judische Geschichte*, 341; Meyer, *Ursprung und Anfange des Mormonen*, 2:406; Lohmeyer, *Urchistentums*, 59ff.; Bruce, *Zeitgeschichte des Neue Testaments*, 32.

24. Matthew knew Jesus' home as Bethlehem, so he could interpret Jesus' travel to Galilee as a flight. However, Mark saw it differently.

## Going to Galilee

Lohmeyer, a pioneer of redaction criticism, noticed the meaning of Galilee in Mark. Marxsen followed and developed his theory; however, he has made a fatal mistake that he intentionally ignored the political and social considerations and tried to study it from the perspective of church history, that is, only as a symbol of theology.[25] Lohmeyer and Marxen suggested that Galilee should be kerygmatically understood as Bultmann did: Jesus was resurrected for the purpose of the *kerygma*. However as Haenchen pointed out, as for Mark, this kind of thinking is unfamiliar.[26] Galilee is the context of Jesus and the context of the minjung. So it should be understood politically, economically, culturally, and socially. From this perspective, Jeon Cheon's criticism and political and social analysis about Galilee is the right move. It is also correct to put Jerusalem and Galilee in opposition; however, he did not get to the roots of the source of the opposition.

Minjung-like character of Galilee has a long history, and it became more vivid during the period of the New Testament and Jesus. In this thesis I intend to divide the political, cultural, and economic backgrounds of Galilee. Such an attempt has many difficulties because they are too tangled to be able to realistically separate. Nevertheless I will try to deal with the economic issue independently, and culture and politics will be dealt with in another section. Here, the word "culture" has a deep relationship with religious evaluation.

### The Political and Cultural Context of Galilee

The reason that people call Galilee the "land of the Gentiles"[27] is that foreigners occupied it for a long time. However, during the time of rabbinic Judaism the meaning takes on religious judgment and discrimination, established through political and cultural contexts.[28]

Galilee was conquered by Assyria in 733 BCE and was forcibly included in Maidu or Megiddo, and came under the direct rule of a foreign nation.

---

25. Both argued that Galilee is the symbol of the territory of Christianity (*Terra Christina*), but has less geographical meaning. So they said Galilee should be understood as the place of *kerygma*. Lohmeyer, *Galiläa und Jerusalem*, 26; Marxsen, *Mark the Evangelist*, 71, 74.

26. Haenchen, *Der Weg Jesu*, 460.

27. Isa 9:2; Matt 4:15–16.

28. The saying, "Galilee! You despised the Torah!" was a curse that Galileans shouted when they attacked Jerusalem.

Since then, the history of trouble was repeated under Babylon and Persia. There is a record during the Maccabean War of a Jewish minority from Galilee who was persecuted and rescued by Simon responding to their plea for help (1 Macc 5:14). After Aristobulus I (104–3BCE) enlarged his territory to Galilee and Edom, Galilee was liberated from six hundred years of the misery of being a "foreign land."[29] However, cities in Galilee had already become colonies of Greek culture by the time of Ptolemy and Seleucid.[30] During the Roman Empire, which inherited that legacy, the twenty-five year old, half-Jewish Herod became governor of that district. By the time of Jesus, people in Judea (Jerusalem) came to despise it again as a foreigner's land. Herod became a Rome-supported ruler of all of Palestine, and when Palestine was divided and ruled according to his will, Galilee became a colony of Antipas (4–39).[31] Galilee, therefore, remained a subject of contempt.

Rome exploited the regionalism between the two regions. A symbolic example of this was the use of different coins. In the Galilee district, they made use of the engraved coin of Caesar Dibelius. Galilee was famous for the minjung's uprisings. The minjung of Galilee had risen up already by the beginning of the first century; the reason was that the Roman governor Quirinius, who was stationed in Syria, took census to increase taxation. What was surprising was that this [the taxation] did not pertain to Galilee, only to Judea, but the fact is the minjung of Galilee fought fiercely with Galilee of Judea at the center. Some people believe that this was due to their pure faith;[32] however, I do not think such an explanation is sufficient. Hengel argued that they stood on the belief that they should reject all authority except for the rule of God, and their aim was social revolution. They were a typical band of proletarian guerillas.[33] They went to Jerusalem and killed the rulers, set Herod's palace and private loan documents on fire because of the belief that they could not accept any ruling authority except God's as the reason given by the authorities in Jerusalem; however, the anger over being marginalized by Jerusalem-centrism also played an important role.

The evidence that Galilee was despised as periphery by Judea (Jerusalem) can be found in the New Testament.[34] The reason for contempt can

---

29. There was no high priest who wielded power in Galilee.

30. Reicke, *Neutestamentliche Zeitgeschichte*, 52.

31. Antipas also devoted all his effort to make the cities of Galilee become Hellenistic. Sepphoris and Dibelius were symbols of that.

32. For example, they bled for removing the golden-eagle statue, which was on the Jerusalem church.

33. Hengel, *Judentum und Hellenismus*, 79, 87, 89, 91ff. 103:108:119ff. 133ff. 288.

34. John 1:46: "Can anything good come from there?"

be understood from political and religious history. It will become clear when we contrast it with Jerusalem and the Davidic Dynasty.

Jerusalem is the city of King David. He became the king of the people of Judah (2 Sam 2:4).[35] He ruled from Hebron, annexed northern Israel— that is the area of Canaan tribal alliance—through cunning and violence,[36] took the city of Jebusites by violence, and made it into the capital (2 Sam 5:6–9). He built a grand palace there and by putting the ark of the covenant in it, which was the symbol of Moses' covenant, he made the city the religious center of Israel. By the eighth century, it became the center of apocalyptic hope. Later apocalyptic literature links the end with David's kingdom and Jerusalem. The city came to be thought of as a godly city.[37] Prophets such as Nathan and Josiah, who towed the government line, connected Jerusalem with the descendants of David and soteriology, influencing the writings of the New Testament. In terms of the significance of Christology in the New Testament, the following are to be considered: 1) that Yahweh came under royal authority, 2) that Jerusalem became the city of the temple for Yahweh religion, 3) the ideological tool of the Davidic kingdom. However, we undercover different understandings of this when reading it with the conclusions drawn from the newest, sociologically critical Old Testament scholarship,[38] directly related to the understanding of the psychological background of Galilee. Recent studies of the Old Testament divide the Mosaic tradition from the Davidic tradition. The Mosaic tradition is based on Exodus, while the Davidic tradition is based on the royal authority of Jerusalem. Brueggemann characterizes these two traditions as follows:

The Royal Trajectory

1. It prioritizes unity

2. It prioritizes fluency (creation) and continuity (dynasty)

3. Its dominant pattern of understanding is cosmic and comprehensive

4. It has a tendency to respect and promote the rich city-dwellers

---

35. Judah did not join the alliance of tribes.

36. His invasion, threats, and tricks are famous. Refer to 2 Samuel 2–5.

37. Maass, "Jerusalem."

38. Mendenhall, "The Hebrew Conquest of Palestine"; Gottwald, *The Tribes of Yahweh*. Brueggeman said, "There are summarized traditions of the OT and sociology about ancient Israel, but there are many scholars who divide the Sinaic tradition and the Davidic traditions." Brueggemann, "The Trajectories in Old Testament Literature and the Sociology of Ancient Israel."

5. It gives priority to safety, so it has a tendency to be conservative

6. It focuses on the glory of God, his divinity

The Liberation Trajectory

1. It prioritizes the stories of liberation

2. It uses the language of war and discontinuity

3. Its dominant pattern of understanding is about historical characteristics

4. It has a tendency to respect and promote the poor

5. It gives priority to change so it has a tendency to be revolutionary

6. It focuses on the justice of God

These characteristics well summarize the features of Jerusalem. Jerusalem became a government patronized under David's kingdom. This was not only for the ruling powers, but also for the periphery as well. This was because they could not give up on the ideology that made Jerusalem a deified city and respect for the Jerusalem temple. The principle of guarding Jerusalem corresponded with the logic of "safety first," and all policies remained unchanged as a result. At the time of Jesus, the Jerusalem party was divided into many groups. Among them were the Hassidim, who participated in the Maccabean War, the Essenes, the Zealots, the John the Baptizer faction, the Jesus Movement belonging to the post-Jerusalem faction, while the priests, the Sadducees, and the Pharisees belonged to the conservative Jerusalem faction who respected the existing system. Although it was the Pharisees who raised the nationalistic movement earlier, it was now the Sanhedrin who had come to power.[39] They replaced rabbinic Judaism and became the ideological leaders of Jerusalem. They collided with Jesus.

Galilee is a part of the tribal alliance of Zebulun-Nephtali, as cited in Matthew. It means that this area was different from Judea, the successor of David's kingdom. The differences are the same as those between Bruggemann's "Trajectory A" and "Trajectory B." Galilee was the symbol of a politically and culturally alienated area during the time of Jesus.

---

39. There is an argument that Pharisees are minjung-like, but this is an error rooted in ideology rather than historicity. Although the Pharisees raised the movement of the practice of law, they were not concerned about minjung. During the Hasmonean period, the ruling authorities persecuted the Pharisees; however, the Pharisees became powerful after the death of Jannäus, who had persecuted the Pharisees for six years. During the period of Herod, they were again persecuted; during Jesus' time, they became the ruling class and executed their power through the Sanhedrin.

This area became the center of an anti-Roman movement and the center of political and military resistance. It is therefore reasonable that it became the target of Roman and Herodian purges. To the people of Judea, "Galilee" came to be equated with "resistance," and Galilee became an area of dread to the people of Jerusalem.[40]

This was because they had connected Galilee with the Zealots.[41] This was an expression by the people of Jerusalem towards the Herodians. We can see this very clearly from the fact that they called Herodians "thieves." They had their reasons. This was because the Herodians detested the Jews of Jerusalem and were tools of Roman oppression.[42] They tried to purge Jerusalem and made the high priest their enemy. As a result, when the Zealots attacked Jerusalem, Menahem set fire to Agrippa's castle and killed Annaniah, the high priest, while Johannes brutally removed the Sanhedrin and the noble families. According to Josephus, there are not many records of the fights between Rome and the Zealots. There are, however, many accounts of purges of the Sanhedrin and the high priest.[43] This shows that Galilee was alienated politically and culturally from Jerusalem, and their misery found a violent outlet.[44]

## The Economic Situation of Galilee

The most realistic problem is, again, the economy. Josephus defined the insurgents in Galilee as "thieves," and he wrote that many people joined the band of thieves for their own safety. There were many thieves all over Galilee who resisted bravely. We need to examine what we mean by "their own safety." The first thing that we need to examine is the fact that many women joined. If the entire family had joined, then we can assume that they were under great financial duress and could not maintain a normal life. Galilee is known as the most fertile ground in Palestine. Palestine was originally an agricultural society,[45] and Judea relied on the output of Galileee because

---

40. Hengel, *Judentum und Hellenismus*, 59–60; Kreissig, *Die sozialen Zusammenhänge*, 124.
41. Hengel, *Judentum und Hellenismus*, 54.
42. Ibid., 88.
43. Kreissig, *Die sozialen Zusammenhänge*, 134.
44. The word *zealot* will be revisited later in this chapter.
45. Kreissig, *Die sozialen Zusammenhänge*, 17ff.

Judea's land was barren and its climate was bad.[46] For this reason, many people came to Galilee, and Galilee was the most heavily populated area.[47]

However, we should take note that Galileans were mostly tenant farmers and day laborers.[48] I do not have all the materials to determine exact details [of this phenomenon], however I think there are several reasons for this. According to Herz,[49] Roman policy towards their colonies followed Ptolemy's policy towards Egypt. It appointed military bases and occupied the surrounding territories as private land and exploited it. These lands were managed by an administration that mobilized peasant labor by force. Second, it gave feudality to a king or a privileged class as the means of control. The temple lands belonged to the second category. This system enforced double cultivation by the peasants. Rome increased taxation of Judea in the amount of six hundred talents.[50] In addition, they required poll taxes for men, women, and slaves, an income tax, a stock tax, and a land tax. Herod, who wielded puppet power under the Roman Empire, earned over one thousand talents per year.[51] However, this is not exact because the figure is estimated from his inheritance distributed to his descendants. According to Josephus, Archelaus inherited 400, Antipas 200, Philippus a hundred, and Salome five hundredtalents. However in other records it is recorded that Archelaus inherited six hundred talents.[52] Maybe it was covered by the income from the farms. It can be guessed from the records that when Archelaus was banished from being a feudal lord, Augustus took Archelaus's territory and management.[53]

In addition, the chief accountant's records show the entire village of Arus as a part of Herod's private holdings.[54] There is a record that Augustus gave the entire Jamain territory to his wife as a gift.[55] This record was not limited to Galilee. Though it is difficult to prove by statistical data, it proves how severe the tyranny was and why the Galilean peasants were

46. Jeremias, *Jerusalem zur Zeit Jesu*, 43, Foakes-Jackson and Lake, *Prolegomena I: The Jewish, Gentile and Christian Backgrounds*, 1.

47. Even in a small town there were fifteen thousand people; see Jeremias, *Jerusalem zur Zeit Jesu*, 52.

48. Baron, *A Social and Religious History of the Jews*, 1:278.

49. Herz, *Grossgrundbesitz in Palastina im Zeitalter Jesu*, 98ff.

50. Schürer, *Geschichte des Judischen Volkes im Zeitalter Jesuchristi*, 1–13.

51. Jeremias, *Jerusalem zur Zeit Jesu*, 10ff.

52. Otto, *Herodes*.

53. Josephus, *Ant.* 18.2; Hengel, *Judentum und Hellenismus*, 341.

54. Josephus, *Ant.*, 17.10.0.

55. Ibid., 18.13.1.

so poor. The normal wages for one day's labor were one denarius.[56] This was the minimum cost of living. One denarius is one-thousandth of one talent. Thus, one talent is the daily living wage for ten thousand families. This shows the gap of tyranny between the ruler and the subjects. Palestinian peasants of 1 BCE were almost tenant farmers and their survival was severely threatened.[57] They were in charge of production, but found living difficult.[58] One person said that in Palestine, especially in Galilee, there were many hired peasants.[59] Josephus said that the tenant farmers were in extreme poverty during the Herodean period.[60] What was the reason for this? Hengel said that it was because of the exploitation, and Baron demonstrated the exploitation in Galilee.[61] The problem was that the peasants did not own land. Economically, farming villages in Galilee were actually satellite towns. The land owners sent "farm bailiffs" and managed the farms.[62]

Then what class did they belong to? Not only the politicians, but also the priests were part of the landowning class.[63] They were pro-Rome, which was politically necessary to maintain the rights to the temple tax and tithes. Harsome, the father of the famous Rabbi Eleazar, had a thousand cities and boats. It is said that while he was patrolling his property, he came across a group of slaves, whom he forced to work on his land.[64] Eka Rabbati said that four rabbis in one town accumulated so much wealth that the entire population of the town could live on it for ten years. Rabbi Eleazar offered thirteen thousand cows per year as his tithe. These distinct examples cannot replace statistical data, but it is clear that there were business magnates in Jerusalem and maybe there were more landowners in Galilee than in Judea. This is a correct assessment since the food supply of infertile Judea was dependent on Galilee, as I have mentioned before.[65]

56. Billerbeck, *Kommentar zum Neuen Testament*, 1:831.

57. Kreissig, *Die sozialen Zusammenhänge*, 27.

58. Dalman, *Arbeit und sitte in Palästina*, 2:197.

59. Hengel, *Judentum und Hellenismus*, 329ff; Baron, *A Social and Religious History of the Jews*, 1:278.

60. Josephus, *Ant.* 17.307.

61. Hengel, *Judentum und Hellenismus*, 431; Baron, *A Social and Religious History of the Jews*, 1:278.

62. Lohmeyer, *Soziale Fragen in Urchristentum*, 55ff.

63. Politicians and priests were important privileged classes. These two have something in common: they were both landowners. This is noteworthy. Hengel, *Judentum und Hellenismus*, 89, 219; Kreissig, *Die sozialen Zusammenhänge*, 99.

64. Kreissig, *Die sozialen Zusammenhänge*, 97.

65. Jeremias, *Jerusalem zur Zeit Jesu*, 52.

This is supported by the fact that the Zealots who first formed in Galilee attacked the Jerusalem city hall and burned all ownership documents and records of debts.[66] Zealots, whose members were bankrupted peasants, targeted the ruling class in Jerusalem before Rome. Galilee was the symbol of the oppressed, alienated, and exploited. It was a place of the minjung, the politically, economically, and culturally alienated class.[67]

### Proclamation of the Coming Kingdom of God

Waiting for the kingdom of God occurs within places of suffering. Daniel is thought to be the quintessential apocalyptic literature. It was written during the period of Selucid Antiochus IV (Epiphanes) (175–64 BCE). This apocalyptic literature was the primary genre until the second century CE, the worst period of Israel's history. During this period [many apocalyptic works were produced]: the *Book of Enoch*,[68] the *Ascension of Moses*, the *Book of Ezra 4*, the *Book of Baruch*, and Revelation, the only New Testament book to be included. Scholars put forth many theories with some good results; however, what cannot be overlooked is that they study the minjung movement, not in the context of the fight for survival, but as a religious phenomenon. It is easy to lose focus when analyzing expressions and ideas of apocalyptic literature scrupulously. It is important to understand that the literature consists of various expressions of the sorrow of an oppressed people. They desire miracles, judges, and a new reign of God, stemming from feelings of anger and revenge, lamentation of their own limitations, hostility towards the world, and also a hope for the world. So it is not worthy of study without the presupposition that it is the cry of the minjung. Some people are content to recite the genealogies of literature and forget the *Sitz im Leben* of the writers. They regard the minjung's wretched cries as mere aesthetics. So we should avoid studying apocalyptic literature from the perspective of the academy. Apocalyptic literatures have many internal conflicts and contradictions, and borrow

---

66. Klausner, *Jesus of Nazareth*, 252–57; Kriessig, *Die sozialen Zusammenhänge des Judäischen Krieges*, 113.

67. Suh Nam Dong, "The Theology of Minjung," 82; Kim Yong-bok, "Social Biography of Minjung and Theology," 61. Suh and Kim defined minjung as those who are politically, economically, and culturally oppressed. Kim Yong-bok especially emphasized the difference between the proletariat and minjung. However, it does not mean the oppressed class in industrial society is ruled out.

68. The book of Enoch has Ethiopian and Slavic versions. The former is a part of the canon of the Ethiopian Church. Textually, it is a work from the Roman period.

expressions from other sources, which are not necessarily Jewish or Gentile. They simply wanted to survive. Their enemies dominated their reality, and they possessed no power to overcome their situation. Therefore, they looked to their belief in God, who created two worlds to save them (the *Ethiopian Book of Enoch*). History had changed and the old history was coming to a close; they had arrived at the conviction that God would establish an eternal kingdom which would be in contrast to the earthly one (Daniel). However, it was difficult to endure the present hardship so they came to count the days. For example, Daniel counts the days of oppression as three and a half years. In Babylon, the number seven was thought to be a divine number, so he wanted to express the belief that they would suffer until death by numbering [the days of tribulation] half of seven as a way to console. During this period of tribulation, the concept of the Kingdom of God [the direct rule of God] became increasingly otherworldly. Eventually, the hope for a revolution became the vision of the millennium.[69] Before God rules directly, the "son of man" will have all authority and bring an end to all oppression (Daniel). This "son of man" will expel kings and people of power, and break the teeth of evil people (The Ethiopian *Book of Enoch*). Also, he will give freedom to the righteous, and lead them to the festival of the Messiah, and rule over them (*The Ethiopian Book of Enoch* 62:9–10; 69:26–29). These are the writings of minjung, who, at a dead end, gave this writing universal trajectory rather than detailed characteristics. This is why it is important. They had a long history of suffering from Epiphanes, the Maccabean War, the colonization by Rome, the tyranny of Herod's family, and the cruelty of governors. Their last cry and appeal was for the new world where God would rule directly over them. Nevertheless, we should seriously examine the faction in Jerusalem who ruled over southern Judeans, who came back from imprisonment after the Northern Kingdom was destroyed. I will divide them into the Jerusalem faction and anti-Jerusalem faction for convenience. The Jerusalem faction is comprised of priests, members of the Sanhedrin, and Pharisees; the anti-Jerusalem faction is represented by Essenes, John the Baptizer's faction, Zealots, and Jesus. The leader of the anti-Jerusalem faction is Chasidim, who had played a critical role during the Maccabean War and became anti-Jerusalem because of the corruption of the Hasmonean Dynasty, established in the Maccabean War. What we should note is that the Jerusalem faction was always used by the government, and it had a strong

---

69. Suh Nam-dong thinks highly of the millennium, but it appeared only twenty times in Revelation. In the book of *Barnabas*, he commented about the millennium.

tendency to reject the advent of the Kingdom of God.⁷⁰ This is easily understandable because it was the privileged class within the existing system. Its members were guardians of the old system and therefore could not help but reject any revolutionary ideas.

Apocalyptic literatures have a functional relationship with suffering, and the privileged class cannot help but deny apocalyptic literatures, regardless of the established dogma. By this, it is clear which class waited for the coming of the kingdom of God. Jewish society's apocalyptic belief was directly related to the poor and the oppressed, whether it was linked to the Messiah or not.⁷¹ Brandon said that the day laborers especially had a strong hope for the Messiah.⁷² The editor of Luke connected the advent of the Messiah and the liberation of the poor and the oppressed (4:18; Isa 61:1–2). "Lift up the stone and you will find me. Break the trees and I will be there" in P. Oxy. 12.6–9 alluded to the relationship between the workers and the Messiah.⁷³ In the Qur'an, there is a prophecy that says, "The poor judged justice so they laughed and disdained the king and men of power."⁷⁴ What is important is that when crisis came to Hellenism, apocalyptic ideas prevailed. The reason was because survival had been threatened and, at the same time, the belief in the end of the old order and the coming of a new world was favorable for them. Baron, especially, had proved that this tendency was found in the lower class.⁷⁵ In the Zealots, particularly, was

---

70. Goppelt, *Christentum und Judentum in ersten und zweiten Jahrhundert*, 64. The high priests denied apocalyptic or messianic beliefs because these threatened their survival. Baron presupposes that those who waited for the Messiah were the lower class people (Baron, *A Social and Religious History of the Jews,*, 2:35) and arrived at the same conclusion as Goppelt. Stauffer, *Jerusalem und Rom*, 103. Pharisees, on the other hand, were a part of the ideological genealogy of Chasidim, which meant that they embraced the apocalyptic literature. Gradually, they moved away from it because of their position as the ruling class in Jerusalem. Hengel agreed that in rabbinic texts, there is nothing about the hope for the Messiah. He conjectures that this was because in 2–3 BCE, when the rabbinic text was completed, it was a difficult period to broach such topics. The presupposition that the Pharisees also had hopes for the second coming was vivid among the Essenes, and the early church was nothing more than their hope. Pharisees believed that the movement in Galilee was heretical, and they denounced Galilee Judea's criticism of the Pharisees for granting divorce for people in power, which exposes their attitude towards the authorities (see Hengel, *Judentum und Hellenismus*, 585).

71. Kreissig, *Die sozialen Zusammenhänge*, 104ff.

72. Brandon, 156.

73. IQSb v. 21.

74. Baron, *A Social and Religious History of the Jews*, 2:35.

75. Hengel, *Judentum und Hellenismus*, 42ff.

the movement of minjung who desired for the Kingdom of God or the advent of the Messiah to rule over them.

It is a movement that rose up after the tyranny of Epiphanes, and was affected by Chasidim, who joined the Maccabean revolt. It would be worthwhile to study their characteristics. The reason that Josephus called the Herodians a band of thieves[76] was not just because they had turned and flattered Rome, but because it was true. He wrote about a "big group of thieves [that] attacked and killed the most powerful people. Ostensibly they said they did it to regain their country but in fact the reason was their own selfish interests."[77] And also it is written that, "demanding freedom was just a mask, and they tried to conceal their brutality and selfish interests. This is proved by their behavior."[78] We do not have to ignore these words of Josephus. They *did* fight for independence and demanded freedom; however, their poverty led them to plunder. There were many bands of thieves and there was very little difference from the Zealots. There were also many other bands of robbers who pretended to be freedom fighters. What becomes clear from Josephus's comments is that people were so poor that they could not live normally. During the Joseon Dynasty when the authorities exerted their power, many poor peasants became thieves, leading to the formation of several famous bands such as *Seo-gang Dan, Pesa-gun Dan*, and *Yu Dan*. They did indeed steal. The bigger robberies among them were the Hong Gyung-rae Revolt and the Jin Ju Revolt. The 1894 Peasant Uprising was made possible because of these revolts. These groups were patriots on the one hand and thieves on the other. The Zealot movement in Galilee was started and developed in a similar way. Poverty was the direct cause, and desire for a new world was their strength. They were a mostly non-landowning class, such as peasants who were expelled farmers from landowner's houses, runaway soldiers, slaves, and shepherds.[79] Among them were small farmers who were the majority, and [their numbers] increased daily.[80] They came together in the forests of Galilee and became an army in the middle of the first century.[81] They were mostly financially oppressed persons, which led

---

76. Josephus, *Ant.*, 18, 7.

77. *Jewish War* 7.256–64.

78. Hengel, *Judentum und Hellenismus*, 335.

79. Josephus, *Ant.* 18.274; 20.256; Hengel, *Judentum und Hellenismus*, 34.

80. Klausner, *Jesus of Nazareth*, 252ff., 259: Kreissig, *Die sozialen Zusammenhänge*, 113.

81. Hengel, *Judentum und Hellenismus*, 26.

them to attack the Roman revenue offices[82] and rape the vineyards of King Herod. Many of them were killed by the landowners or were arrested by the government.[83] The Zealots were made up of these kinds of persons. They had an ardent hope for the kingdom of God or the Messiah, and these [acts] were the cry of their lives and the conviction that a new world would be on their side. Simon, a slave, and Anthronges, a shepherd, were representative leaders of the revolts. They wore crowns and pretended to be kings, but the minjung followed them without much resistance.[84] Judas the Galilean was held in high esteem as the messiah.[85] Many people followed his son, Menahem, who entered Jerusalem and acted out messianic rituals.[86] For minjung, they have no presupposition that the Messiah should be born to royalty. Nor did they expect him to have supernatural powers. Persons who sought to gather people through such promises failed,[87] rather it was normal people who were held in high esteem as the Messiah. This means that the minjung's perspective of the Messiah is different from the concept defined by theologians. I will deal with this topic again later; for now, what is clear is that Zealot-centered Galilee was where people longed for a new world, and this was the same place that Jesus preached that the kingdom of God was coming. This was the best way out of suffering for the minjung of Galilee and at the same time it was a mark of the influence of Rome-Herod-Jerusalem.

## Acts of the Minjung

Mark 1:14–15 is considered the economic and cultural background and the cornerstone of Mark's minjung theology. To examine the entire Gospel of Mark through this lens is the presupposition of this thesis. There is another presupposition: that Jesus as described in Mark, his acts and his destiny, is not just a personal biography, but is a "social biography." Whether he is called Jesus, the Son of God, Messiah, or Son of Man, it does not refer to the personal life of Jesus of Nazareth but towards his sociability.

82. Ibid., 38; Ziegler, *Die Konigsgleichnisse*, 93.

83. Josephus, *Jewish War* 5.27–28; *Ant.* 17.273ff. Farmer, "Judas, Simon and Athronges," 147–55.

84. Josephus, *Ant.* 17.271ff.; Stauffer, *Die Botschaft Jesu*, 112.

85. Josephus, *Jewish War* 2.434.

86. Theudar claimed that he could divide the Jordan River (Josephus, *Ant* 20.97ff). Josnas Sopherot said he would run to Jericho by a miracle (*Ant.* 20.169–72), and Dositheus of Samaria said he would discover articles needed for the Gerizim Church by a miracle (Kriessig, 109); however, minjung did not follow him.

87. About this analysis, see Tödt, *Der Menschensohn*, 13–53.

Bultmann considered Jesus as one existence, and he argued for existential solidarity with Jesus and us. It means that he adhered to the perspective of existentialism. However, in this essay, I want to consider him socially so that we can collectively experience him historically.

Jesus called himself the "son of man." The "son of man" is sometimes in the first person and sometimes in the third, with different corresponding meanings. I do not want to treat the matter here,[88] but only seek to find out the possibility of sociability. It is a common view that "son of man" in the New Testament is based on Daniel chapter 7 verses 13–14. However, whether or not he is the same person as in Daniel is not important. What is important is whether or not it can be interpreted socially. Daniel 2:44–45 and 7:13–14, and verse 27 are related to each other, and the phrase "one who like a human being" is identified with holy people. In 7:13–14 it says, "one who like a human being . . . was given dominion and glory and kingship, that all peoples, nations, and languages should serve him," and in verse 27 these things will belong to people of the most high. The Hebrew, "one who likes a human being" can be interpreted collectively (*Korporative Interpretation*).[89] North considers this a collective concept and he said that "people" does not mean Israel but "heavenly people." Zimmrli holds the same position, but he adds that "people" refer to the "people of God in this world."[90] Hengel states that "eternal Kingdom" in Daniel chapter 7 refers to the "sovereignty of people of God." F. Hahn also stated that Daniel 7:13–14 and 27 can be interpreted collectively in relation to Psalm 110:1,[91] while this interpretation is impossible in the New Testament. E. Schweizer also presupposed that the "son of God" was a collective concept that referred to the people of Israel, and he agreed that the "son of man" is also a collective concept,[92] holding the same opinion as Hahn that in the New Testament, it refers just to a personal Jesus. However, he agrees that the way of Jesus becomes the way of the community; however, the fact that he denies the collective interpretation of the New Testament does not mean that he contracts the fact that the Son of God at the end of the world has a deep relationship with his people. He recites the supporting materials.[93] It is difficult to agree with Hahn when he says that the "son of God" is

---

88. Porteous, *Das Danielbuch*, 23, 38ff., 94.
89. Noth, "Heiligen des Hochsten," 274 ff.
90. Zimmerli, *Grundriss der alttestamentlichen Theologie*, 300.
91. Ibid., 17.
92. Schweizer, *Erniedrigung und Erhohung bei Jesus*, 89.
93. Ibid., 90.

understood collectively in Semitic languages. He agreed that Mark 8:38b, 13, and 2cf rely on Daniel 7:13–14,[94] but he tried to avoid that interpretation. Is this not a problem of a Westerner who is locked into the concept of individualism, [and] possessed by the concept of "personality?"[95] Hanh relates Mark 16:45 with Daniel 7 and the "son of man" in Daniel indicate the suffering of the former people. He said that the "son of man" will represent people and suffering instead of them.[96] To arrive at such a conclusion, would not it be more reasonable and realistic to see "son of man" collectively? What is the meaning for a person from outside to intervene and suffer in the minjung's place? Why on earth are people caught up in a religious stereotype that someone of another level must suffer instead of the people?[97] C. H. Dodd argues that the "son of man" is originally a collective concept but it is consigned to Jesus. So he says we should relate the

---

94. Ibid.

95. In Hebrew perspective there is no clear separation between one person and the group. For example, is the Suffering Servant of Isaiah 53 a person or the whole people of Israel? Westerners have discussed this over and over again; I do not think Isaiah 53 itself suggests this argument, but it takes effort to interpret it as referring to a personal Jesus. Does not Yahweh indicate sociability? God is not personal but the subject of the worship of a group; he is a liberator of the group, so there is no doubt that this is a collective concept. Westerners have argued for "personality" since the Enlightenment; they cannot escape from the concept of personality, but what on earth is personality? In Hebrew or Asian perspectives, as not brainwashed by the West, there is no concept of personality. Lee Seung-hoon defined the meaning of personality in the Korean dictionary as "dignity of person, unity of personal intelligence, soul, will, and physical aspect," and religiously it is defined as "dignity of God, who has a personality." However, is this kind of definition Oriental? Do not Orientals figure things out comprehensively? When we define wise men or saints, are these not different expressions of comprehensive understanding? Someone argues that the distinction from nature is difficult because there is no concept of personality; is this not a great proof that Orientals figure things out comprehensively? Without this basic understanding, the concept of *In Nae Cheon* (the theme of 1894 Peasants' Uprising, which means person is heaven) could not have developed. In this case, *In* ("person") is not an individual but a group. I want to ask whether the basic concept of Buddhism holds the same ideas or not. Is Buddha Siddhartha? When the term is used cosmologically, then it is universal being, and when it is used sociologically, then it is a social being. Apparently, the New Testament worried about this problem. The reason that Paul interpreted *church* as Christ or the body of Christ, and attempted not knowing Jesus *according to the flesh* was because Jesus cannot be thought of individually. At the same time, using Jesus as a proper noun by adding an article to *christos* is to reverse this phenomenon. Paul's *christos* and John's "I am in you, you are in me" can only be understood when sociability is presupposed. Westerners, who presuppose individuality (personality) in their interpretation are stuck in their interpretation.

96. Schweizer, *Erniedrigung und Erhohung bei Jesus*, 59.

97. Dodd, *According to the Scriptures*, 499.

concept of the son of man to the people. T. W. Manson relates the "son of man" in the Synoptic Gospels with Daniel, and he says Jesus was preparing for the passion as the collective "son of man" when disciples disappointed him before the event. Although there are some differences in their points, there are a considerable number of scholars who argue this.[98] So if we study Jesus' behavior from this perspective, we find new aspects. Within this premise, when we examine Jesus' acts, we will study events as they happen to the group rather than pursuing Jesus' personal life. I especially want to examine Jesus and the minjung within the categories of host and guest. I want to find minjung in the relationship between them.[99] I cannot further this argument in this paper but I will suggest a few important topics and directions:

1. Jesus was minjung in his makeup and behavior. Every Gospel emphasized that Jesus was the descendent of David, and had royal authority; though Mark emphasized that Jesus was from Galilee, the nameless land had nothing to do with his birthplace or blood ties, where even Josephus did not comment. Mark clarified that when Jesus went back home, he was just a carpenter, and his home was hostile (6:1–3). Sometimes patients and the mob of Jerusalem said that he was the descendent of David, but Mark transmitted materials that argued that the Messiah (of course Mark assumed that this was Jesus) in Jerusalem could not be a descendent of David (12:35–37). It is very different from the Gospel that wrote about the pre-existence of Jesus[100] or his ascension. There is only the story of the transformation in the mountain, but it is material that was transmitted before Mark. Jesus was minjung who followed him, not different from *ochlos*.

2. There is no record that Jesus went to the city from Galilee, but the location of Jesus' life in the country. The fact that he used rural language is telling. An example is that as Jesus was known to be a Galilean, people who followed Jesus were also Galileans. Peter was a Galilean and a follower of Jesus (14:70). The women who witnessed Jesus' passion and the vacant tomb were also with Jesus in Galilee (14:67). "Let's meet at Galilee" (14:28; 16:7), which Marxsen thought was the key, was closely

98. Taylor, *The Gospel according to St. Mark*, 84; Rowley, *The Relevance of Apocalyptic*, 121.

99. Suh Nam-dong, "The Theology of Minjung": "The subjective of Minjung theology is not Jesus but Minjung." However, I think if we divide the two, there is no answer.

100. Gnilka *Das Evangelium nach Markus*, agreed with Bultmann and said that Mark did not accept the preexistence of Jesus.

related to Galilee, minjung, and the New World. That is the new *Sitz im Leben*, which is the context of Mark: minjung and the community. The editor of Mark commented on Galilee thirteen times. The reason that he commented on it over and over again, even when it was not necessary, was that it has a deep relationship with historical consciousness as a writing of minjung.

3. Jesus is where the minjung are, and the minjung are where Jesus is. Although the minjung are nameless, and their function is unlike the background that plays up Jesus, the minjung come alive through the relationship. There is no record that Jesus went around to cities which had already become Hellenistic, but he went from countryside to countryside. Just as the minjung were the poor, he also had nothing. The reason that he said to his disciples when he dispatched them, "have nothing but a staff," (6:7ff.) was the exact image of his life,[101] and it is the same with minjung's life. He did not associate with the minjung unconditionally, awaken their powers, or declare the "minjung, united!" to push them to fight.[102] Nor did he suggest any conditions, but accepted them as sons and daughters of God. Jesus ignored the fact that they were condemned sinners. That is why it is hard to find verses that admonish them as sinners, rather it is transmitted that he chastised those who castigated the oppressed and the poor sinners. It is important for Mark that Jesus gave food and healed them. Is it not more reasonable to see these acts as the desire of the minjung or an expression of the minjung's capacities rather than Jesus' supernatural abilities? Is this not an exercise of power to move beyond self-limitation through "existence with you?" These are not individual acts of Jesus, but social acts. That is why it is possible for Jesus to say, "I cannot do miracles," when people did not believe him in his own hometown; and it is why he is able to declare, "Your faith has made you well"; and this is the reason why his powerlessness is suggested all the way to the cross without much protest.

Jesus used the minjung's language from start to finish. It was his own language, and it is narrative in nature (Erzählung). Anyone who was illiterate or uneducated could understand. It is the language from the whole of life and not merely of the mind.[103] The language of

---

101. Theissen, "Die Straken und Schwachen in Korinth."

102. Kim Yong-bok, "Social Bibliography of Minjung and Theology." He repeatedly refused to see Minjung as an object in this context.

103. Ahn, "Christianity and Minjung's Language." Hyun Young-hak expressed it as

the minjung is Jesus' "house of existence." Oral tradition is its nature. The fragments of minjung's life and wisdom were collected and converted into a language by Mark.[104]

4. Passion of the minjung: Jerusalem is the place where Jesus was arrested and executed. Jerusalem wanted to kill Jesus from the beginning by colluding with Herodians. Like the minjung of Galilee his passion was processed in complete isolation. Nobody was on his side. He was deserted by minjung, disciples, and was betrayed by one of them. If we place Jesus and minjung into subject-object divide, then we need many explanations about how the minjung of Galilee and the minjung of Jerusalem are different,[105] or how Judas Iscariot betrayed Jesus because he was ideologically disappointed with Jesus. However, if we consider Jesus' passion as the compression of the minjung's experience then no other explanation is needed. Trials and lonely execution, which Jesus embodied, reflected the minjung's fate. It was not Jesus of Nazareth who was deserted, unduly judged and executed on the cross, but minjung.[106] Jesus (the "son of man") in this passion is the symbol of the whole group. Here, Mark saw the destiny of the minjung in their *Sitz im Leben*. He may have seen Jesus' passion become present in the minjung's destiny. Further, nothing the theists expected happened from Gethsemane to execution on the cross. But Jesus, who suffered when he was beaten, shed blood and died when pierced, starved when he did not have food, and died when he reached his limit, hopeless, and abandoned even by God, is born again in the place of the minjung of Galilee where no miracles happened. If not, how could Mark depict such a complete and bleak darkness?[107] As Israel was defeated by Rome, as Jerusalem had not one stone left on top of another without a single miracle, these minjung died powerless without any protec-

---

"Minjung's language lived through the body." I think this is a more proper expression. See Hyun, "Attempt to Interpret Korean Masque."

104. Kim Yong-bok, "Minjung's Social Biography and Theology." He said, "There are not many records about Minjung's social biography. So Minjung's social biography became a concealed one. Our task is to find Minjung's social biography and to participate it." Is not Mark the pioneer of this task? Hyun Young-hak found minjung's language beyond the mask and saw the insight and wisdom of "Ugly and foolishness of Minjung who live in the body." See Hyun Young-hak, "Attempt to Interpret Korean Masque."

105. Tagawa Kenzo, *Genshi Kirisutokyō shi no ichidanmen*, 133ff.

106. Suh Nam-dong considers Jesus as the symbol of minjung. See "The Task of Minjung."

107. Ahn Byung-mu, "Mark's Theology Considered from His Passion," 3.

tion. So the minjung of Mark can see their own death from his death. They thought Jesus died instead of them. In this sense, the story of the Last Supper was transmitted. However, Jesus, who was executed on the cross, did not say, "I did it for you." Actually, it was his bitter struggle, like the wretched the minjung, that his death became a death of a hero. It was the death of the abandoned. In this sense, Jesus' last cry in Psalm 22:1, "why have you forsaken me?," can be understood only in the place of the suffering minjung. If his death had been superhuman, then minjung following Jesus would have despaired from the loneliness of abandonment. However, there is another important thing. This was a deeply despised and a miserable event, and from this event of dereliction, minjung theologian Mark saw death as the end to the vicious cycle of reality which is from strength for strength and violence to violence.[108] The suffering Jesus, even though he was put in that position through the Roman authorities, confronted God as if it was God who was trying to kill him. This should be considered the purest, and therefore, the most powerful form of death to the vicious cycle. The sword of violence loses its grip because he did not respond to the sword with a sword but responded to it by dying by the enemy's sword. Such resistance exposes the ugly face of the people who were trying to kill him. Jesus was silent to the end. All these things are acts of death.

5. Jerusalem swallowed up Jesus. However, the tomb that buried him threw him up. This event means the resurrection of the Galilee minjung, including Peter, who was in despair. The promise to meet at Galilee (14:28; 16:7) and not Jerusalem presupposes their resurrection. Mark does not introduce the site in which the event took place forty years before, but he ends his writing with the promise to meet in Galilee. Why? The resurrection of Jesus forty years before was thought to be the beginning of a new world; however, in reality, it was not true. So Mark did not see this as history, but made it as the starting point of the new hope by suggesting the coming *parousia* to the minjung of Mark. And Jesus, who will meet us, will come to Galilee, the place of the minjung. However, this is the Jesus who already brought down the curtain on death. He is not one who will come on the clouds, but one who was executed in Jerusalem, and will return after achieving victory over death there. This is the Jesus of Galilee.

108. Suh Nam-dong (Ibid.) considers Kim Ji-ha's "severing" as dialectic of *han* and claims that this is different from social revolution. He said, "It is a cutting of the vicious cycle sublimated by a higher spiritual power."

# 6

# Minjok, Minjung, and Church

—Ahn Byung-Mu

The broad-ranging but important themes of *minjok*, minjung, and church are the topics of this essay, written upon the request of a newspaper. Under these themes, I will reflect on the historical role of Christianity in our nation and propose its desirable role in our society. In our history we have a sense of minjok (similar to nation) but not of minjung (the masses). If we think about it from a different perspective, what actually exists is minjung, while minjok is only a related concept; however, what was continually emphasized was minjok and the minjung that made up the minjok were exploited and neglected under the auspice of benefitting minjok.

We have a strong national-consciousness because our history is a history of constant invasions and persistent external threats. The minjung were absolutely obedient to the government and emphasized the destiny of the minjok because they considered love of the minjok their top priority; in return, the very government they supported spurned the minjung. Minjok was established by the minjung, and the minjung entrusted the government with authority for safekeeping. However, since its establishment, the minjok has exploited and subjugated the minjung. This finally means that there is no minjok or minjung—there is only a government that institutionalizes both. This has resulted in humiliating negotiations with the Chinese and the Japanese annexation of Korea, which were decided by a small number of individuals in power without the minjok or minjung's participation. Due to their love of the minjok, the minjung were obedient to the government that held power over the minjok; however, the dormant indignation over their exploitation and backbreaking work, which was the only remuneration for minjung's loyalty to the minjok, found expression in modern history's Hong Kyong-nae Incident and the Donghak Peasant Revolution of 1894. These fanned the flames of a broader minjung revolution, especially among the peasants, who had been repressed in the name of the minjok.

If we examine the Donghak Revolution in isolation, we find two characteristics. First, it was rooted in an attempt to save the beloved of the minjok who were at risk. Second, it was a movement to recover minjung's lost rights. The emphasis, however, was on saving the minjung. They claimed the slogan *jepok gumin*—"elimination of tyranny and saving the minjung." However, this minjung movement that placed the minjok at the center was not only repressed mercilessly, but also crushed by mobilized foreign militaries, and its participants were labeled as rebels.

Today is the anniversary of the March First Movement. This movement protested Japanese aggression, led by the minjung, without aid from the government, which had sold out its own minjok for profit. This movement justified minjung's power that had lit the fire of the Donghak Revolution. The declaration of independence unveiled the higher level of minjung spirit and maturity to the world. First, the declaration was the proclamation of the freed minjung and the voice of twenty million people. This was not a simple explosion of emotion but an articulation of the ideology of world peace and a keen sense of history. The ideology of peace came under the premise of human equality, consistent and continuing development of liberty, the elucidation of lasting peace of Asia, and the will to change the world; they sang of the demolition of imperialism and authoritarianism, which are heritages of the passing age. The new world is here before our eyes. The age of power is gone and the age of justice is come. The spring of the new world is come and quickening the renewal of everything. If the winter crawling beneath the earth with the breath that freezes the water and befalls cold snow is a passing situation, then the rising energy of hot wind and warm sunlight is today's situation. The March First Movement expressed to the world the maturity of our minjung, although they were repressed and nameless. The minjung, however, were crushed terribly by a cruel, invading power.

The minjung were liberated from a thirty-six yearlong darkness and enraptured with joy at the independence of their country. Their joy at regaining the nation was translated into a passion for minjok's independence. The minjung established their government by their own hands for the first time. However, the first government that was established in such a manner changed as soon as it came into power. They became only concerned about the government, and thought nothing of the minjung who had established it. As time passed, the minjok disappeared and only government remained; the government deceived, repressed, and threatened the minjung to maintain their authority. Minjung's anger finally exploded into the April Revolution, rekindling the fires of the Donghak Peasant Revolution and the March First Movement.

The Democratic Party, which was founded for the minjung, was destroyed by a military coup before it could integrate the voice of the minjung into national policy, which was unsympathetic to the cause of the minjung. The government that took control of power asserted the minjok as new political ideology; slogans such as "national democracy" and "modernization of the minjok" are examples. The term 'national' only makes sense with the premise of a minjok, and democracy makes sense only with the premise of the minjung. Because the government gave no thought to the minjung, what remained was the minjok; however, the government rendered the term minjok meaningless under the auspice of modernization by drawing Japanese money and military power. It was during this period that the same spirit that lit the fire of the Donghak and April Revolutions also resisted the government that sold out the minjok. In response, the government trampled minjung's voice by force. For the following ten years, the minjung became silent, like a tamed pet.

Only students spoke on behalf of the minjung from time to time. Students struggled for the cause of the minjung alone, often scattered by force, only to rise up again. The government tightened its control of the minjung by a series of repressive policies: the Garrison Decree, the declaring of a state of emergency, and finally, *Yushin*, the revitalizing reform system that controlled minjung's voice.

Even a worm will squirm. How much longer will the minjung, who began the Donghak Revolution, the March First Movement, and April Revolution, play dead? Some who had seen the students' protest as merely an unorganized response to the government decided to become the voice of the minjung. They are the voices of Kim Changuk, Ji Haksun, and Park Hyunggyu. For speaking out, they were put in jail with 200 of their colleagues and sentenced to fifteen years in prison. They did nothing more than to voice the concerns of the minjung.

What was the purpose of their imprisonment? What good does it do to cover their mouths when the fury rooted in deep dissatisfaction of the minjung has not dissipated? The minjung has eyes, hands, and feet! Even if they remain silent, stones on the street will cry out.

Part II: Selected Writings by Ahn Byung-Mu

The government should have rewarded rather than imprisoned those capable persons because they were the pressure valve for the minjung whose growing anger could easily have turned into anti-government activities. They were not like Choi Suwoon, who could not stand the tyranny of the corrupt government and started a reform movement, or Choi Haewol, or Jun Bongjun who started riots, burned government offices, and refused to pay taxes. Unlike them, they were merely conveying minjung's frustration.

We can only conclude that this government, by throwing them into prison, was not capable of hearing minjung's voice. The Dong-A Daily Affair supports this point. If Dong-A was unlawful in its dealings, then the government should have taken legal action. Instead, the government tried to carry out secret assassinations of those involved, which proves the point that the government was not ready to listen to the voice of the minjung. Imprisonments, which symbolically represented minjung's situation, became a great opportunity for the movement. This peaceful petition fell on deaf ears, so it became a civil rights movement. The situation and process are very similar to the Donghak Uprising, which was started because the government refused to grant amnesty to Choi Haewol. However, this movement was not the Second Peasant Uprising.

How the minjung were persecuted for a simple request for the release of political prisoners! Although some were released, the minjung continued to petition the government for Choi's amnesty by lying down in front of the palace. If such peaceful demonstration is considered sin resulting in arrests, not many can be as bold as one student who said, "I am honored" at the news of his death sentence, but many will gloriously choose imprisonment as a means of speaking for the minjung.

## What Is the Role of the Church?

The church is the gathering of Christians; the people who were put in prison were members of the Christian Professors' Association. Why did they stand on the side of the minjung?

First, the Christian church in Korea is repenting of its past. People say that participating in society is outside of the church's mission, but all the church did was to repent. Historians all agree that the Korean church played a decisive role in the formation of the minjok during its infancy. Playing a leading role in the March First Movement was a concrete expression of the church's involvement in society, and nobody had denounced it as a violation of the separation of church and state. What was the state of the church after the independence?

The church had the minjok in its mission purview but not the minjung. So the church did not have eyes to see how Lee Seungman's regime trampled on the minjung. They were blinded by the slogan provided by Lee's government—the minjok—and they unconditionally supported the government while closing their ears to minjung's mourning rising from the oppressive policies of Lee's regime.

When I think about the attitude of the church during the April Revolution, I cannot hold up my head due to shame. When the minjung were oppressed and suffered under the muddy stream of corruption, the Korean church did not even know the terms 'human rights' or 'justice.' When the young students rose up and carried on a bloody war, the Christian church was silent like a mute who had a spoonful of honey in his mouth. Even when the famously spineless professors reluctantly joined the student movement, the Korean church remained silent as if they were dead. Such cowardly behavior betrayed the teachings and actions of Christ. Jesus clearly was not for the powerful or the rich, nor was he on the side of model citizens or the intellectuals of the society. He was a friend of the minjung, sided with the minjung, and died for the minjung. In the bible there are two different terms for the minjung. One is *laos* and the other is *ochlos*.

*Laos* has a similar meaning to *minjok*: it refers to people who have rights and protection and those belonging to a certain group. *Ochlos* refers to people who are deprived of their rights or protection. We should pay close attention to the fact that in the first written gospel, Mark, the people whom Jesus cared for, who followed him unconditionally, and anchored their hopes in him, were not the *laos* but the *ochlos*.

## *Ochlos*

They are the minjung who are weary and burdened, the lost sheep, the uninvited, the poor, the disabled, the blind, the crippled, the mistreated prodigals wandering the streets and alleys of towns; they are the unemployed roaming the streets, the oppressed, the imprisoned, the hungry, the naked, the moaning and the persecuted. In social stratum, they are the fourth class. It was those in authority and the so-called elites who resisted Jesus, and eventually accused and crucified him. Christians after Jesus, as Paul mentions, were "not wise by human standards, not many were powerful, and not many were of noble birth" (1 Cor 1:26). In the initial stage of the Korean church, it was the *ochlos* that had gathered, and the Nevius Mission Plan made the *ochlos* the central missional target. However, the Korean church eventually became a gathering place for those who ate and dressed well, and the *ochlos*, who were friends of Jesus, were too ashamed to even enter the church. This is the reason that the Korean church became, not only powerless and alienated from the minjung, but also the reason for its estrangement from Jesus. However, recently, as awakening from sleep, the church began listening to the voice of the *ochlos*.

As a result, the church began taking an interest in the oppressed, becoming their mouth, hands, and feet, and regaining their lost position gradually. This was not an anti-government or a political movement, but a process of recovery and identifying with Jesus' original spirit. However, we are faced with a new situation—a mandate for radical and swift reform of the existing identity of the Korean church and its structures. This realization began with the discovery of the fact that, without true freedom, there is no freedom in mission or freedom to love. This began with many Christians who were imprisoned for their words and actions on behalf of the poor and the oppressed. What we discovered in prison was political and economic structural evil. In this context, the Christian church needs to clearly establish its direction. But how? I do not have the blueprint. I only want to suggest some possibilities for our basic posture. First, the church is not a political party; therefore, the church cannot be directly concerned with who should be in power. Instead, the church's administrative and institutional interests should be consolidated and concentrated on the minjung. This means devoting all of the church's energy to building a democratic society. This is the way *for the* minjung *and by the* minjung.

Second, Christianity needs to develop a new way of reasoning for the establishment of a new value system. The ethical base of Christianity is love. However, love needs to be grounded and concretized from its abstractions. This should be performed from the side of poor and oppressed *ochlos* recovering their rights. The only way to disarm the communists is by recovering Christianity's original message, which was seized by the communists.

Such a movement of love for the *ochlos* needs to be systematized and a blueprint that would transform their resignation to hope needs to be introduced. The blueprint should not only be a vision of a wealthy society, but one that would bring the entire society together. Systematization means to create joint responsibility, which simply means creating a sense that "whatever happens to you also happens to me." Systematization is necessary because the evil that oppresses people is structural. This is the way to avoid episodic explosions of anger or criticism for the sake of criticism and prevent political and economic tyranny.

Third, any Christian movement should resist violence. Therefore, we oppose the use of violence as a means of resisting violence. We believe Jesus' words, "for all who draw the sword will die by the sword" (Matt 26:52). In order to rescue history from this vicious cycle of violence, we have to find a new way. We know that violence is easier to use than law.

Fourth, at the same time, because we believe that the final decision of history is up to God, we should keep the faith that we "do our best but leave the decision to God." So, rather than choosing violence to confront violence, like Jesus who chose to be crucified, we follow the way of suffering—like the thirty-three representatives of the March First movement who read the Declaration of Independence and waited for imprisonment while holding out their hands to be cuffed. This is the vision of the minjung, who would rather be dragged away while standing up for what they believe even as they live lives of oppression. This is the teaching of Jesus: "If any want to become my followers, let them deny themselves and take up their cross and follow me" (Matt 16:24).

# PART III

Critical Responses to Ahn Byung-Mu's Minjung Theology

# 7

## Minjung, the Black Masses, and the Global Imperative

### *A Womanist Reading of Luke's Soteriological Hermeneutical Circle*

—Mitzi J. Smith

"I know I got it made while the masses of black people are catchin' hell, but as long as they ain't free, I ain't free."

MOHAMMAD ALI

"The concept of love is inextricably interwoven throughout philosophy and religion. And it is in the context of the modern world that faith, love and action based upon one's own personal responsibility to all other [human beings] and to the future of all [hu]mankind becomes most important."

SHIRLEY CHISHOLM[1]

---

1. Chisholm, "The Relationship between Religion and Today's Social Issues," 183.

# Part III: Critical Responses to Ahn Byung-Mu's Minjung Theology

## Introduction

I AM AN AFRICAN American female employed with Ashland Theological Seminary, which is the graduate branch of Ashland University, both of which are primarily white and rural. However, I teach at the seminary's Detroit metro area center. Most of my students are black females, but I also teach white and Asian students. I grew up in a loving and nurturing single-parent Christian household. My mother, Flora Ophelia Carson Smith, (1929–2009) personified and embodied godly ethics and values that I seek to emulate. Flora loved taking care of her four children and her household meticulously and did so even after a debilitating and undiagnosed disease left her wheelchair bound. She could no longer work as a nursing assistant caring for older people or as the "salad girl" in a well-respected Columbus, Ohio, restaurant. My mother also loved other people; she "thought it not robbery" to feed, dress or encourage others, whenever she could. In word, and practice, she showed my siblings and me that we should love ourselves, love each other, and other people. My mother embodied, and we inherited a womanist *materology* (Greek: matēr; translated *mother*) of how to incarnate a living God in a black mother's body baptized in suffering but anointed by an undying Spirit of love and perseverance, despite and because of living among the masses. Flora fell into a fireplace, headfirst, at age five; struggled with narcolepsy in high school; found herself homeless, with one child in her arms and two hanging on her dress-tail, upon returning from work and having failed to get a rent receipt from a unconscionable landlord, to name a few of her experiences.

I grew up poor and many times did not have what I wanted especially as a teenager, yet I remember feeling more slighted by the loss of my mother's presence at school when she could no longer walk than by our economic circumstances. Despite our poverty and my premature determination to forego college and obtain a good paying job, I matriculated at five schools, finally earning my PhD in religion (specializing in New Testament) from Harvard University. Nobody in my immediate family had yet earned a college degree, but they encouraged, praised, cosigned, and prayed for me. In fact, it was my mother and a former neighbor from the projects, Mrs. Slocum, who made sure I had bus fare and money in my pocket when I first left home for college. You see, out of her own poverty, my mom sometimes fed Mrs. Slocum's children. Materology says I cannot let my neighbor's children starve if I can help it. A circle of people, some we know and some we do not, put their hands, monies, hearts and prayers together with our dreams and hard work to help us achieve what might otherwise be impossible. So I believe in putting back and paying forward into that circle. I am not free to turn my back to the masses while they stand with their "backs against the wall."[2]

As a black female and womanist biblical scholar, I prioritize black women's experience and artifacts as a starting point for engaging in biblical interpretation and theoethical reflection. In her 1979 essay "Coming Apart," Alice Walker described a womanist as a "feminist, only more common"[3]; that is, I suppose, more like or having more in common with ordinary black women. Walker recognizes that black and white women's experiences differ. Historically, when white women asked black women to choose between the women's suffrage movement and the abolition of slavery, black women chose the latter. They recognized experientially and ontologically the inextricable bond between black men and black women's freedom. In her 1983 book *In Search of Our Mothers' Gardens,* Walker, while defining the terms "womanish" and "womanist," describes black women's individual and communal loyalties: "Also: A woman . . . [c]omitted to survival and wholeness of entire people, male *and* female. Not a separatist, except periodically, for health. Traditionally universalist, as in: 'Mama, why are we brown, pink, and yellow, and our cousins are white, beige, and black?' Ans.: 'Well, you know the colored race is just like a flower garden, with every color flower represented.' Traditionally capable, as in: 'Mama, I'm walking to Canada and I'm taking you and a bunch of other slaves with me.' Reply: 'It wouldn't be the first time.'"[4] A womanist perspective is concerned for the masses or the "entire people" but not at the expense of her own health. Black women's concern for self health and for a communal and universal wholeness is the womanist materological interpretative lens through which I shall read the crowds in Luke's Gospel and engage minjung theology.

I shall first briefly discuss minjung theology and compare it with black and womanist theologies. Second, I discuss some historical ideologies about the relationship between individual mobility or success and the deliverance of the crowds/the masses in terms of black peoples' experiences and history. I further address the contemporary situation of the black masses in America in relation to the success of individual African Americans. Third, I review Ahn Byung-Mu's observations about the crowds in Mark's Gospel and his literary social construction of minjung in relation to Jesus. Finally, I explore some texts in Luke's Gospel where I observe what I call a *soteriological*

---

2. Thurman, *Jesus and the Disinherited*, 11.
3. Walker, "Coming Apart," 3–11.
4. Walker, *In Search of Our Mothers' Gardens*, xi–xii.

Part III: Critical Responses to Ahn Byung-Mu's Minjung Theology

*hermeneutical circle* operative; namely, the salvation/deliverance of individuals is inextricably connected with the crowds.

## Minjung Theology

The noun minjung is a literal Korean pronunciation of a Chinese word. Generally, *min* means "people," and *jung* connotes "the mass." Minjung is a difficult term to interpret; it is open to more nuanced translation. Minjung signifies the Korean people's history of oppression, colonization, and alienation. Thus, minjung as theological reflection is "contextual and indigenous."[5] Indigenous Korean people who compose the minjung are the poor, women, ethnic groups, workers, farmers, and peasants who are politically, socioeconomically, intellectually, and/or culturally alienated, discriminated against, marginalized, and oppressed masses.[6] The Korean peoples' oppressors have been both foreigners and their own indigenous elite. From 1910 to 1945, the Korean people were feudal peasants under Japanese colonization; from 1945 to 1990 the minjung were industrial workers, peasants, and the urban poor under Korean dictatorship; and from 1990 to the present Korean people continue to experience oppression under so-called democratic governments. The minjung movement ignited in 1970 when Jeon Tae-Il set fire to himself in solidarity with his fellow exploited factory workers. Consequently, Christian leaders acknowledged the severity of the situation and began to stand for and with the poor and exploited minjung.[7] Minjung theology is critical reflection on the minjung's struggle for liberation.

For minjung theology, the Jesus event is the ultimate liberating phenomenon. The Jesus-Event is Jesus' suffering, death and resurrection. It is "holistic, dynamic and changing," unlike the kerygma (proclamation) of Jesus, which is "ideological, static, and unchanging."[8] An inclusive and holistic minjung theology incorporates "indigenous cultural and religious elements as part of divine revelation." All of the minjung's experiences and/or history of struggle for liberation are sacred and holy; this includes

---

5. Lee, "Minjung Theology: A Critical Introduction," 3–29.

6. Kyung, "'Han-pu-ri': Doing Theology from Korean Women's Perspective," 52–62.

7. Kim, "The Problem of Poverty in Post-War Korean Christianity," 43–50.

8. Lee, "Minjung Theology," 5, 11, 15; Jinkwan, "Minjung (the Multitude), Historical Symbol of Jesus Christ," 153–71.

the good and evil and the moral and immoral.⁹ By characterizing himself as the "servant of the minjung," Christ becomes the object of salvation history and the minjung become its subject. In or through Jesus, God sides with the minjung as the oppressed of society.¹⁰ God's preference for the oppressed minjung functions to engender salvation for all of humanity.¹¹

## Minjung Theology, Black Theology, and Womanist Theology

Both black theology and minjung theology emerged in periods of protest. Black theology, as a systematic reflection on and articulation of black people's experience of slavery and oppression in light of their belief in a just and loving God, was constructed during the civil rights and black power movements of 1960s and 1970s. According to James H. Cone, the father of black theology, God stands on the side of the oppressed.¹² The paradigmatic biblical event that demonstrates God's preference for enslaved and oppressed peoples is the exodus from Egyptian slavery. As James Deotis Roberts argues in his 1988 essay "Black Theology and minjung theology: Exploring Common Themes," the Exodus event allows black people to be the subject of God's liberative acts in black religious history. Thus, black people's political liberationist response to oppression should decisively be nonviolent and constructive and seek to make black people the subjects of their own history.¹³ Roberts argues that "When a people change from being objects of history to being subjects of their history, they become a force to reckon with. They are motivated from within and are prepared to confront any odds in the quest for liberation."¹⁴ For minjung theology the Exodus event is similarly paradigmatic and empowering. Cyris H. S. Moon asserts that in "the Exodus event the minjung can be clearly understood as a force that stands in opposition to the powerful."¹⁵

Minjung and black theology, Roberts asserts, focus on the experience of suffering and connected with suffering is the theme of theodicy. Theodicy seeks to understand the justice of God in the context of suffering. "The problem of structural evil and the consequence of mass suffering"

9. Lee, "Minjung Theology," 20, 21.
10. Ibid., 19.
11. Ibid., 22.
12. Cone, *God of the Oppressed*.
13. Roberts, "Black Theology and Minjung Theology," 99–105.
14. Ibid., 103.
15. Moon, "A Korean Minjung Perspective," 241.

are unavoidable.[16] Thus black and minjung theologians contextualize suffering and attempt to transform it. The cross is central to both but "the cross is not a symbol of escape; it is rather a symbol of engagement with evil and suffering. Christ's victorious resurrection is seen in relation to the cross as its sequel and ultimate vindication."[17] Womanist theologian JoAnne Terrell cautions against placing too much attention on the cross lest we find ourselves glorifying suffering especially for black people and others who have endured so much unnecessary evil.[18] Suffering can be the consequence of ministry and god-like living, but suffering is not the goal. Some suffering results from evil acts and omission or silence regarding injustice. Not all suffering is redemptive.[19]

Like minjung theology, black theology is holistic and inclusive regarding the culture and tradition of indigenous peoples as legitimate sources of theological reflection and divine revelation. This includes black people's religious and/or political histories, traditions, ways of knowing, God-talk, and artifacts. Roberts argues that "black theology should be broadly conceived, encompassing a strong emphasis upon history and culture, without toning down the essential, political liberation thrust."[20] This "political liberating" thrust continues to be important since many gains made in the past are being eroded; "blacks still live in the shadow of slavery."[21]

Black people and their allies have won hard-fought civil rights battles and other victories since the Emancipation Proclamation, and we have proudly witnessed individual accomplishments (most recently, the first African American president and first lady, President Barack Obama and First Lady Michelle Obama). But we continue to live with lagging income, employment, education, and health-care statistics as well as the threat of eroding civil and human rights. Black communities struggle with internal and external injustices. Womanist theologians confronted black theology's lack of self-critique with respect to sexism, classism and heterosexism. Jacquelyn Grant argued that black men ignored black women's unique experiences rendering them invisible in their theological reflections,[22] a

16. Roberts, "Black Theology and Minjung Theology," 103.

17. Ibid., 104–5.

18. Terrell, *Power in the Blood?*. See also St. Clair, *Call and Consequences*.

19. St. Clair (*Call and Consequences*, 83, 132) distinguishes between pain and suffering as forms of agony.

20. Roberts, "Black Theology and Minjung Theology," 99.

21. Ibid., 100.

22. Grant, "Black Theology and the Black Woman," 418–33; see also Delaine, "Womanist Theology," 290–99.

Mitzi J. Smith—*Minjung, the Black Masses, and the Global Imperative*

critique to which black theologians conceded and corrected. Womanist theology continues to strive to be an inclusive theology interested in the health and welfare of the whole community.

Given this theological emphasis on inclusivity among black, womanist and minjung theologians (male and female), Jesus' relationship with the crowds in Luke's Gospel provides a useful paradigm for conceptualizing the importance of the masses and for rejecting a concentration on the success of a few as a synecdochical substitute for deliverance of the masses from disease, hunger, and inequalities.

## Individual Achievements and the Black Masses

With the election of the first black president of these United States of America in 2008, political pundits and commentators (primarily Anglo) asked whether we could now think of America as a postracial society. Similarly, one of my white male students asked me whether we should legitimately continue talking about racism as a reality, given that he (the student) is sitting in a class taught by an African American Harvard-trained PhD, and given the election of the first black president. I answered with an unequivocal Pauline "by no means!" When masses of black peoples continue to subsist anywhere near the superficial poverty line, are subjected to systemic profiling and racism, do not earn a living wage, have limited or no access to quality education or health care, and are inequitably treated within the justice system, we cannot begin to claim that we live in a post-racial America.

The struggle to articulate and address the connection between individual responsibility and the plight of the masses is as old as Moses, the son of Pharaoh, whom God chose to lead a mass of people out of Egyptian bondage in the Old Testament. That struggle has long existed within the black community. Should we encourage those who have been able to achieve a certain socioeconomic status despite the status quo to reach back and help elevate their oppressed brothers and sisters while attempting to obliterate oppressive systems? Or should we advocate for a widespread contentment among the masses without a political liberative agenda to change the status quo, advocating for a "pull yourselves up by your own bootstraps" mentality? Two early twentieth century American "Negro" leaders articulated two different solutions to this dilemma. The sociologist, scholar, author, and political activist W. E. B. Du Bois (1868–1963), the first African American to graduate from Harvard University with a doctoral degree in 1895, wrote: "The Negro race, like all races, is going to be saved by its *exceptional men*. The problem of education, then, among Negroes must first of all deal with the *Talented Tenth*; it is the problem of *developing the best of this race that they may guide the mass away from the contamination and death of the worst, in their own and other races*" (emphasis mine).[23] Du Bois seems to call for the salvation of a representative mass within the masses by the gifted few. Martin Luther King Jr., over 150 years later criticized Du Bois's vision as not for the uplift of the "whole people" but for an "aristocratic elite" who would benefit while they left behind the ninety percent.[24]

Booker T. Washington (1856–1915) was born a slave and became the leading educator among African Americans in the 20th century, the first principal/teacher of the famous Tuskegee Institute, and author of his best-selling autobiography *Up from Slavery*. Washington, it appears, wished to impact the masses but within the status quo, as reflected in his famous quote "cast down your buckets where you are."[25] In 1949 the theologian, mystic, scholar, author, and pastor Howard Thurman (1899–1981)[26] wrote that masses of people constituting "the poor, the disinherited, and the dispossessed" still "live with their backs constantly against the wall." Thurman ask what does religion or the religious offer them?[27]

Black women activists in the late 19th and 20th century recognized that "their fate was bound with the masses," as expressed by the National Association of Colored Women's Motto "Lifting as We Climb." A prevailing perception existed that black women's "womanhood" was judged by "the masses of our women."[28] Many black women activists understood from experience that "opportunity and environment" and "not circumstances of birth or previous experience separated them from the masses."[29] Middle-class black women could be elitist, but many were guided by a moral imperative to liberate and educate the masses. Rosa Bowser (1855–1931), Richmond, Virginia's first "colored" teacher, wrote in *The Woman's Era* that "Race progress is the direct outgrowth of individual success in life"; "The

23. Du Bois, "The Talented Tenth," 31–75 (italics added).
24. King, *Why We Can't Wait*, 19.
25. Washington, "Atlanta Compromise Speech."
26. Howard Thurman first published an essay titled "Good News for the Underprivileged" while he was Dean at Howard University's Rankin Chapel in 1935, and that essay became the core of his book *Jesus and the Disinherited* as noted in the Forward of said book.
27. Thurman, *Jesus and the Disinherited*, 13.
28. Giddings, *When and Where I Enter*, 97–98.
29. Ibid., 98.

race rises as individuals rise and individuals rise with the race."[30] Many black women educator-activists, such as Anna Julia Cooper (1858–1964), worked with one high heel planted in the Booker T. Washington camp (supporting industrial education) and the other in the Du Bois school (promoting higher education and earning PhDs).[31]

The Reverend Dr. Martin Luther King Jr. (1929–1968; pastor, civil rights leader, theologian, and author) connected injustice perpetrated against black people with its global impact. King famously asserted that injustice anywhere (particular) is injustice everywhere (universal). The transformation of one or a few lives should not excuse or obscure justice everywhere else. In 1963 King expressed his disappointment with both political parties when President Kennedy failed to sign a key housing bill that would end housing discrimination in financing by financial institutions. King wrote that "While Negroes were being appointed to some significant jobs, and social hospitality was being extended at the White House to Negro leaders, the dreams of the masses remained in tatters. The Negro felt that he recognized the same old bone that had been tossed to him in the past—only now it was being handed to him on a platter, with courtesy."[32]

Shirley Chisholm (1924–2005), the first female to seriously run for president of the United States of America, asserted that the civil rights movement did not achieve the goal of integration. Individual achievements, she argued, are insufficient and often come at the price of minorities becoming "pseudowhites." Chisholm wrote that "successful blacks who are proud of their own accomplishments should not disregard the fact that despite their own efforts, they owe most of their success to the momentum of their group, to actions taken before they came of age."[33] In order to engender "real progress," Chisholm argues, "we must all move ahead together, and we must do it ourselves."[34] Chisholm referred to Washington's industrial education program as "mind-deadening" and called for fully trained black professionals and for black control of black institutions. She advocated nonviolent and pragmatic fighting within the system to change the system.[35]

---

30. Ibid., 102.

31. Ibid., 105. Ann Julia Cooper earned a doctorate at age sixty-seven after she retired.

32. King, *Why We Can't Wait*, 6.

33. Chisholm, *Unbought and Unbossed*, 151.

34. Ibid., 154.

35. Ibid., 157–58.

## Part III: Critical Responses to Ahn Byung-Mu's Minjung Theology

When he served in the US Senate, President Barack Obama (first African American president of the USA, former US and Illinois state senator, U.S. Constitution scholar, and author) addressed the state of black masses and other minorities, and our continued individual responsibilities to them:

> Still, when I hear commentators interpreting my speech to mean that we have arrived at a "postracial politics" or that we already live in a color-blind society, I have to offer a word of caution. To say that we are one people is not to suggest that race no longer matters—that the right for equality has been won, or that the problems that minorities face in this country today are largely self-inflicted. We know the statistics: On almost every single socioeconomic indicator, from infant mortality to life expectancy to employment to home ownership, Black and Latino Americans in particular continue to lag behind their white counterparts. In corporate boardrooms across America, minorities are grossly underrepresented; in the United States Senate, there are only three Latinos and two Asian members (both from Hawaii), and as I write today I am the chamber's sole African American. To suggest that our racial attitudes play no part in these disparities is to turn a blind eye to both our history and our experience—and to relieve ourselves of the responsibility to make things right.[36]

Black political, educational, and religious leaders have struggled with the plight of the masses that still live with their backs against the wall in light of the few who have climbed over and face the wall. What is the individual's responsibility to the masses from which she emerged and thus to whom she is related by provenance, common humanity, and a remembered oppression? We shall attempt to address these questions through an analysis of the Lukan Jesus' relationship to individuals and the masses. In the process, we shall identify the masses or minjung in Luke. But first we shall discuss Ahn Byung-Mu's characterization of the masses and Mark. Ahn's analysis will serve as a point of departure for our analysis of Luke.

### Ahn Byung-Mu's Analysis of the Social Construction of the Minjung in Mark's Gospel

In Ahn Byung-Mu's seminal essay, "Jesus and the Minjung in the Gospel of Mark," he attempts to interpret the "crowd(s)" (Greek: *ochlos*, sometimes

---

36. Obama, *The Audacity of Hope*, 232–33.

*pantes*; *laos* is not found in Mark) in Mark from the perspective of minjung theology. Ahn's literary reconstruction of the crowds in Mark is foundational for understanding the minjung in relation to Jesus. Ahn argues that since little attention has been given to a social construction of the crowds that followed Jesus, his "words and deeds have been desocialized." Much of what Jesus said and did occurred in the context of the crowds.[37]

Ahn observes that the crowds form the background for Jesus' activities as they follow him. The crowds are differentiated from the disciples whom Jesus rebukes.[38] Jesus does not rebuke the crowds even though they consist of the so-called sinners and outcasts. The crowds, the "minjung of Galilee," take an "anti-Jerusalem" stance, according to Ahn, and are distinguished from the Jerusalem ruling class. Finally, the crowds are represented as strong and susceptible to manipulation since the rulers attempt to mobilize them on their side.[39] Despite their attempts to manipulate the crowds, "the unjust and powerful" fear them. Yet, the crowds do not organize themselves into a power bloc, and neither does Jesus. Therefore, Ahn argues, we cannot regard the crowds as "a political bloc," but only "existentially as a crowd. They are minjung not because they have a common destiny, but simply because they are alienated, dispossessed, and powerless."[40]

Ahn found no qualitative evaluation of the crowds and no attempt to judge them on the basis of "an established religious or ethical standard or in terms of a new ethic."[41] Like Jesus, the crowds were peripatetic. Therefore, they likely held no established social positions and were not "members of an identifiable economic class."[42] Nevertheless, "Minjung belong to a class of society which has been marginalized and abandoned"; they do not belong to the People of God (*laos*) nor are they the baptized crowd.[43]

Mark provides a paradigmatic representation of the crowds that follow Jesus. The crowds are composed of sinners, the sick, the socially alienated, and/or those who committed religious sin. The fact that tax

---

37. Ahn Byung-Mu, "Jesus and the Minjung in the Gospel of Mark," 85–86

38. Lee, "Minjung Theology," 21–22. Lee posits no idealized or romanticized view of the crowds; the minjung are not sinless. Whether Ahn concludes therefore that the minjung are sinless is unclear. Perhaps, the ethical and moral character of the crowds is not the focus since to do so would shift attention from the crowds as victims of oppression to them as perpetrators.

39. Ahn, "Jesus and the Minjung," 88–89.

40. Ibid., 101–2.

41. Ibid., 90.

42. Ibid.

43. Ibid., 101.

collectors are among the crowds demonstrates the crowds or minjung are not limited to the economically and politically alienated.[44] *Ochlos* (Greek translated *crowd*) is a relational and fluid concept.[45]

Ahn described Jesus' attitude toward crowds as protective, welcoming, and familial. The crowds are "sheep without a shepherd," a metaphor that served as a critique of the leaders. The crowds were alienated from their rulers. Jesus accepted the crowds as members of his spiritual or fictive family. Jesus took pleasure in teaching the crowds, and they were fascinated by his teachings. Jesus unconditionally accepted and supported the crowds, who were the "alienated and despised class in the community."[46] Ahn asserts that "Jesus' attitude toward the minjung was never limited to people who were politically oppressed," but they included "the aggrieved, and the weak."[47] Jesus promised the future kingdom of God, which represents God's love and justice. God wills to stand with "minjung completely and unconditionally."[48]

## The Gospel of Luke and the Crowds/Minjung: A Soteriological Hermeneutical Circle

Much of what Ahn discovered about the crowds in Mark applies to the crowds in Luke, particularly Jesus' attitude toward them. Jesus welcomed them, embraced them, and provided for their needs. The minjung/crowds have real needs, which Jesus meets unconditionally. However, I wish to complete the hermeneutical circle that Ahn began. While Ahn examined the crowds solely in relation to Jesus, I analyze the relationship between individuals and the crowds and between Jesus and individuals that Jesus encountered in or out of the crowds. In Luke, I observe an organic or wholistic movement in which the whole gives meaning to the individual parts and individual parts derive meaning from the whole. This does not mean that individuals have no identity apart from the minjung/crowds, but that without the voice and testimony of individuals who emerge from the crowds we could not know the minjung. Protowomanist voting rights activist Fannie Lou Hamer often quoted Luke 4:18 as proof that God was not just interested in liberating black people but the ubiquitous masses: "Jesus was talking about people."[49]

44. Ibid., 91–96.
45. Ibid., 101.
46. Ibid., 89–90, 94.
47. Ibid., 95–96.
48. Ibid., 102.
49. Grant, "Civil Rights Women," 39–50, 46.

## Mitzi J. Smith—*Minjung, the Black Masses, and the Global Imperative*

Individuals present to us the multifaceted, multidimensional, and human nature of the crowds. From individuals we learn something about the whole. Womanist theologian Jacquelyn Grant argues that "a wholistic analysis is a minimal required for a wholistic theology."[50] A wholistic theology seeks to liberate women, men, and children or the entire black community, as well as the human race. A wholistic theology also recognizes that we live in and are part of the larger world. The Yahwist account of the creation story (Gen. 2:4b–24) reminds us that all humans draw substance, meaning, and life from the earth (*adamah*) and from God. Karen Baker-Fletcher argues that our sense of "interconnectedness moves [us] out of prisons of individualism to relearn compassion, to know experientially and to understand that injustice anywhere is a threat to justice everywhere, that when one suffers all suffer, that when one rejoices all rejoice."[51] Womanist biblical interpretation should concern itself with the individuals that emerge out of the crowds to experience wholeness and the crowds they leave behind that continue waiting for their change to come. As Layli Phillips explains, "womanism allows everyone to move toward the same place along different paths: that place is universal community; that path is whatever uniquenesses they have acquired by birth and all their successive travels through different experiences since that time. While this perspective may be unsettlingly nonracial for those who view womanist as merely another name for black feminism or a black women-centered perspective, the reality is that one hallmark of womanist is Black women's and other women of color's expression, vision, and articulation of universal sentiments and aspirations."[52]

The womanist interpretive framework I employ is organic. I am concerned with the socioeconomic dilemma of masses of black people and other peoples (male and female), the minjung, and other people locally and globally who live marginalized, alienated, and oppressed lives. My analysis, unlike Ahn's, does not concern redaction criticism. I explore Luke's narrative as an organic whole. Luke provides a literary paradigm for conceptualizing the relationship between the masses/minjung and individuals who experience salvation, wholeness and/or mobility. Most if not all of the individuals who experience God's salvation through Jesus' ministry do so within the context of the masses, as part of the minjung. The salvation, deliverance, or wholeness (Greek: *sotēria* or *hygiēs*) of individuals is inextricably connected with the minjung, and the minjung benefit from the salvation or wholeness

---

50. Grant, *White Women's Christ and Black Women's Jesus*, 221.
51. Baker-Fletcher, *Sisters of Dust, Sisters of Spirit*, 20.
52. Phillips, "Introduction—Womanism: On Its Own," xxxvii.

that individuals receive. I call this phenomena inscribed in the text a *Soteriological Hermeneutical Circle*.[53] The Greek noun *sotēria* is translated salvation. Hermeneutics refers to the art or process of interpretation or translation.

In Luke, as Ahn observed in Mark, much of what Jesus said and did occurs in the context of crowds. Individuals that Jesus heals emerge from the crowds and thus were originally minjung. When Jesus heals or restores an individual to wholeness, this individual act of deliverance affects the minjung. Jesus, in Luke, intends to impact particularly those that some, including the elite religious right(eous), label "sinners." The term "sinners" is a designation that the elite religious right(eous) employ signifying people who do not interpret or practice the Mosaic law and/or religious rituals to the same extent or in the same manner as they prescribe or who belong to groups stereotypically associated with certain social positions (e.g. tax collectors or publicans).

This phenomena of stereotyping and thus categorizing people as "sinners and tax collectors" can be observed in contemporary rhetoric. It casts blame on the masses for their poverty and accuses them of collecting or receiving government tax aid undeservedly. Consequently, many individuals who once lived among the minjung will distance themselves from the minjung to avoid guilt by association. Recently, some persons associated with the contemporary so-called "religious right" blamed the masses who live in poverty for their situations. For example, Newt Gingrich stated that "Really poor children in really poor neighborhoods have no habits of working and nobody around them who works, so they literally have no habit of showing up on Monday. They have no habit of staying all day. They have no habit of 'I do this and you give me cash' unless it's illegal."[54] And some like the American Center for Law and Justice's David French believe people are poor because of deep spiritual deficiencies that result in bad choices and they should not be able to rely on the government or the church for assistance.[55] According to US Census Bureau statistics released September, 2011, 46.2 million Americans live below the poverty line.[56] Currently an estimated 15.7 million American children (ages 0 to 17 years) live in poverty.

---

53. See Martin Heidegger, *Being and Time*, 153. Context informs text, and text informs context in what is known as the hermeneutical circle.

54. Newt Gingrich, candidate for the Republican Presidential nomination, fundraiser in Iowa, December 2, 2011.

55. Mantyla, "Why the Religious Right Opposes Government Assistance for the Poor."

56. United States Census Bureau Report, September 13, 2011; online: http://www.census.gov/prod/2011pubs/p60-239.pdf/.

These figures do not include those who live near or around the superficial poverty line.⁵⁷ White children have the *highest poverty numbers* and black children have the *highest poverty rate* with 25.6 percent children in poverty. Black children are only 14.4 percent of the US population. Black families continue to earn the lowest median income of about two-thirds of the average white family.⁵⁸ Globally, billions of people live in poverty. Fallacious and biased ideologies cast masses of people as "sinners and tax collectors" without regard for factors that contribute to mass poverty, such as colonialism, post- and neocolonialism, systemic racism, sexism (and other isms), deregulation, and capitalistic greed and materialism of which many of their accusers are perpetrators or participants. The circle goes both ways, in the direction of salvation and in the way of destruction.

In Luke, we can observe a soteriological hermeneutical circle operative. I shall analyze seven stories (7:1–10; 7:11–17; 8:19–21; 8:40–56; 9:10–17; 15:1–32; 18:9–14; 18:35–43) through a womanist soteriological hermeneutical lens, which I believe shall assist us in understanding the relationship between the crowds/minjung and individuals.⁵⁹ At 7:1–10 (// Matt. 8:5–13) the story about the healing of the centurion's slave is framed by the presence of people/crowds (v.1, *laos* and v.9, *ochlos*). Jesus uses the centurion's example of transformative faith to exhort, teach, and rebuke the masses, which includes Israelites: "to the crowd that was following him he said, 'I tell you, not even in Israel have I found such faith.'" Because of the centurion's faith, which compels him to enter among the crowds to seek Jesus, his slave was restored. As an oppressed and marginalized person, the slave we would identify the slave with the minjung. But since the slave cannot be present to speak and seek Jesus for himself, his master becomes his voice. Similarly, the Lukan story of the encounter between Jesus and the widow of Nain (7:11–17) is framed by the presence of a great crowd/people (v. 11, *ochlos polus*; v. 12, *ochlos*; v. 16, *laos*). When Jesus resurrects the widow of Nain's son, both Jesus and the widow arrive with their crowds. She is a part of the crowds and emerges from the crowds. She speaks for her son. And as one of the most vulnerable in society, subsisting in a patriarchal context without adult male protection, she is the voice and

---

57. Smith, "The Problem of the Color Line and the Poverty Line."

58. United States Census Bureau, "Child Poverty in the United States 2009 and 2010"; online: http://www.census.gov/prod/2011pubs/acsbr10-05.pdf/.

59. I do not generally distinguish between the two Greek nouns *ochlos* (primarily translated "crowd") and *laos* (generally translated "people") in my analysis of Luke because I am more interested in the distinction between larger groups of people as opposed to individuals.

## Part III: Critical Responses to Ahn Byung-Mu's Minjung Theology

embodiment of minjung. After Jesus raises the widow's son, *all* are impacted; the people erupt in praise, viewing the miracle as God's favor upon them too. Jesus demonstrates God's solidarity with the minjung and God's ability and willingness to meet the needs of the minjung who are often *voiceless* and vulnerable people who need physical and/or socioeconomic transformation or wholeness.

At Luke 8:19–21, Jesus' family visits him but cannot reach him because a crowd (*ochlos*) has surrounded him. Jesus takes advantage of this familial visit as an opportunity to conceptually expand family relations beyond biology: "*My mother and my brothers are those people who hear and do the word of God,*" v.21. Jesus' biological family, as the particular, becomes a metaphor for a fictive family, the universal or whole. The part informs the whole and the whole informs the part. But the part and the whole are never synonymous and should not be monolithically or stereotypically construed. Jesus neither excludes his family nor prioritizes them at the expense of the masses. Compare this pericope with 11:27–28 where a woman announces that Jesus' biological mother is blessed. Jesus affirms her proclamation, but he expands her blessing: It is those who hear and keep the word of God that are blessed. Again, the particular of his biological mother becomes a metaphor incorporating the minjung. The minjung are Jesus' kinfolk; they are children of God.

The context for Jesus' healing of Jairus's dying daughter and the woman with the chronic hemorrhaging is the crowded city (8:40–56// Matt 9:18–26; Mark 5:21–43).[60] At v.40 a crowd awaits Jesus' return when Jairus emerges from the crowd seeking Jesus' help for his daughter. Yet Jairus is not the only person in the crowd seeking restoration. While on his way to Jairus's house, a crowd continues to follow and press Jesus. It is as a part of and from within the crowd that the chronically hemorrhaging woman manages to touch the fringes of Jesus' garment. Despite the crowd's density, Jesus is concerned to know who from among the crowd grabbed the fringes on the hem of his garment. The minjung or the masses are the dying and diseased, young and old, with and without advocates who need to be whole.

The woman speaks from the crowd identifying herself. By calling her out compelling her to identify herself, the entire crowd is made aware of the situation. The crowd is drawn into her story because on some level her story is their story; she is one of them. Thus, all of the people (*pantos tou laou*) are

---

60. Luke follows Mark in this regard.

blessed when Jesus makes her whole. Because what Jesus can do for her, he can do for them. God is active in Jesus restoring hope among the minjung.

When the apostles return from their commission (9:1–6), Jesus takes them into Bethsaida to spend some alone time with them (9:10–17; Matt 14:13–21; Mark 6:30–44), but the crowds (*ochloi*) find out and invite themselves to the private gathering. Jesus welcomes (*apodechomai*) the crowds.[61] Generally, Jesus does not engage individuals to the exclusion of crowds or vice versa. We move from the particular to the whole again when Jesus takes the one lunch of two fishes and five loaves to feed a crowd. All roads lead back to the crowds. The mention of the left over twelve baskets full of food also signifies a movement from the universal (the satisfied crowd) back to the particular (the remnants). The story moves from the twelve apostles to the crowds; from the crowds to five loaves and two fish; then from a meager lunch to the actual feeding of the multitude; and from the fulfilled crowd to twelve remaining baskets full of food, representing several turns of the soteriological hermeneutical circle. We see this pattern in terms of feeding, healing, resurrecting the dead, and teaching. Luke's Jesus creates and maintains a connectedness, rhetorically and pragmatically, between individuals and the masses; the salvation or wholeness of individuals is inextricably connected with the minjung.

Only Luke uses three parables to make the point that even if one individual or item is lost, one must attempt to rescue or find him or it (15:1–32; Matt 18:12–14). Luke sets Jesus' sharing of the three parables within the context of a gathering of "*all* the sinners and tax collectors," 15:1. In Luke, the phrase "all the sinners and tax collectors" seems to represent a certain group of people stereotypically understood by some Pharisees and scribes (15:2; cp. 5:29–30; 7:39). The parables show that we should value any individual (or the metaphorical coin or sheep) that is lost or finds herself in an annihilating situation. The lost son, coin, and sheep in this context represent "all the sinners and tax collectors." The gospel is about making people whole and not about exalting those we consider whole or who have "made it" as a synecdochical substitute for the suffering or lost minjung. This point is also made in the Lukan parable of the Publican and the Pharisee (18:9–14). Jesus chastises the Pharisee not because he lives a good ritual and moral life but because of his attitude toward "the rest of the human beings," 18:11. Jesus is not opposed to the Pharisee's lifestyle. But he singles himself out as the one who has achieved as opposed to others who have not obtained a certain

---

61. Mark and Matthew say Jesus had compassion (*esplagchnisthē*).

lifestyle. This sounds all too much like a rhetoric common in contemporary religious circles, especially where the prosperity gospel prevails.

At Luke 18:35–43 (Matt 20:29–34; Mark 10:46–52) even as Jesus journeys to Jerusalem a crowd (*ochlos*) accompanies him. As they pass by, a blind man sitting along the roadway works himself into the crowd. From out of the crowd, the blind man cries out to Jesus for mercy, v.38. He is part of the crowd; he is *a* voice of the crowd. That Jesus took the time to heal this man on his way to his own death demonstrates the priority Jesus places upon the cries and oppressions of the minjung. Again, when Jesus heals the blind man, the minjung are encouraged because God has healed one of them. And this event increases the probability of their healing: all the people praise God, v.42.

The soteriological hermeneutical circle we find inscribed in Luke demonstrates that the minjung are the voiceless, oppressed, suffering, and marginalized people who sometimes have advocates and at other times stand alone "with their backs against the wall." They are women, children, and men who need to speak about their conditions, to be heard, and to be made whole. The minjung live among the masses, emerge from the masses, and they are the masses. Yet, individuals who emerge from the masses are not synonymous with the masses in a stereotypical sense. The minjung are composed of real flesh and blood people with real needs and a desire for wholeness. By journeying among the crowds and allowing the crowds to follow him, Jesus provides space and place for people who make up the crowds to be seen, heard, and made whole. God views the minjung as part of God's family; they are the children of God. We should view the world and our relationship to it organically regardless of how high we have climbed up the socioeconomic ladder. We who arise from the masses should not view ourselves as distinct from the masses. The wholeness that God has engendered through Jesus for individuals that emerge from the masses witness to the possibility of wholeness for all minjung. When an individual experiences salvation or wholeness, it is not for the purpose of exalting herself above the local or global minjung. The historical and contemporary story of the minjung is our story. Yet, no one story exhausts the story or oppressive experiences of the minjung. The crowds are not monolithic; their experiences and their socioeconomic, ethnic, religious and gender statuses differ. But they share in common a need to be delivered from some physical, social, and/or spiritual oppression. In Luke 4:18–19, God's Spirit commissions and anoints Jesus to deliver good news among the poor, to announce the release of the colonized, and restoration of sight to the blind, and to liberate the oppressed. And the minjung will recognize in this the favor of God.

## Conclusion

Today God has anointed us to announce the favor of God upon the poor, the marginalized, the neglected, the voiceless, and those who suffer because of injustice perpetrated against them by church and governments alike. We are not anointed to proclaim a Gospel of prosperity that demonizes and objectifies the poor. God has anointed us to stand in solidarity with the contemporary minjung. Today's minjung include people who live in poverty; exist without shelter/homes; suffer without access to (good) medical treatment; are stigmatized and bullied for being different; and are trafficked and sexually abused in church, home and neighborhood. The minjung are people locally and globally who strive to survive in the rubble and ashes of colonization, deracination and enslavement, Apartheid, holocaust and genocide, Jim Crowism, disenfranchisement, racism, sexism, heterosexism, and unbridled capitalistic greed. The minjung are flesh and blood people cast into the streets and rendered homeless in the midst of a global recovery from a recession caused by Wall Street and disproportionately felt on main street. They are the people who increasingly find themselves languishing on the lower end of a socioeconomic gap continually widening in favor of the rich to the detriment of the underemployed and unemployed poor. They are the mothers who are arrested for sending their children across district lines to receive a better education. We continue to live in a racialized society in which one is ostensibly or physiognomically black or white. The minjung are people who are more likely to be treated unjustly because of the color of their dark skin and who are the objects of laws like "Stand your Ground" that allow a white Latino to hunt down and kill a young black kid carrying candy and iced tea. That same law justifies the imprisonment of a young black woman who fires a warning shot into the air to protect herself from an abusive mate. We are called to take a stand with God in solidarity with the minjung in the struggle for justice, restoration, and wholeness. I am minjung. The minjung are God's children.

# 8

# "The Inhabitants of the Earth" in Revelation
## Ordinary People in Imperial Context
—Greg Carey

"Life, Liberty, and the pursuit of Happiness."

"Christ has died, Christ is risen, Christ will come again."

## Introduction

There are two simple creeds: "Life, Liberty, and the pursuit of Happiness" and "Christ has died, Christ is risen, Christ will come again." Each consists of three items, and each is open to interpretation, but each is demanding absolute loyalty. To these we might add another, "Peace and security," the slogan of Roman imperial theology. This essay, written within the context of a divided and decaying American empire,[1] investigates how the Book of Revelation characterizes ordinary people, "the Inhabitants of the Earth," amidst a conflict between "the testimony of Jesus" and fidelity to Roman imperial religion.

Political orthodoxy in the United States defines the acceptable boundaries of social and political discourse. Though orthodoxy itself can change, a speaker invites hostility and forfeits a public audience by transgressing these boundaries. Commonly held understandings of "Life,

---

1. The adjective *American* would properly refer to the Western hemisphere. In the absence of a felicitous adjectival form for things having to do with the United States of America, I am employing the conventional usage.

Liberty, and the pursuit of Happiness," a phrase taken from the second sentence of the Declaration of Independence, reflect those boundaries. Right to life movements thrive in the United States, even (or especially) among those who have no qualms regarding the execution of political criminals or wars that have led to hundreds of thousands of deaths in Iraq and Afghanistan. In the United States appeals to liberty resound among those who condemn government as a problem rather than a resource, even as the nation incarcerates more of its citizens than any other nation in the world.[2] Opponents of a national health care program appeal to individual freedom (the pursuit of happiness), despite a health insurance industry that dictates how people may access medical care. The acceptable boundaries of public discourse enable such contradictions to thrive.

Americans may disagree concerning the death penalty, abortion, public prayer, foreign policy, labor issues, and free trade. But in those conflicts, even the suggested qualification of individual liberty lies outside the bounds of legitimate public discourse. Meanwhile, ordinary people suffer as the United States experiences its greatest income disparity since the Great Depression and one-third of American families with children live below the poverty line. In short, ordinary people who value life, liberty, and the pursuit of happiness support policies that contribute to their own exploitation. Politicians and business interests embrace "free trade," while working Americans suffer from both un- and underemployment as a result of corporate imperialism. Why pay a fair wage in the United States when labor is cheap in other parts of the world?

All international systems of exploitation, or empires, must discern how to deploy human resources (or labor) to their advantage without diminishing the masses' efficiency or arousing critical levels of resistance.[3] The book of Revelation describes an imperial economic system that generates wealth and luxury for rulers and merchants: gold and silver, jewels and pearls, fine fabrics and scents, livestock and weapons, even slaves (18:12–13). Yet the exploited masses, the "Inhabitants of the Earth," sing praise to the empire and dedicate themselves to it. Pitting the Followers of the Lamb against the Inhabitants of the Earth, Revelation testifies to the divided loyalties created by Roman imperial culture, a pattern that persists in many global contexts to this day.

---

2. Forman, "Why Care about Mass Incarceration?," 998.
3. Hardt and Negri, *Empire*.

Part III: Critical Responses to Ahn Byung-Mu's Minjung Theology

## Minjung Interpretation

Our interest in the Inhabitants of the Earth reflects the influence of Ahn Byung-Mu's minjung hermeneutics, but it takes Ahn's work in a new and complicated direction. In his reading of Mark, Ahn asserts that Mark's Jesus sides with the minjung in their common resistance to the ruling authorities of their day. Reading Mark with perhaps too much historical confidence, Ahn characterizes Jesus' disposition toward the masses: Jesus "accepted and supported them without any conditions."[4] In his reconstruction of early Christian proclamation, Ahn contrasts the formulaic kerygma (or abbreviated proclamation) of emerging Christianity with the story-oriented narration of the Jesus event that emerged among the minjung.[5] Again Ahn emphasizes Jesus' solidarity with the minjung in their common resistance to Roman imperialism and collaboration by Judean elites. Whereas emerging institutional Christianity sought to make peace with the powers of its day, Ahn asserts, the minjung treasured and passed along the more populist Jesus traditions.

With respect to the Gospels, Ahn characterizes the minjung as the common people who follow and support Jesus. Not necessarily impoverished, though most minjung would be poor, these people constitute "the alienated and despised class" in society.[6] Mark denotes the minjung with the Greek term *ochlos* rather than *laos*. *Ochlos* conveys a populist sense, as in *crowd, mob,* or *"the" people*, whereas *laos* particularly refers to the community of Israel. Ahn observes that one frequently encounters the phrase, *ochlos laou,* or "the crowd of the people/Israelites."[7] Though the category is fluid rather than stable, Mark's use of *ochlos* points to the common or despised people who are at once marginalized and feared by the powerful. Likewise, the minjung correspond to ordinary masses of marginalized and alienated persons who have not yet organized themselves.

Ahn roots his work in the Korean movement of minjung theology, or theology from the point of view of "politically, economically, and culturally alienated persons."[8] I claim no competence to assess minjung theology as a movement, but I do find it essential to examine how Ahn characterizes it. Ahn claims that Korean public discourse emphasizes "a

---

4. Ahn, "Jesus and Minjung in the Gospel of Mark."
5. Ahn, "The Transmitters of the Jesus-Event Tradition."
6. Ahn, "Jesus and Minjung in the Gospel of Mark."
7. Ibid.
8. Ahn, "Minjung Theology from the Perspective of the Gospel of Mark."

sense of nation but no minjung." Although the minjung build up and constitute the nation, nationalistic discourse has turned the minjung to its own purposes. In his words, "there is no nation or minjung—there is only government that instrumentalizes both."[9] Though Ahn died in 1997, and though Korea's cultural and economic dynamics change rapidly, minjung theology continues its effort to interpret Scripture from the point of view of the marginalized masses.[10]

Minjung theology speaks specifically from an evolving Korean context, but it has attained global influence. Though Ahn and other minjung theologians have not explored how the concept of minjung might inform theology in other contexts, my reading of Revelation suggests a significant qualification. In contexts marked by imperialism and domination, the minjung do not constitute a homogenous category. Rather, as the Apocalypse "reveals," oppressive dynamics divide ordinary people over against one another.

## Revelation: General Context

As the New Testament's only literary apocalypse, Revelation relates the visionary experience of its narrator, who identifies himself as John. John encounters the risen Christ, who dictates brief letters to seven churches located in the Roman province of Asia, now western Turkey. These seven letters provide a key to the interpretation of Revelation, as they characterize each of the seven churches according to the perspective favored by John. The letters reflect diverse circumstances among the churches. Some live in comfort, while others struggle with poverty. Some are faithful, while others are infected with competing teachings or lethargy. Some churches are experiencing persecution or conflict with local synagogues.

John then ascends into the heavenly realms, where he encounters the Lamb, Revelation's distinctive symbol for Jesus. Before God's throne he witnesses history's climatic conflicts through a series of remarkable images and symbols. As the vision concludes, the New Jerusalem descends to earth, creating a realm of healing and wholeness. He closes the apocalypse with a final exhortation to the churches.

Most interpreters regard Revelation as a call to faithful witness in the face of immense cultural pressure. Nearly every detail of Revelation's

---

9. Ahn, "Minjok, Minjung, and Church."

10. Yim, *Minjung Theology towards a Second Reformation*; Yeong Mee Lee, "A Political Reception of the Bible: Korean Minjung Theological Interpretation of the Bible"; online: http://sbl-site.org/Article.aspx?ArticleID=457/.

interpretation is disputed, but most interpreters agree that Revelation envisions a period of persecution for Followers of the Lamb in Asia. Several references to faithful witness, suffering, and persecution populate the book.

- John himself resides on the island Patmos, perhaps as an exile, on account of "the testimony [*martyria*] of Jesus" (1:9).
- Revelation 2:9–10 refers to conflict with the synagogue, the threat of prison, and suffering.
- Revelation 2:13 mentions "Antipas my faithful witness," who has been killed. This may mark the first occasion in Greek literature in which being a witness (*martys*) takes the connotation of dying for one's faith.
- Revelation 6:9–11 envisions the souls of those who have died on account of their testimony. These cry out for vengeance. (See Rev 20:4.)
- Revelation 12:11 alludes to those who have conquered Satan through their testimony (*martyria*), thereby risking their lives.
- Revelation 13:7 describes the Beast who receives permission "to make war against the Saints and to conquer them."
- Revelation 17:6 depicts the Harlot as "drunk with the blood of the Saints and the blood of the witnesses (*martyrōn*) of Jesus.

Historians debate whether an actual persecution broke out in Asia during the late first century. Within a few decades of Revelation's probable composition, we have Pliny the Younger's account of persecution (*Letters* 10.96–97) in nearby Bithynia. Pliny notes that while he lacks experience regarding trials of Christians, some locals are accusing their neighbors of being Christians. Pliny does not seek them out—thus, persecution is not official Roman policy—but he does require the accused to curse Christ and offer sacrifices on behalf of the emperor. This practice suggests that Pliny, and perhaps the Christians themselves, perceived a conflict between loyalty to Jesus and loyalty to the emperor. Many interpreters link Pliny's report to Revelation 13:12, which may indicate compulsory worship of the emperor. If some Asian cities indeed required participation in the imperial cults, such pressure could explain Revelation's concern regarding persecution. We simply cannot know for sure.

In any case, Revelation calls its audience to witness to Jesus regardless of the cost. It calls for "endurance and faith" (or "resistance and loyalty"; 13:10). It encourages its audience to "come out" from the wicked city (18:4) and to keep their garments clean of profanation (3:4, 18; see 7:13–14). John bears *witness* (1:1; 1:9) to Jesus the faithful *witness* (1:5; 3:14), honoring those who have died on account of their own *witness* (2:13; 12:11; 20:4) and identifying Jesus' followers as those who *witness* to him (12:17).

One readily imagines that those who followed Revelation's program experienced rifts with their neighbors, colleagues, and households. Exclusive witness to Jesus required people to abstain from public meals and festivals, where groups honored various deities. Even adoration of the household gods would be out of bounds. That Revelation employs the language of "coming out" (18:4) and remaining clean (3:4, 18) suggests a suspicious outlook on the larger society. When Revelation characterizes that society as "the Inhabitants of the Earth," we see a rift among dominated peoples. Within the sphere of imperial hegemony and regional hierarchy, Revelation divides the minjung into the Saints and the Inhabitants.

## The Inhabitants of the Earth and the Elites of Asia

Revelation 13 is best known for its characterization of the Beast, the astonishing creature that rises from the sea to dominate the world. "Like" a leopard, with feet like a bear's and a mouth like a lion's, and adorned with ten horns, the Beast evokes the series of kingdoms similarly depicted in Dan 7:1–7. Daniel relates a series of world empires that rule over Israel; Revelation's Beast encompasses all of their power and destructiveness into one force of imperial domination. Deriving its power from the Dragon, Satan (12:9), the Beast evokes worship from "the whole earth" (13:4).

The Beast divides the earth's population into two groups, the Inhabitants of the Earth, whose names are not recorded in the Lamb's book of life, and the Saints, upon whom the Beast wages war (13:7–8). Interpreters often overlook the Inhabitants. Their role is largely passive, yet they are critical for any serious engagement with the situation to which the Apocalypse responds. Coerced and deceived by an Other Beast, the Inhabitants worship the Beast. Their worship includes building images of the Beast. Loyalty to the Beast is rewarded by access to commerce: no one can buy or sell unless one bears the Beast's Mark.

Most interpreters agree as to the basic dynamics of Revelation 13. Just as the beasts of Daniel 7 represent a series of great empires, Revelation's Beast depicts Roman imperial power. Interpreters vary in the level of detail they assign to Revelation's characterization of Rome. For example, the mortal wound of Rev 13:3 (see 17:7–14) convinces many interpreters that Revelation fears the return of the emperor Nero, the first great persecutor of Christians: Revelation may stand among those ancient texts that imagine either Nero's personal return or the rise of an emperor as deadly as he.[11] Nevertheless, most interpreters understand the Beast's arrogance and blasphemy as pointing to the cult of the Roman emperor. Throughout Asia, temples and festivals dedicated to the emperor and to Rome sprouted and flourished during the first century CE. Rome's great power indeed evoked worship, and it rested on both domination and generativity. The Inhabitants proclaim, "Who is like the Beast, and who can make war against him?" (13:4), but they also rely upon the Beast for their commerce. In building roads, developing civil engineering, driving pirates from the coasts, and providing general security against invasion, Rome generated the potential for significant economic growth.

But what of the Other Beast? Unlike the Beast, who arises out of the sea, the Other Beast emerges from the earth. This distinction suggests that the Other Beast represents something indigenous. Again, interpreters generally agree as to a basic understanding. The Other Beast calls attention to the indigenous elites from the Asian cities. Acknowledging their dependence, the Asian elites literally competed to demonstrate their devotion to Rome. Asia's cities petitioned the Roman Senate for the privilege of hosting festivals in the emperor's honor and erecting temples to the emperor himself. The elites further supplied the resources for festive worship, all the way down to the robes and crowns adorning the local choirs (see Rev 2:10; 3:11; 4:4, 10). As modern cities compete to host the Olympic Games and other significant events, Asian cities competed for imperial recognition.[12]

Beneath the elites reside the Saints and the Inhabitants. Two things alienate the Saints from the Inhabitants: loyalty and access. The Saints' loyalty to the Lamb, Christ, precludes them from joining the Inhabitants by worshiping the Beast. Furthermore, the Saints' refusal to join the Inhabitants in worship excludes them from access to commerce, which the Inhabitants enjoy.

Revelation represents this alienation graphically. The Inhabitants, whether of high status or low, wealthy or impoverished, free or enslaved, receive a mark on their right hand and forehead. This mark, "the name of the Beast or the number of its name" (13:17, NRSV), qualifies people to participate in the market, to buy and to sell (13:16–18). This same mark

11. See Carey, *Ultimate Things*, 97–98.
12. On the imperial cult in Asia, see Friesen, *Imperial Cults and the Apocalypse of John*.

also dooms the Inhabitants to judgment (16:2; 20:4). God's slaves reject the Beast's mark, for they have already received a mark on their foreheads that indicates their service to the Lamb (7:2–4). Their resistance at once marks them for martyrdom and for salvation (20:4).

Not all of the Inhabitants benefit equally from imperial commerce. In addition to the Beast, Revelation presents the Great Whore. Decked out in splendor, the Whore rides the Beast. Like the Beast, she executes violence against the Saints (17:1–6; 18:24). We should avoid overly specific identifications, but Revelation associates the Whore with both diplomacy and commerce. Revelation 18 dramatizes how some people lament the Whore's collapse. Kings mourn. Merchants mourn. Sea captains and sailors, all those who do commerce by sea, also mourn. They grieve because the system that has generated luxury and wealth has met its end. Imperial commerce produces items such as gold, silver, jewels, fine fabrics, and weapons—even slaves (18:12–13).

And there lies the essential point. Roman imperial commerce made a very few people fabulously rich, and it benefitted other elites and merchants as well. Yet enormous masses of people, the minjung if you will, toiled to produce that wealth without actually benefitting from it. Their number included millions of slaves. All of these people, whether slave or free, poor or rich, stand among the Inhabitants. The Whore is dangerous not only to the Followers of the Lamb but also to all sorts of other victims (18:24).

Imperial culture divides people from one another. Rome divides the Inhabitants into the few rich and the many poor. But Rome also provides the context in which the Saints separate themselves from the Inhabitants. The Saints' refusal to worship the Emperor not only alienates them from the benefits of imperial order, it also alienates them from their neighbors.

## Interlude: Empire and the Minjung

Revelation reflects a division among ordinary people, the minjung, within Roman Asia. Such division results from the pressures imposed when an imperial culture undermines traditional social bonds and creates new structures that benefit some people at the expense of others. James C. Scott, an anthropologist and political scientist whose work on everyday peasant resistance still informs postcolonial biblical interpretation, observes how subordinate groups experience enormous pressure from their elites. For example, employers may reward subordinates by offering substandard jobs. While such jobs undermine the larger labor market, desperate people accept them

Part III: Critical Responses to Ahn Byung-Mu's Minjung Theology

as a means of survival. This pattern threatens solidarity among laborers and reduces overall compensation in the job markets. Subordinate classes can look after their own interests only by resisting such external pressures—a reality that implies coercion and conflict among subordinates.[13]

Similar dynamics play out in an influential series of novels by the Nigerian author Chinua Achebe. The first and most famous of these, *Things Fall Apart*, involves the first encounter between a set of Ibo villages and their European colonizers. The colonizers bring new religion and new commerce, backed by military might. Predictably, things "fall apart." Some villagers adopt the new ways for themselves, while others resist. Inevitably, families and villages experience division. Achebe declines to offer a one-dimensional characterization of colonialism. Along with their ignorance, violence, and arrogance, the colonizers bring some good things. These gifts include medicine, technology, and some compelling cultural values, but of course they also lead to the dissolution of an ancient way of life.[14]

One readily imagines that Roman imperial culture elicited mixed responses in ancient Asia. Several interpreters of Revelation discern stresses among the believers in Asia concerning status, economics, and loyalty. Where John refers to wealth, poverty, and weakness among the seven churches (2:9; 3:8; 3:17), Paul B. Duff perceives divisions that involve economics and social practice. Some upwardly mobile believers find it necessary to participate in groups and public events that involve sacrifices to patron deities, while the more disadvantaged condemn them as apostates. Condemnations of "Nicolaitans," "Balaam," and "Jezebel" for promoting sexual sin (*porneia*) and eating idol-food (*eidōlothuta*) reflect these tensions (2:6, 14–15, 20–25). As the biblical prophets employed the imagery of sexual sin to condemn idolatry, so John excoriates these competing prophets for accommodating idolatry within the churches.[15]

Just as it does in 1 Corinthians and Romans, the question of diet (idol-food and meat) divides the churches along lines of status. Unlike Paul, however, Revelation links these debates among believers with the larger cultural and economic context of the Empire. The question of idolatry relates to worshiping the Beast. Those who worship the Beast and receive its mark also participate in the economic system (13:16–18). The Whore who rides the Beast generates cargo that ranges from luxury items

---

13. Scott, *Domination and the Arts of Resistance*, 130–31, 85n38.

14. Achebe, *Things Fall Apart*. Later novels in the series follow the process of progress and alienation into global modernity: *No Longer at Ease*, and *Arrow of God*.

15. Duff, *Who Rides the Beast?*

to slaves (18:12–13). Revelation rejects the notion that matters of piety and diet constitute internal debates. On the contrary, one cannot separate worship from Empire and resistance.

John's concerns extend beyond the churches, targeting another group more specific than the Inhabitants. Revelation twice refers to the "synagogue of Satan" (2:9; 3:9). Revelation 2:9–10 identifies slander from "those who call themselves Jews but are not," possibly associating this group with persecution and imprisonment for the church in Smyrna. Revelation 3:9 envisions a moment in which this group will bow before the feet of faithful Saints in Philadelphia—an apparent vindication after conflict. Interpreters have long wrangled over this group's identity. In my view these passages indicate a tension between the churches—still owning their Jewish identity—and their Jewish neighbors.[16] As to the true nature of this tension we can only speculate. Again we recall Pliny's correspondence with Trajan: the Bithynian Christians faced accusations from their neighbors, not from the authorities. Given the precarious situation in which some Jewish communities found themselves, perhaps the dangerous "slander" to which John refers (2:9) amounts to pointing out the distinction between followers of Jesus and the synagogues. Some Jews likely disavowed John's "Saints" as followers of a failed messiah who had been crucified as a seditionist. Whatever the specific complaints, pressure from the Roman imperial context expresses itself in polemics between church and synagogue.[17]

Revelation features multiple divisions due to tensions between the Followers of the Lamb and the Inhabitants of the Earth, conflicts within the churches, and potentially dangerous polemics between synagogues and churches. All of these divisions reflect what I would call 'symptoms' of resistance to Roman imperial culture and commerce.[18]

## Revelation and the Inhabitants

The tension between John's loyalty to Christ and his neighbors' loyalty to Caesar manifests itself in Revelation's portrayal of the Inhabitants. The Apocalypse stages the Inhabitants under an unflattering light. There's no

---

16. The language of "Jews" and "Christians" creates inevitable anachronisms. "Christianity" did not yet exist as a world religion, and the relationship between the Asian churches and the synagogues remains unclear to us. See Marshall, *Parables of War*.

17. For discussion of this problem, with references to the relevant scholarly literature (up to 1999), see Carey, *Elusive Apocalypse*, 18–21.

18. Greg Carey, "Symptoms of Resistance in the Book of Revelation," 169–80; Carey, "The Book of Revelation as Counter-Imperial Script," 157–76.

## Part III: Critical Responses to Ahn Byung-Mu's Minjung Theology

escaping their complicity in the imperial network. Marvelling, they worship the Beast (13:2, 8; 17:8). They commit *porneia* with the Whore, participating in her network of power and commerce (17:2). And they engage in all sorts of idolatrous and immoral behavior (9:21). One might partially excuse these behaviors, as the Other Beast has thoroughly deceived the Inhabitants (13:14; see 18:23; 20:3, 8). Perhaps they do not appreciate the full implications of their behavior.

Excuses only go so far, however. The Inhabitants not only participate in the Beast's network, they execute that system's violence. They exult when the Beast slaughters the Two Prophets who prophesy in the Great City. They rejoice and celebrate, even bestowing gifts to one another in their glee since the Two Prophets had tormented them by causing drought, turning water into blood, and sending plagues (11:10). Moreover, the Inhabitants worship the Beast while it makes war against the Saints (13:7–8), so that the martyrs direct their cry for vengeance against the Inhabitants (6:10). When the sea turns to blood, an angel praises God for judging the Inhabitants: "Because they have poured out the blood of the Saints and the Prophets, you have given them blood to drink—they deserve it!" (16:6).

The devastating judgments we encounter in Revelation specifically target the Inhabitants. Confronted with the first outbreak of disasters, elite and ordinary people alike recognize the Lamb's wrath. They do not cry out to God but to the rocks, asking the rocks to fall on them and hide them from God and from the Lamb (6:16–17). Meanwhile the Saints receive divine protection (7:3). In the midst of Revelation's trumpet judgments, an eagle pronounces, "Woe, woe, woe to the Inhabitants of the Earth" on account of the coming judgments (8:13). Again people seek death in the face of such horrific punishments while the Saints receive protection (9:4–6).

Revelation essentially denies the Inhabitants their humanity. If the capacity for repentance constitutes an essential dimension of what it means to be human, the Inhabitants do not demonstrate this faculty. We have seen how the Inhabitants acknowledge that their suffering amounts to divine judgment, but in their distress they do not turn to God (6:16–17; 9:4–6). Indeed, Revelation explicitly stipulates that those who survive do not repent of their misdeed (9:20–21). One wonders if they cannot. Things escalate to the point that even as people bite their tongues in pain, they manage to curse God rather than to repent—a point Revelation repeats for emphasis (16:9–11).

Many interpreters have noted that, despite these elements, Revelation may hold out hope for the Inhabitants. "All nations" will worship

God, Revelation insists (15:4). In the New Jerusalem a tree bears leaves that bring healing to the nations (22:2; see 21:24–26). Joseph L. Mangina asserts that "the new Jerusalem rests securely in the generosity and the peace of God."[19] Other interpreters are less optimistic. The hope Revelation offers to the nations apparently extends only to those whose names are recorded in the Lamb's book of life (21:27; 22:3). Craig R. Koester offers a theologically attractive option:

> At first glance, we might wonder where these kings and nations come from [in 21:24–26], since the kings of the earth and the nations were said to have been destroyed by the word of Christ and by heavenly fire (19:17–21; 20:7–10). John, however, is not outlining a simple sequence of events, but presenting readers with contrasting visions that include warnings of judgments and promises of salvation.[20]

I remain not fully convinced that Revelation holds out hope for the Inhabitants. Its insistence that, though recognizing God and the Lamb, they do not repent of their violence suggests a less optimistic scenario. This grim sensibility extends to Revelation's clear desire for vengeance, which is voiced by the martyrs (6:10) and celebrated by heavenly choirs (15:3–4; 16:4–7). The nations' presence in the New Jerusalem does extend a measure of hope for the Inhabitants. They too suffer at the hands of the Beast and the Whore (13:4; 18:13, 24), but they also participate in the violence against the Saints.

## Reading the Inhabitants from the Contemporary United States

Revelation's depiction of the Inhabitants of the Earth demonstrates the value of minjung interpretation, but it also reveals that minjung interpretation requires contextualization. If by minjung hermeneutics, we mean to include a sympathetic focus upon the marginalized masses of people, a minjung interpretation of the Apocalypse proves "revelatory." Revelation's imperial context divides the minjung against one another, pitting those who witness to Jesus over against their neighbors, the Inhabitants of the Earth. Revelation points out how the masses of people may be complicitous in deadly systems, even to the point of violence against their neighbors and even when their complicity undermines their own interests.

---

19. Mangina, *Revelation*, 242.
20. Koester, *Revelation and the End of All Things*, 198.

Part III: Critical Responses to Ahn Byung-Mu's Minjung Theology

Revelation voices some sympathy towards the Inhabitants of the Earth. They suffer from both deception and exploitation. Yet the opposition between the Lamb's Followers and the Earth's Inhabitants also uncovers the limitations of an unqualifiedly positive assessment of the minjung—at least in some contexts. Wherever we may land in our theological and ethical assessment of the Apocalypse, it challenges readers to discern the forces that divide ordinary people against one another and lead them to participate in systems that ultimately degrade their own welfare.

Contemporary readers in the United States routinely express frustration with Revelation. Many reject its alleged otherworldliness, its "pie in the sky" hope for deliverance beyond this life. Yet nothing about Revelation suggests disengagement with the present order. Yes, Revelation promises conquest even to the martyrs—but martyrs die precisely because of their "resistance" (1:9; 3:10; 13:10; 14:12) and "testimony" (*martyria*) to Jesus (1:9 again; 2:13; 6:9; 12:11, 17; 20:4). Revelation's ultimate hope lies not in a rapturous escape but in the New Jerusalem coming *down* from heaven.

Other readers find Revelation opaque, with its challenging symbolism and obscure allusions. For modern readers Revelation indeed poses many challenges. Yet ancient readers easily recognized Revelation's direct critique of Roman arrogance and oppression—and, one imagines, ancient readers would also have perceived its bleak assessment of the earth's Inhabitants.

Still other readers object to Revelation's theological and ethical outlook in several respects. Many argue—and I agree—that Revelation voices a desire for violence, along with a rigidly sectarian outlook, and its deployment of feminine imagery belies an ugly misogyny. I will not minimize those objections. Yet contemporary readers need not turn to Revelation, or to other biblical literature, for direct answers to our modern questions. Instead, Revelation's gift may reside in provoking questions we are not yet asking.

Thus this contemporary reader wonders what questions Revelation and minjung theology may address to the heated American political climate of this age. As the Occupy Wall Street movement protests disparities of wealth and income that have achieved historic levels, how do the Inhabitants of the West assess their own situation? Do they yet worship and stand in awe of the imperial and commercial Beast? And as the Tea Party movement, inhabited by countless, mostly white middle-income citizens, applies the "socialist" epithet against reform efforts in the areas of finance, taxation, and health care, one wonders whether the Inhabitants of the West have devoted themselves to the very systems that guarantee their own demise. Those few Christians who regard the current wealth divide between rich and ordinary citizens—not to mention the poor—as a sign of a corrupt and even idolatrous system must confront the question: How does one engage the Inhabitants of the West, who are at once victimized by and perpetuators of their own oppression and the exploitation of countless others?[21]

21. I am grateful to Jin Young Choi of Colgate Rochester Crozer Divinity School, in Rochester, New York and Patrick McCullough of the University of California, Los Angeles, for their careful reading of this essay and their wise comments.

# 9

# Ambivalence, Mimicry, and the *Ochlos* in Gospel of Mark:

## *Assessing the Minjung Theology of Ahn Byung-Mu*

—David Arthur Sánchez

## Introduction

On New Year's Eve 2011, I accompanied a group of students from Loyola Marymount University on an eight-day pilgrimage to Mexico City and environs. As a Mexican born in the United States, I find these trips are often painful encounters with the colonial past of Mexico, in relationship to Spain—and Mexico's neocolonial present, in relationship to the United States of America. Our first stop was in the colonial city of Cuernavaca. I was immediately overwhelmed by the palace of the Spanish conquistador, Hernán Cortés, and the expansive Spanish cathedral in the heart of the city that had displaced the indigenous Aztec edifices that had previously occupied those spaces. The architectural landscape of Mexico City similarly reflected the same Spanish colonial imposition on once Aztec territories. The histories and artifacts of the indigenous peoples of Mexico were either relegated to the National Anthropological Museum or peripheral archaeological sites. What was most prominently foregrounded in the visual landscape of Cuernavaca and Mexico City was the acute Spanish colonial history of Mexico's past.

## David Arthur Sánchez—Ambivalence, Mimicry, and the Ochlos in Gospel of Mark:

Our trip culminated with a physical crossing of the border back into the United States. The majority of US citizens returning to the United States do so via automobile. We chose as a group, however, to encounter the border by legally reentering the United States on foot at the Otay-Mesa border crossing in California. It was a more genuine—albeit safer—attempts to recreate the physical border crossing that thousands of Mexican immigrants attempt each year. Even as U.S. citizens we encountered a series of dehumanizing events in our northern journey. We stood in line for hours in the heat without food, water, or restroom facilities. When we finally entered the US Immigration and Customs Center, we were interrogated and had our bodies physically searched. Our luggage was opened and x-rayed. At the end of the process, I recall a US Border Patrol agent coldly looking at me and saying, "Welcome home."

This recollection of my recent trip to Mexico is a vignette of how I perceive myself ethnically, politically, and theologically. My ethnic identity is fraught with ambivalence because my ancestry is both Spanish and native Mexican. I am both colonizer and colonized, rapist and raped, dominant and marginal. Politically, I straddle the border between the land of my ancestors, Mexico, and the only geographic home I have ever known, the United States of America. Further complicating the issue is the fact that the region in the US where I reside, California, was at one time Mexican territory! As a result, my theology is always informed by the complex negotiation of religious expressions that are imposed (Spanish Catholicism) and those that are indigenous (spiritual and religious practices native to the Americas).

The border crossing also facilitated a painful mimetic compromise in my own perception of self, especially in relationship to the United States *and* Mexico. My pilgrimage into the heart of Mexico demonstrated that I am also "other(ed)" there. Not fully Mexican and not fully "American." I am in-between and interstitial, an exilic border crosser on both sides of the divide. Mimicry was and continues to be a tool of survival in this negotiation. As I re-entered the United States I was expected once again to become the colonial mimic: "adopting the cultural habits, assumptions, institutions and values"[1] of the United States. While in Mexico I spoke only colloquial Spanish, trying to mask my identity as a *pocho*.[2] There too, I strategically adopted the country's cultural habits, assumptions, institu-

---

1. Ashcroft et al., *Post-Colonial Studies*, 139.

2. *Pocho* is a derogatory term used by Mexican nationals for Mexicans born in the United States.

Part III: Critical Responses to Ahn Byung-Mu's Minjung Theology

tions, and values. To be perceived and perform as a non-"other" on both sides of the border allows me (and other "others") to negotiate a hostile world with a sense of invisibility, blending in—all the while negotiating the inner tensions of ambivalent notions of self and national identity.

This essay will employ the postcolonial language of mimicry and ambivalence in assessing the work of Ahn Byung-Mu, especially as they relate to his construction of the *ochlos* in the Gospel of Mark. In my estimation, the *ochlos* in the Gospel of Mark are also in the vulnerable position of being "border-straddlers" between ethnic Galilee and colonial Jerusalem.[3] Therefore, this essay will highlight the constructed identities and activities of the *ochlos* in the Galilee and compare it to their identity and activities in Jerusalem. It is my desire that the language of mimicry and ambivalence will shed light on the painful shift in identity and activities of the *ochlos* in relationship to both Galilee and Jerusalem. The assessment of their identity shift will attempt to shed light on the *ochlos* as colonized (and/or imperialized) actors in the world who performed according to postcolonial (survival) cues. This assessment will also allow for a thicker description of their performance in Jerusalem that Ahn Byung-Mu briefly alludes to when he notes: "then we may need many explanations about how minjung of Galilee and Minjung of Jerusalem are different."[4] This essay will serve to place in critical contrast the *ochlos* of Galilee (which Ahn spends the majority of his focus) and the *ochlos* of Jerusalem. I too will argue that the *ochlos* of Galilee and Jerusalem are different, but not in identity. I propose that the *ochlos* that followed Jesus during his ministry and made the Passover pilgrimage from Galilee to Jerusalem are only different in their negotiation of colonial power between the two locales. I propose that the Galilean *ochlos* are transformed in Jerusalem into ambivalent colonial mimics once removed from the colonized "shelter" of the Galilee. Therefore, the bifurcation between the Galilean and Jerusalem *ochlos* is not one of composition (although I would argue that the Jesus movement may have indeed recruited a few members in Jerusalem), but rather one of performance in relationship to proximity of colonial power.

3. This essay will use the terms *colonialism* and *imperialism* interchangeably in the Saidian sense. See Said, *Culture and Imperialism*, 8. Here Said posits: "The term 'imperialism' means the practice, the theory, and the attitudes of the dominating metropolitan centre ruling a distant territory; 'colonialism', which is almost a consequence of imperialism, is the implanting of settlements in distant territories."

4. Ahn Byung-Mu, "Minjung Theology from the Perspective of the Gospel of Mark." It should also be noted that Ahn uses the terms minjung and *ochlos* interchangeably in his theological construction. For example, see Ahn, "Jesus and Minjung in the Gospel of Mark."

## Mimicry and Ambivalence

According to postcolonial theorist, Homi Bhabha, the notions of mimicry and ambivalence are intertwined. The orientation (and subversive nature) of the colonial mimic is always an ambivalent disposition towards those who have colonized the subject in the subject-object (i.e. colonized-colonizer) relationship. Therefore, Bhabha posits the following relational definition:

> Colonial mimicry is the desire for a reformed, recognizable Other, as a subject of difference that is almost the same but not quite. Which is to say, that the discourse of mimicry is constructed around an ambivalence; in order to be effective, mimicry must continually produce its slippage, its excess, its difference. The authority of that mode of colonial discourse that I have called mimicry is therefore stricken by an indeterminancy: mimicry emerges as the representation of a difference that is itself a process of disavowal. Mimicry is, thus the sign of double articulation; a complex strategy of reform, regulation and discipline, which 'appropriates' the Other as it visualizes power.[5]

As a result, the colonial mimic is perpetually in a state of ambivalence, simultaneously "wanting one thing and its opposite."[6] In one assessment of Bhabha's definition of ambivalence it is noted that:

> Ambivalence disrupts the clear-cut authority of colonial domination because it disturbs the simple relationship between colonizer and colonized. Ambivalence is therefore an unwanted aspect of colonial discourse for the colonizer. The problem for colonial discourse is that it wants to produce compliant subjects who produce its assumptions, habits and values—that is, 'mimic the colonizer. But instead it produces ambivalent subjects who mimicry is never far from mockery. Ambivalence describes this fluctuating relationship between mimicry and mockery, an ambivalence that is fundamentally unsettling to colonial dominance.[7]

In this essay, the terms mimicry and ambivalence will be employed to assess the actions of the *ochlos* in both Jerusalem and the Galilee. The argument that will be promoted is that the Galilean *ochlos* are ambivalent in that the colonized are always simultaneously attracted to and repulsed by the power structures that subjugate them. This would be true of the *ochlos*

---

5. Bhabha, *The Location of Culture*, 85–86.
6. Ashcroft et al., *Post-Colonial Studies*, 12.
7. Ibid., 13.

in both the Galilee and Jerusalem. On the other side of the equation, I will argue that the attribute of mimicry is less acute in the Galilee than in Jerusalem because the colonial expectation of mimicry is not as relevant as the distance increases between the subjugated *ochlos* and the imperial epicenter of Jerusalem. To employ the nomenclature of James Scott, the *ochlos*' "hidden transcript"[8] is much more observable in the Galilee because imperial surveillance is not as concentrated there. However, when the Galilean *ochlos* moved towards Jerusalem, the performative aspect of "public transcript"[9] becomes their *modus operandi* especially after the arrest of Jesus of Nazareth. Therefore, fluctuation is allowed in performance because of the constant counter-pulls of ambivalence; however, mimicry is either magnified or decreased in relationship to proximity of power. As a result, the actions of the *ochlos* as either faithful followers of Jesus in the Galilee or part of the *ochlos* that cries out for his crucifixion in Jerusalem are readily decipherable through the lens of postcolonial theory.

## Minjung Theology and Postcolonial Criticism

For this project, I have been asked as a *Chicano*[10] postcolonial critic to respond to the work of Ahn Byung-Mu. Initially, I would like to introduce two preliminary observations on our methodological dispositions. The first responds to the intentionalities of both postcolonial and liberation agendas. Postcolonial criticism shares the emancipatory commitment of liberationist criticism inasmuch as it:

---

8. See Scott, *Domination and the Arts of Resistance*. Here Scott argues, "Every subordinate group creates out of its ordeal, a "hidden transcript" that represents a critique of power spoken behind the back of the dominantit is a discourse that cannot be spoken in the face of power." On the other hand, "public transcript is a shorthand way of describing the open interaction between subordinates and those who dominate. The public transcript, where it is not positively misleading, is unlikely to tell the whole story about power relations. It is frequently in the interest of both parties to tacitly conspire in misrepresentationsthe more menacing the power, the thicker the mask."

9. Ibid.

10. The term *Chicano/a* is multivalent. I use the term primarily as an ethno-political designation. From an ethnic perspective, it designates people of Mexican ancestry who are born in the United States. Its employment is also an overt rejection of the label *Mexican American*. From a political perspective, it is first and foremost a term of resistance similar to the African American employment of "Black." In my worldview, to designate oneself Chicano/a is to take a political posture of resistance to the continuing neocolonial policies of the United States as it relates to Mexicans and Mexico.

> Offers a space for the once-colonized. It is an interpretive act of the descendents of those once subjugated. In effect it means a resurrection of the marginal, the indigene and the subaltern. It is an act of reclamation, redemption and reaffirmation against the past colonial and current neocolonizing tendencies which continue to exert influence even after territorial and political independence has been accomplished.[11]

However, while both postcolonial and liberationist orientations share some common aspirations, postcolonial (biblical) criticism is:

> Deeply suspicious of the liberationist tendency to give the Bible the unquestioned benefit of the doubt, to regard the Bible itself as *the* place where the message of liberation is to be found, and to excuse the Bible from the critical analytical gaze which other texts (including other readings of the Bible) are subjected.[12]

The by-product of these two observations is that while Ahn and I may share the same emancipatory goals from our unique ethnic and national contexts, the methodologies we employ to critique the power-structures we seek to dismantle are different (i.e. liberationist vs. postcolonial hermeneutics). However, it is quite possible to argue that while Ahn specifically employs a liberationist hermeneutic, he does so in a postcolonial biblical critical manner. In other words, his interpretive work of aligning the *ochlos* in the Gospel of Mark—in conversation with his understanding of modern minjung peoples—is a postcolonial maneuver in that it defines a category of people over against the ruling classes of *both* Jerusalem and Korea. Therefore, like the postcolonial biblical critic, Ahn also focuses, "on the whole issue of expansion, domination, and imperialism as central forces in defining both the biblical narratives and biblical interpretation,"[13] albeit from a contextualized, liberationist perspective.

However, the differences in our reading of the *ochlos* in Jerusalem may indeed be the result of our positionality to the Bible as a liberation theologian and a postcolonial theorist. Ahn spends minimal time in deciphering the actions of the *ochlos* in Jerusalem. This is understandable because from a liberationist perspective, the *ochlos* of Jerusalem seem hardly redeemable. This is especially true in the Gospel of Mark that contains no post-resurrection appearances to redeem them. It is also a difficult and painful maneuver to equate the Galilean and Jerusalem *ochlos* seamlessly to the

---

11. Sugirtharajah, *The Bible and the Third World*, 250.
12. Jean-Pierre Ruiz, "Taking a Stand on the Sand of the Seashore," 124.
13. Sugirtharajah, *Postcolonial Criticism and Biblical Interpretation*, 25.

Part III: Critical Responses to Ahn Byung-Mu's Minjung Theology

modern minjung peoples of Korea. Are we/they—the faithful followers of Jesus—the same minjung/*ochlos* that called for his crucifixion in Jerusalem? How do we connect the faithful *ochlos* of Galilee to the post-resurrection *ochlos* that encounter the risen Jesus in Galilee (again!) as described in the other Synoptic Gospels and John when Mark leaves us with animated cries of the *ochlos* advocating for his crucifixion (Mark 15:13–15)? Is the compression and conflation of the passion of the minjung with the passion of Jesus the only tenable solution to this inconsistency in loyalty?[14] Are we able to frame a people (minjung or *ochlos*) with whom God has a preferential option for in this manner? Perhaps this is not the case from a liberationist's perspective. But, from a postcolonial critical perspective, it is essential. It is a reading that demands a non-innocent reading of our histories. It is a reading that demands that as physical, ideological, and theological border-crossers we recognize the polyvalent aspects of our identities; both positive and negative, righteous and sinful, Galilean-centric and Jerusalem-centric. The resultant postcolonial theology that would emerge is one that validates us in our sin rather than one that validates us in our privileged (i.e. preferential option), perceived righteousness. It is a theology that allows us to be both with Jesus in Galilee *and* Jerusalem.

## Minjung and *Ochlos*

Any broadening of the identity and description of the *ochlos* in the Gospel of Mark requires an assessment of the minjung peoples in modern Korea. Ahn makes the explicit connection between the two groups in his writings. My first exposure to the *ochlos*–minjung theology of Ahn Byung-Mu occurred on my recent pilgrimage to Mexico. It was a reading strategy that I conscientiously employed. My suspicion was that I would be encountering a form of Korean liberation theology and reading it in a Latin American context would amplify my initial encounter with it because of my pre-existing exposures to Latin American theologies of liberation. I was also aware of, but not yet entirely conversant in, the complex colonial history of the Korean Peninsula. What I discovered in my initial exposure to the scholarship of Ahn Byung-Mu was a complex theological system that foregrounded a people: the minjung; and a corollary theological presupposition that understood "God's will is to side with the minjung completely and unconditionally."[15] At first glance, minjung Theology reso-

14. Ahn, "Minjung Theology."
15. Ahn, "Jesus and Minjung."

nated with other forms of liberation theology I had encountered in that it posited that God maintained a "preferential option" for a specific category of people: the minjung of the world.

So who are the minjung to which Byung-Mu refers to and what is their relationship to the *ochlos* mentioned in the New Testament text, the Gospel of Mark—an association quite prominent in Ahn's work? The writings of Ahn were somewhat illusive in offering a specific definition of the minjung. Perhaps, as a contextualized Korean theologian, the author assumed that the reader would understand the meaning matrices from which he wrote. Ahn does, however, offer the following brief description of the Galilee as the site of ancient minjung peoples who are, "the politically, economically, and culturally alienated class."[16] The definition of minjung can be expanded to include the:

> Politically oppressed, economically exploited and culturally alienated. Minjung does not have to satisfy all of these categories. Some intellectuals claimed that if you are politically oppressed, even though you are not poor economically, you are minjung. Similarly, if you are culturally alienated, like women suffering from the patriarchal society, you are minjung women. Nowadays, most migrant workers in Korea might be called "postcolonial" minjung who are certainly politically oppressed, economically exploited, and culturally alienated. In this way we could identify minjung in our society individually and collectively.[17]

Essentially, the minjung are the masses of society that occupy marginal and marginalized spaces in relationship to those perceived as the dominant, centered, and "powerful" class(es), both in antiquity and modernity. The sociologist, Han Wan-Sang, defines the minjung as, "people who are oppressed politically, exploited economically, alienated sociologically, and kept uneducated in cultural and intellectual matters."[18] From a specifically Korean context, the minjung are the "ordinary people" and true subjects of Korean history.[19]

According to Volker Küster, the rise of minjung theology is directly related to political events in Korea during the 1970s in which intellectual circles counteracted the consolidation and perceived abuses of political power by then President Park Chung-Hee. This political-theological

---

16. Ahn, "Minjung Theology from the Perspective of the Gospel of Mark."
17. Küster, *A Protestant Theology of Passion*, xii–xiii.
18. Quoted from Hyun Young-Hak, "Minjung," 4.
19. Küster, *The Many Faces of Jesus Christ*, 155.

Part III: Critical Responses to Ahn Byung-Mu's Minjung Theology

response was especially evident after Park's drafting of the Yushin Constitution which granted the leader unlimited political power. It should not go unrecognized that the impetus for the formal development of minjung theology occurs in the 1970s but the notion of the minjung as a minoritized people precedes the theological worldview and is embedded in the complex, colonial history of Korea.

What I have found most noteworthy in the specific type of minjung theology developed by Ahn is his correlation between the minjung of twentieth-century Korea and the *ochlos* of the first-century Gospel of Mark. This sophisticated theological proposal allows Ahn to derive his emerging ecclesiology from a specific Biblical *topos*. As a result, contemporary minjung peoples are reciprocally defined through the lens of the first-century *ochlos*.

In its most basic form, the Greek term *ochlos* can be defined as: crowd, throng, populace, the (common) people, and a large company.[20] More specifically, Ahn defines the *ochlos* through the lens of the author of the Gospel of Mark whom he argues depicts them as: the non-disciple followers of Jesus (he also notes that the *ochlos* are never rebuked by Jesus while the disciples are)[21]; tax collectors and sinners; widows, children and the sick; oppositional to the ruling class of Jerusalem; feared as a group by the ruling authorities; they are the minjung of Galilee; and they are a class of society which has been marginalized and abandoned.[22]

In true liberationist form, Ahn extrapolates that Jesus never showed what might be termed "universal love." He loved people with partiality. He always stood on the side of the oppressed, the aggrieved, and the weak."[23] Therefore, "[Jesus] stands with the minjung, and promises them the future of God[Like Jesus], God's will is to side with the minjung completely and unconditionally."[24] Consequently, it is not a tremendous ideological leap to conclude that like the liberation theologies that precede it, minjung theology unequivocally posits that Jesus/God have a "preferential option" for a particular category of people, in this particular case, the minjung/*ochlos*. However, as already cited in this essay, if Ahn is to claim this unconditional love and preferential option on behalf of minjung peoples through the lens of the *ochlos* of the Gospel of Mark, he must be prepared to do so collectively as ambivalent, sinful mimics in both the Galilee and Jerusalem.

20. Bauer et al., *A Greek-English Lexicon*, 600–601.
21. Ahn, "Jesus and Minjung."
22. Ibid.
23. Ibid.
24. Ibid.

David Arthur Sánchez—*Ambivalence, Mimicry, and the Ochlos in Gospel of Mark:*

## The Minjung-Ochlos of the Galilee and Jerusalem

One of the most significant contributions of Ahn's work on the *ochlos* in the Gospel of Mark is his foregrounding of Mark's deployment of the term in relationship to the Hebrew Bible and the rest of the New Testament. He specifically notes that in the Septuagint, the term *laos* is used to translate the Hebrew term '*am*, "as many as two thousand times."[25] Ahn also recognizes that in the Septuagint, as well as other Greek sources, the term *laos* is "mostly used to denote a national group and often means belonging to some ruling community."[26] Ahn goes on to note a shift in the deployment of *laos* in the Septuagint when cited in the plural form:

> *Laos* is used specifically for "God's people" '*am*. Another characteristic usage of the Septuagint is that *laoi*, plural of *laos*, is used 140 times, and it has the meaning of "crowd" or *ochlos*. In this case, there is not the substantial meaning of *laos*. This is a significant characteristic, since ordinary people hardly make an appearance in the use of *laos* in the Septuagint.[27]

The shift in deployment of *laos* (national group belonging to some ruling community) in the Septuagint to the plural, *laoi* (crowd or *ochlos*), is significant. According Ahn, the term *ochlos* is used in the Septuagint sixty times with the general meaning of "the mass" but does not suggest a Hebraic term for which it translates. He goes on to argue that:

> *Ochlos* is a descriptive term [whose] precise meaning varies from context to context. It could mean "insurgents," "tactical troops," or just refer to the majority. It sometimes designates a crowd of children and women.[28]

In the New Testament and the Gospel of Mark specifically, Ahn makes the following observation:

> It is certain that in the New Testament, Mark is the first writer to introduce the term *ochlos*. It does not appear in any New Testament writing before Mark, but documents written after Mark, such as the other Gospels and Acts, contain this word many times,

---

25. Ibid.
26. Ibid.
27. Ibid.
28. Ibid.

## Part III: Critical Responses to Ahn Byung-Mu's Minjung Theology

proving the influence of Mark. All of these factors indicate that we must pay close attention to Mark's use of the word *ochlos*.[29]

It is indeed significant that Mark is the first New Testament author to employ the term *ochlos* in that it is never mentioned in the writings of Paul or the Pauline tradition which make up almost half of the New Testament. Ahn attributes this terminological lacuna to Paul's interest being kerygmatic rather than focused on the historical Jesus. The absence of the term in Paul functions to enhance the reader's reception of Mark's overt deployment of the term in his Gospel.

According to Ahn, there are five general characteristics of the *ochlos* in the Gospel of Mark: 1) they form the background of Jesus' activities (Mark 2:4, 13; 3:9, 20, 32; 4:1; 5:21, 24, 31; 8:1; 10:1); 2) Mark applies the term specifically for "tax-collectors and sinners," (2:13–17); 3) They are occasionally differentiated from the disciples (4:36; 6:46; 7:17, 33); 4) The *ochlos* took an anti-Jerusalem position and were clearly on the side of Jesus. They were the minjung of Galilee (2:4–6; 3:2–21; 4:1; 11:18, 27, 32); and 5) Because the *ochlos* were against the rulers, the rulers were afraid of them and tried not to arouse their anger (11:18, 32; 12:12; 15:8, 15).[30] As a result of these general characteristics, Ahn goes on to posit Jesus' general disposition towards the *ochlos*: 1) He has compassion on them (6:34); 2) Jesus declared them his mother and brothers (3:34); and 3) Jesus taught the *ochlos* (2:13; 4:11–12; 7:4; 10:1; 11:18).[31]

From a relational perspective, the *ochlos* are posited in the Gospel of Mark as contrasted, condemned and alienated by the ruling class. They are the "colonial other" having to negotiate the complete imbalance of power distribution in first-century Palestine. In relationship to Jesus, the *ochlos* are accepted unconditionally, who anxiously await the promised Kingdom of God. Jesus is in solidarity with the *ochlos* of the Gospel of Mark. He is part of the *ochlos*; he is minjung.

What is somewhat perplexing in Ahn's article, "Jesus and Minjung in the Gospel of Mark," is his relative silence on the Jerusalem *ochlos* (Mark 15) especially in light of his very thick description of the *ochlos* prior to the arrest of Jesus. What can we learn about them—about us—from their actions? How do we come to terms with the *ochlos* that was ever present in the ministry in Galilee and transformed in Jerusalem that fateful Passover

---

29. Ibid.
30. Ibid.
31. Ibid.

weekend? Is it fair to differentiate them as two separate entities and what are the ramifications—both ancient and modern—of integrating the two?

## A Postcolonial Reading of the Jerusalem Ochlos of Mark 15

In the Gospel of Mark 15:6–15 the *ochlos* is both visible and vocal. In the scene before Pilate, stirred by the chief priests, the *ochlos* advocate for Barabbas, while simultaneously antagonizing Jesus, proclaiming, "Crucify him." If indeed the Galilean *ochlos* are to be differentiated from the Jerusalem *ochlos*, why is the term *ochlos* used both before and after the Passion sequence? If Mark was the first New Testament author to employ the term *ochlos* for a specific category of people, it must be the case that this term is used consistently throughout the entirety of the Gospel of Mark to signify the same group of people. The *ochlos* of the Galilee are the *same* exact *ochlos* in Jerusalem, albeit transformed. It then becomes the work of the exegete to come to terms with the significant transformation of the *ochlos*. It should be noted that even the Galilean apostles are transformed in Jerusalem as seen in Peter's denial (Mark 14:66–72) and Judas' act of "betrayal" (Mark 14:43–50).

The question the exegete is required to ask is why the transformation? Returning to the language of postcolonial theory, colonized peoples are always inclined to a state of ambivalence in relationship to their colonizers. The oppressed are simultaneously attracted to and repulsed by their oppressors. In the buffer zone of the Galilee and environs, where Roman occupation was less concentrated, Jewish people (*ochlos*) were more inclined toward the repulsion aspect of the ambivalence equation (see e.g. Mark 5:1–20). The "hidden transcript" of the occupied could be playfully and critically exhibited apart from the controlling eye of Roman authority; hence, the reputation of the Galilee as a locus of rebellious activity. The messianic language of the Jesus movement is demonstrative of that anti-imperial sensibility (cf. Isaiah 45, where Cyrus of Persia is called God's anointed (messiah) in contrast to occupying Babylon).

Yet in Jerusalem, the *ochlos* is presented in complete camaraderie with the Jerusalem authorities (15:6–15) and eventually with the Roman punitive authorities. The *ochlos* that once stood in solidarity with Jesus also sought his execution. In the face of Roman authority in conjunction with Jewish Temple leadership, the Galilean *ochlos* transformed into the Jerusalem *ochlos*. Messianic enthusiasm withered under the hand of Roman authority. The Galilean *ochlos* shifted from its prior state of repulsion toward dominating authorities on the ambivalence scale towards attraction. This attraction need not be a shift in previous loyalties but rather a defensive strategy that allowed the survival of the group—or more precisely—the individuals that composed it. Covert imperial-critical language (hidden transcript) so readily apparent in the Galilee, gave way to the language of colonial mimicry (public transcript). And that public transcript—that conspiracy of misrepresentations—was observable in Jerusalem that Passover weekend. It is observable in the apostolic colonial mimicry of Judas and Peter and is acutely observable in the cries of "crucify him" uttered by the *ochlos* at the trial scene. From a postcolonial perspective, the *ochlos*—like the apostles—were transformed in Jerusalem into defensive colonial mimics. It is a scenario not hard to imagine given the military intimidation factor of Rome and their complicit Temple authorities. Therefore it should come as no surprise that when the women discover the empty tomb in Mark 16, they are directed to, "go, tell his disciples and Peter that he is going ahead of you to Galilee; there you will see him, just as he told you" (Mark 16:7). The Gospel according to Mark required a (*re*)transformation of the *ochlos* and apostles, a (*re*)transformation that required their return to the Galilee—a (*re*)transformation that could not take place in Jerusalem.

## Conclusion

I am appreciative of the scholarly and theological contributions of Ahn Byung-Mu, especially in relationship to the Gospel of Mark and the minjung peoples of Korea. It is not difficult to imagine all subaltern, minoritized, oppressed, colonized, and "othered" peoples in a similar manner and the fluidity of his work allows for those comparisons. His reading of the *ochlos* in the Gospel of Mark and application to modern minjung is a powerful demonstration of the appropriation and application of Christian Scripture for modern interpreters. The correlation of the *Sitz im Leben* of the *ochlos* in antiquity and the minjung in modernity is foundational for theologies of liberation today, especially—but not limited to — minjung theology. I am deeply appreciative of his commitment to readings of Christian Scripture dedicated to the promotion of social justice.

The postcolonial reading that I have offered is meant to supplement Ahn's theological endeavor. I am in agreement with, and completely supportive of, his liberative reading of the *ochlos* in the Gospel of Mark and its application for minjung peoples today. The supplement that I have added from a postcolonial perspective is that even in this privileged position

(God's preferential option for the *ochlos* and minjung) there is still a tremendous amount of accountability left to shoulder by marginalized and oppressed communities. With privilege comes responsibility, lest we become transformed into hostile *ochloi* as persuaded by the economic lure or modern empires. That, in my estimation, is the complete message of the Gospel of Mark. You are privileged in your positionality as a Galilean *ochlos* but transformation into a Jerusalem *ochlos* is always a potentiality. Persuasion of the powerful is always attractive when you position yourself proximate to it. Fluctuation of loyalties is always vulnerably unstable based on our positive psychological ambivalence towards wealth and power. The Gospel of Mark, in its totality instructs us to always remember the declaration at the empty tomb of Jesus, "he is going ahead of you to Galilee; there you will see him, just as he told you" (Mark 16:7).

# 10

## The Freedom to Just Peace

*Revisiting Minjung Theology for a Current Ecumenical Discourse*

—Fernando Enns

### Introduction

IN THE EARLY 1980s, a student of one famous faculty of theology in Germany proposed to do his exam in systematic theology on Korean minjung theology. He did not pass the exam because of the simple fact that the examining professor knew of no literature about such a thing as minjung theology.[1] Yet, for those of us, who studied theology in Germany during the 1980s and early 1990s—the very place where Ahn Byung-Mu spent nine important years (1956–65) of theological training and reflecting—it was almost impossible not to come across this inspiring person and theological approach.[2] Contextual and liberation theologies were erupting around the globe. By listening to the confessing voices from churches in the midst of political struggles we realized that the story of Jesus was not just a

---

1. Major works in the German language were only forthcoming, most of all: Ahn Byung-Mu, *Draussen vor dem Tor*.

2. Most of all the friend and colleague Volker Küster, who has contributed immensely to the reception of minjung theology in Germany and beyond. Cf. Volker Küster, *A Protestant Theology of Passion*. In addition, Hoffmann-Richter, *Ahn Byung-mu als Minjung-Theologe*; Wieczorek, *Reden von Gott in Afrika und Asien*.

subject of scientific research but also an empowering event that continued to draw persons into its reality in order to provoke remarkable changes in societies. Of course we knew about the impact the gospel can take on biographies, if theologians allow the Christ-realness ("*Christuswirklichkeit*") to interpret social realities, like Dietrich Bonhoeffer and others did. With persons like Ahn Byung-Mu we became aware that this is not simply a fact of the past but that the God-story continues with our generation, in our own context. I share the personal, summarizing account of Jürgen Moltmann for Ahn Byung-Mu and Korean minjung theology: "I was fascinated by the fact that one exegetic discovery—the active role of *ochlos* in the story of Jesus after Mark—provoked a current Christian liberation movement. Since Luther's discovery of the justifying gospel this had not happened very often".[3] We felt encouraged to ask about the relevance of theology for political orientation—a question that had been abandoned from some theology faculties in Germany.

Without doubt, Ahn himself had been inspired by the stories of the German "*Kirchenkampf*," the active resistance against Nazi-terror, and the church's role in social-political rebuilding of society after World War II. And yet, it takes a strong intellectual power, a believing heart, a love for the church and your own people as well as a deep spirituality of longing for the wisdom of God's will to translate theological convictions into an active approach to change social and political realities. And it takes true friends. None can do this alone. Dorothea Schweizer, the first German co-worker at the Korean Theological Study Institute (founded in 1972 by Ahn Byung-Mu), recalls Ahn's passion: "In light of the cruel fact having to live and to breathe in a totalitarian nation-state and being confronted with injustice, human rights violations, restrictions to personal freedom, violence and terror on a daily basis, it was without question for Professor Ahn that a spiritual as well as theological contest with this cruel reality would become a permanent task and challenge ."[4] Dorothea Schweizer

---

3. Moltmann, "Politische Theologie in ökumenischen Kontexten," 9. ("Ich war fasziniert von der Tatsache, wie eine exegetische Entdeckung—die aktive Rolle des ochlos in der Geschichte Jesu nach Markus—eine gegenwärtige befreiende christliche Bewegung hervorgerufen hatte. Das war seit Luthers Entdeckung des rechtfertigenden Evangeliums nicht oft geschehen.")

4. Schweizer, "Das Koreanische Theologische Forschungsinstitut und Prof. Dr. Ahn Byung-Mu."
"Angesichts der schrecklichen Tatsache, in einem totalitär geführten Staat leben und atmen zu müssen und sich täglich mit Ungerechtigkeit, Menschenrechtsverletzungen, Einschränkung der persönlichen Freiheit, bis hin zu Gewalt und autorisiertem Terror konfrontiert zu sehen, war es für Prof. Ahn keine Frage, dass eine geistige

continues to explain that for Ahn it became a clear goal to overcome such cruelty by non-violent means, to give a chance to healing and reconciliation as well as to promote democratization and reunification: "The biblical texts and the readiness to follow Jesus have always been the criterion for him."[5] Only "prophets" like Ahn seem to have the strength to develop a theological approach that is driven by the simple yet most difficult to answer question; how can Christian theology, that carries the message of healing and reconciliation as its center, unfold that liberating power amongst the suffering people, the minjung? As with Bonhoeffer and many other theologians, the encounter with the suffering, the imprisoned, the wounded, had become key-experiences for developing such a powerful theological approach. Moltmann says: "Minjung-theology is a perception of the gospel, experienced in resistance and persecution."[6]

It is true, Ahn has been trained, influenced and inspired by Western (German) university-theology but many in the West (Germany)—like myself—have been reinspired by the way theology can become a life-changing experience, as with minjung theology. This proves that the relevance of any contextual theology is never limited to one single context if the text itself comes to life by the reception of a suffering people. Such a contextual theology becomes a messenger of truth for all other contexts, I believe, in order to be shared in the wide ecumenical family of faith. This article aims at "harvesting" some insights from minjung theology for the current ecumenical debate on "just peace." Following the approach that experience shapes theology—and vice versa (!), I will start by reflecting on some experiences within the German context.

## Minjung Experience in Germany

"We Are the People!"

"Wir sind das Volk!" (We are the people! / We are *ochlos*!) This has been the rallying cry of the people in former East Germany, as they marched on the streets of Leipzig and other cities in the fall of 1989, tens of thousands of them. This chant became the center of the demonstrations. All frustration,

---

und theologische Auseinandersetzung mit dieser grausamen Wirklichkeit permanente Aufgabe und Herausforderung für das KTSI sei."

5. Ibid. "Die biblischen Quellen und die Bereitschaft zur Nachfolge waren für ihn dabei immer der Maßstab."

6. Moltmann, "Vorwort," 12, in Moltmann, Minjung: "Minjung-Theologie ist eine im Widerstand unter Verfolgungen erfahrene Erkenntnis des Evangeliums."

all pain, all suffering of years of oppression found a single concentration in these simple words which everyone could understand. The slogan was a summarizing, empowering and self-assuring expression for all the hopes for a different future: democracy, human rights, freedom!

There are moments in the histories of people when everything comes together. The limit of frustration with the existing political system is reaching a climax, and too many people have suffered injustice under the ruling powers. The group who was able to come to terms with the system is diminishing, and the majority does not see a future for themselves any longer. Yet there are "prophets" (sometimes martyrs) who symbolize and proclaim a possible, a just alternative. This is the *kairos* for change in a society. People of all kinds, young and old, rich and poor, educated and non-educated, men and women, believers and non-believers are forming one big movement. That one single issue of becoming aware of who you are can be found in *ochlos* who join hands in solidarity. For the people of East Germany that moment of awareness of its own power came in the fall of 1989. "*We* are the people!"

There are no promises that change will really come, and no guarantees that a better future will in fact arise. It is more likely that "the system" will fight back, as it has done so many times before, without grace, making things even worse, legitimizing the use of massive violence by calling "those people" terrorists, anarchists, accusing them of being influenced by foreign hostile powers. For the sake of security and stability violent abolition of the people's movement seems politically defendable. Still, in a real *kairos*, the people do not buy into that rational of violent, oppressive power any longer. The collective cry for freedom seems to be stronger than the fear that things could get worse for the individual.

Today we witness movements like these in many different Arab countries. None of all the political experts had foreseen these developments. It seems that it is really the people themselves who decide when time is fulfilled. Is not this the reality of the *ochlos*, described in the Gospel of Mark and pointed out by minjung theology?

## "No Violence!"

In East Germany, there was another slogan, as famous as "we are the people," that was chanted in all the mass demonstrations towards the end of the struggle: "Keine Gewalt!" ("no violence!"). As simple as the other slogan, again, this one had a uniting, strengthening, disciplining force: it

## Part III: Critical Responses to Ahn Byung-Mu's Minjung Theology

reminded all demonstrators that they agreed not to use violence of any kind. They would not accept to be caught into the vicious circle of violence. And it was a clear signal to the representatives of the political system, police and military forces: we are not threatening you personally, we will not fight against you, and we know that—in the end—you are part of the people as well. Many analysts of those days say that this chant was crucial for the peaceful outcome of the struggle. No bullets were shot, and the system simply collapsed by the non-violent power of the people, *ochlos*.

The interesting question is: How in the world could such a diverse crowd agree on that chant "no violence"? Here the churches played a decisive role. The churches had been one of the few places in society that provided a space for gatherings without allowing the government to control the contents of their meetings. One should not become too romantic; the churches were not the driving forces of the "revolution." Of course there had been collaborators in the churches as well, and of course the churches were always at risk to loose their limited freedom. But the churches had become marginalized minorities in the system as well. There were enough courageous congregations who understood themselves as places *of* the people: a place to assemble in order to share their sorrows, a place to interpret their situation in light of the gospel, a place for comfort and encouragement, without conditions for entering that space. This is fulfilling the priestly as well as the prophetic calling of the church. All major demonstrations in the fall of 1989 in Germany started with a prayer in the churches, candles were lit and the beatitudes of the Sermon on the Mount were translated into the *kairos* situation: "no violence!" Is not this the very character of a minjung church?

There is one more dimension that I want to highlight here since it seems to have been crucial for the churches to become such places.[7] After the fall of the iron curtain, those churches became minority churches again. But during the *kairos* they were at the center of the people's movement. For decades these churches had been searching for a way to confess the gospel truth within an atheistic and discriminating political system—by searching for help and support of the international ecumenical family. They had become truly ecumenical spaces, not so much concerned about denominational boarders or membership numbers. Over the years they had strengthened their ties with the ecumenical world. The Conciliar Pro-

---

7. Among the literature by people who have been personally affected and actively involved in the struggle, cf. Falcke, *Wo bleibt die Freiheit?* Subklew-Jeutner, *Der Pankower Friedenskreis*.

cess for Justice, Peace, and the Integrity of Creation (JPIC) of the World Council of Churches (WCC)[8] during the 1980s helped them to express a clear vision of a just and peaceful society. In retrospect, it seems this was a necessary preparatory process for what was yet to come. The actors themselves were surprised by the sudden "reality check" of all their fine ecumenical documents for which they were not unprepared![9] After the collapse of the political system, these ecumenical documents gave some guidance for the important discussions on how to construct a new society. Some formulas have even found their way into programs of political parties. To become a minjung church in East Germany, three factors seem to have been crucial: the presence and the openness to people of all kinds, a healthy distance and independence from the political powers in order to be credible, and strong ecumenical relations beyond one's own nation state (for support as well as for possible corrections from nationalistic ideologies or sectarian and fundamentalist tendencies). Minjung theology might be a Korean, contextual theology. Still this very experience of the churches in East Germany allows for a cross-contextual, cross-cultural, ecumenical reading of minjung theology. I believe this is the experience of so many churches in situations of injustice, violence, and oppression. *Ochlos* is a global phenomenon!

## "Freedom!"

Towards the end of the 1980s when major changes took place in South Korean society and former opposition leaders moved into political power, I asked Paul Schneiss,[10] who had been part of the political struggle, what the role of the church would be in such a situation when "the battle is won," and when former dissidents and theologians become politicians in power? His surprising reply was, "forming opposition again!" I have been thinking about that ever since. The current president of the Federal Republic of Germany is Joachim Gauck, a former pastor of those churches in East Germany, who became a politician after Germany's reunification. His central message is, we have been longing for freedom so desperately. And we have

8. Cf. Niles, comp., *Between the Flood and the Rainbow*.
9. Cf. Brown, *Von der Unzufriedenheit zum Widerspruch*.
10. I am most grateful to my father-in-law, Reverend Paul Schneiss (who worked on behalf of the Evangelische Kirche in Deutschland in Japan and Korea during the times of severe political struggle 1975–1984), for having introduced me to the Korean context, the political struggle of his friends and their theological approach. This has provided me with some insights that I did not find in any of the books on minjung theology.

Part III: Critical Responses to Ahn Byung-Mu's Minjung Theology

gained freedom—*from* oppression, *from* restrictions, *from* injustice. What we have to learn now is to make good use of that freedom: the freedom *to* get engaged in political affairs, the freedom *to* responsibility for one another.[11]

Drastic changes have been experienced in many different societies after the so-called end of the cold war.[12] Military regimes, which had been supported strongly by the ideological blocks, went away (like in South Korea and other parts of Asia, as well as in Latin America) the Apartheid system in South Africa was overthrown. And yet, a world so drastically changed, still witnesses oppression of masses of people, living in unjust poverty and exploitation, killing each other for all kinds of reasons, waging wars—often civil-wars within a society, and ruining the means of livelihood for future generations. The excitement of the possibility for a bright future under democratic conditions, respecting human dignity and rights for all was soon overshadowed by the realities and results of a one-sided neo-liberal globalization that seemed to replace the old political ideologies.

Of course, in every single context there are many different factors that need to be taken into account. Injustice and violence seldom have one single root-cause, and it is the composition of economic, political, and cultural, sometimes even religious dimensions that lead to new suffering. And yet, from an "ecumenical perspective"—the experience of exchange between many different contextual perspectives, the church as the community of all believers in Christ needs to confront those realities collectively. "If one part suffers, the whole body suffers".

## The Freedom to Responsibility: Just Peace As an Emerging Ecumenical Paradigm

For the churches in the WCC reflecting on these new circumstances it became clear that a new joint effort had to be made in order to pick up the "freedom to responsibility" for justice, peace and creation and take that to Conciliar Process to its next step. As a result of many interdenominational and intercontextual deliberations a "Decade to Overcome Violence—Churches Seeking Reconciliation and Peace 2001–2010" (DOV) was proclaimed at the Assembly in Harare/Zimbabwe. Of course, the historic

---

11. Cf. Gauck, *Freiheit: Ein Plädoyer*.

12. I hesitate to use this phrase, for two reasons: in many parts of the world this period from World War II to 1990 was not been a time of cold war but of hot, vicarious battles; maybe we should not speak of an end of the cold war unless we witness the reunification of Korea.

peace churches (like the Mennonite Church, of which I am member; the Society of Friends—Quakers; and the Church of the Brethren) had been at the forefront in promoting that decade. It became a true ecumenical movement; many churches in different cultural and political contexts took the opportunity to (re-)connect their efforts in building just and peaceful communities. New programs and discussions were started in many regions, in Korea as well as in Germany and many other parts of the world. The WCC served as a platform to bring all these initiatives together in order to provide a space for joint learning and discerning. Many solidarity visits ("Team Visits")[13] were organized, and expert consultations[14] on chosen topics brought the much-needed depth to the ecumenical discussions and reflections. Toward the end of the DOV, an extra effort was made to formulate together what the churches see as their call and duty after those ten years: *An Ecumenical Call to Just Peace* was issued, based on the churches´ ten-year experience. The International Ecumenical Peace Convocation (IEPC) in Kingston, Jamaica, in 2011, marked the culmination of that common journey (similar to that World Convocation 1990 in Seoul at the end of the JPIC). It issued a message[15] as well as a broad study document on Just Peace (the Just Peace Companion),[16] which "presents more developed biblical, theological and ethical considerations, proposals for further exploration and examples of good practice."[17] It is hoped that these materials will assist the WCC to reach a new ecumenical consensus on justice and peace.

In what follows I will make the attempt to revisit minjung theology in order to see how this contextual theology could enrich and contribute to that emerging new paradigm of Just Peace. I do not feel to be in the position of criticizing minjung theology since I am not Korean, I do not speak Korean. I prefer to listen as carefully as possible to those theological insights/experiences and ways of theological reflection of a people in another context that offer that knowledge to be shared in the ecumenical

13. Cf. http://www.overcomingviolence.org/en/peace-convocation/preparatory-process/living-letters-visits.html/.

14. Cf. http://www.overcomingviolence.org/en/peace-convocation/preparatory-process/expert-consultations/past-events.html/.

15. "Glory to God and Peace on Earth." The Message of the International Ecumenical Peace Convocation, Kingston (Jamaica): World Council of Churches 2011. Online: http://www.overcomingviolence.org/en/resources-dov/wcc-resources/documents/presentations-speeches-messages/iepc-message.html/.

16. World Council of Churches, *Just Peace Companion*.

17. World Council of Churches, *An Ecumenical Call to Just Peace*. Online: http://www.overcomingviolence.org/fileadmin/dov/files/iepc/resources/ECJustPeace_English.pdf/.

family of faith. If that new paradigm of Just Peace is going to be an ecumenical one, it needs to be reflected and enriched by many different contextual theologies. I am convinced that the upcoming Assembly of the WCC in Busan/South Korea in 2013 will provide an excellent forum to deepen these encounters.

## Just Peace—A Holistic Approach

In connecting the ecclesiological challenges of unity in reconciled diversity (*koinonia*), Just Peace has emerged as the key concept towards a common and coherent ecumenical theological ethics: "The Way of Just Peace is fundamentally different from the concept of "just war" and much more than criteria for protecting people from the unjust use of force; in addition to silencing weapons, it embraces social justice, the rule of law, respect for human rights and shared human security."[18] Just Peace may be comprehended "as a collective and dynamic yet grounded process of freeing human beings from fear and want, of overcoming enmity, discrimination and oppression, and of establishing conditions for just relationships that privilege the experience of the most vulnerable and respect the integrity of creation."[19]

Just Peace is an overarching concept that overcomes the old dichotomy of non-violent peace building and fighting for justice. In the ecumenical movement too often we have pursued justice at the expense of peace, and peace at the expense of justice. During the DOV we have learned that "to conceive peace apart from justice is to compromise the hope that 'justice and peace shall embrace' (Ps 85:10). When justice and peace are lacking, or set in opposition, we need to reform our ways."[20] The Ecumenical Call recalls the biblical wisdom, that justice is the inseparable companion of peace (Isa 32:17; James 3:18). "Both point to right and sustainable relationships in human society, the vitality of our connections with the earth, the 'well-being' and integrity of creation. Peace is God's gift to a broken but beloved world, today as in the lifetime of Jesus Christ."[21] We catch a glimpse of that gift of peace, "wherever there is forgiveness, respect for human dignity, generosity, and care for the weak in the common life of humanity."[22] And we lose that peace when injustice, poverty and disease

18. Ibid., 10.
19. Ibid., 11.
20. Ibid., 1.
21. Ibid., 3.
22. Ibid., 5.

"inflict wounds on the bodies and souls of human beings, on society and on the earth."[23] By revisiting the writings of Ahn Byung-Mu, I discover that holistic view as well. As a New Testament scholar, who interpreted the Jesus narrations in light of the situation of Korean minjung, Ahn discovered that a sociohistorical reading of those biblical testimonies was needed in order to grasp the liberating power of the gospel.[24] Reducing the gospel to a *"kerygma"* theology (like some of his teachers did in Germany) was to lose that holistic understanding: It is the social, political, economic, religious, and cultural reality of *ochlos* that is the key to reading the gospel of Mark. Justice and peace are announced to the people of Galilee who suffered under the very conditions of real oppression, real poverty, and real discrimination. The proclamation of the kingdom of God is addressing these very realities. Separating the spiritual from the economic or the political dimension of life would be a misreading of the Jesus narration.

## Perspective Is Key: Becoming the Subject of History

In the current ecumenical debate on Just Peace, the situation of the poor and the oppressed is a focus: "Let the peoples speak" is a phrase in the Ecumenical Call. "There are many stories to tell—stories soaked with violence, the violation of human dignity and the destruction of creation. If all ears would hear the cries, no place would be truly silent."[25] The document continues to list some of the current challenges[26] and asks the churches to advocate "for the full implementation of economic, social and cultural rights. Churches must promote alternative economic policies for sustainable production and consumption, redistributive growth, fair taxes, fair trade, and the universal provisioning of clean water, clean air and other common goods."[27]

In a recent discussion of the results of the IEPC, it was De Chickera Geetha, a theologian from Sri Lanka, who made the following point: "We need to be aware of the fact that there is a real difference which plays into all our ecumenical theology—the difference between those who sit in the boiling pot and those who look into that pot." Ahn Byung-Mu has made this point more than once and provokes the question of whether there can

23. Ibid.
24. Cf. Ahn, *Jesus of Galilee*, chs. 5 and 6.
25. World Council of Churches, *An Ecumenical Call*, 2.
26. Ibid., 30.
27. Ibid., 38.

be a real understanding between those who are sitting in the boiling pot and those (like me) who are looking into the pot.

Minjung theology seems to be convinced that it is the *ochlos* sitting in the pot whom Jesus sought and shared meals with. They became his family (cf. Mk 3:31–35). Jesus' liberating and empowering presence amongst them led them to understand: We, the suffering, the imprisoned, the sick, the so-called sinners are in fact subject of history, not just objects of the ruling political, economic and religious powers.[28] We are the first addressees of God's message. It is therefore primarily the *ochlos* who needs to interpret the gospel.

For the ecumenical debates on Just Peace this has far reaching implications. Unless the churches (usually it is the church leaders and delegated theologians) invite, welcome, and listen to the voices of the *ochlos*, we will probably not be able to interpret the realities in light of the reality of Christ (*Christuswirklichkeit*). Even with the best intentions, our calls for more just and peaceful relations might end up revealing a perspective of those in power who try to speak on behalf of the marginalized instead of providing spaces for them to express themselves. It is an unchangeable fact that the church contains suffering members and those who cause suffering. What we need to see (by listening to minjung theology) is the fact that Jesus did not speak on behalf of the marginalized, did not call the authorities to change but first and foremost shared communion with *ochlos*. The church shall not simply advocate for the marginalized. The church is where the marginalized are; otherwise, it is not the church of Jesus Christ. *Ochlos* is not just a sociological term but also a theological category.[29] How do we assure that the one's sitting in the boiling pot takes a leading role when we discuss the issues of Just Peace in light of the Gospel?

## Methodology: Orthopraxis Preludes Orthodoxy

Inseparably connected to the question of perspective is the question of methodology. The DOV was inspired by people who were directly involved in situations of violence. The ecumenical campaign "Pace to the City" connected people cross-culturally: Seven cities around the world were chosen as examples and focal points of severe violence. In all these

---

28. Cf. Commission on Theological Concerns of the Christian Conference of Asia, Minjung Theology.

29. Cf. David Kwang-Sun Suh, foreword to Küster, *A Protestant Theology of Passion*, xiii.

places we identified people who shared the lives of the most marginalized and depressed from violence, still carrying within themselves the vision, that another world is possible, that situations can change, and that those changes can be brought by the *ochlos* themselves, nonviolently.[30] Without the creative methodologies used by these "saints," the WCC would not have found the inspiration for a Decade to Overcome Violence. During the DOV we have continued to incorporate as many voices and contexts of people who are in the midst of the struggles to overcome direct and indirect (systemic) forms of violence.

And yet, the challenge remains, for (classical) theology as well as for the church (leadership) in general, who discuss that ecumenical framework of Just Peace: Are we aware of methodologies that are used and offered by the *ochlos* to shape that emerging ecumenical concept? For Ahn it was self-evident that a lively connection to *hyunjang* (the place where it happens) was a precondition of doing theology.[31] "We did not have minjung theology in our head first, and then went out into the streets and acted," David Suh recalls.[32] Reflection comes after action and leads to new action. Minjung theology is "*inductive* and not deductive, *descriptive* and therefore not normative, *story telling* and not system building, *biographical* and not theological construction, and it is open to *dialogue* and not closed and final as in dogmas and fundamentalism. Minjung theology is not a theology of the Word, but a theology about the world and for the world. It is to change the world and not to explain the world."[33]

Revisiting this approach, I see the need to invite a much greater variety and creativity in theological methods for the current ecumenical debates. This would help the discourse itself to be less exclusive and more integrative, connected to real lives of real people, open to new insights and corrections of traditional dogmas that have led the churches to end up at the side of the political powers more than once. This of course includes giving up some control over the theological discourse—in the end to become more ecumenical. Cross-cultural encounters have taught us this lesson for quite some time (especially in the West), and still we hesitate to value and incorporate different methodologies within the institutionalized circles of the ecumenical movement. The absence from ongoing discourses of some

---

30. I have described this campaign in more detail in Enns, *Ökumene und Frieden*, 180–94. See the English version: "Breaking the Cycle of Violence."

31. According to Dorothea Schweizer; see note 4.

32. David Kwang-Sun Suh, foreword to Küser, *A Protestant Theology of Passon*, xiii.

33. Ibid., xiv.

Part III: Critical Responses to Ahn Byung-Mu's Minjung Theology

contextual approaches to theology (in the end there are only contextual ones, I believe) is not so much a sign of *their* weakness but rather a symbol of the weakness of the ecumenical movement.

### The Relevance of the Suffering Jesus

When churches feel empowered to confront situations of injustice and violence, they refer to the life and teachings of Jesus Christ, of course, whom they confess as their Lord and Savior. "Through the life and teachings, the death and resurrection of Jesus Christ, we perceive peace as both promise and present—a hope for the future and a gift here and now," the churches confirm in a rather general manner.[34] Insight is growing that this is not just *kerygma*, as Ahn would probably call this language and way of thinking, but it is relevant for those who suffer from injustice and violence. "Despite persecution, he (Jesus) remains steadfast in his active nonviolence, even to death. His life of commitment to justice ends on a cross, an instrument of torture and execution. With the resurrection of Jesus, God confirms that such steadfast love, such obedience, such trust, leads to life. This is true also for us."[35]

In traditional theology, the death and the resurrection of Jesus the Christ is often interpreted as one big movement. That is not incorrect, I believe, as we look at the Jesus-narrations and interpretations of the various New Testament accounts, from Matthew to Paul. Still, when we debated this "Ecumenical Call to Just Peace" with representatives from other religions during the IEPC in Jamaica, it was a Muslim from South Africa who raised the most important question: "I see a lot of very good and helpful political analysis, affirmation and moral calls in your paper, which I share. And yet I wonder: Does the suffering person on the cross, whom you refer to in your confessions so strongly, have anything to do with your call to justice and peace? I do not find that in your paper."

Ahn has pointed out time and again: If we move too quickly from death to resurrection, we will miss very important aspects of the gospel message. Referring to the Gospel of Mark—often in opposition to the Pauline Letters, because of the interpretation of his German teachers,[36] Ahn

34. World Council of Churches, *An Ecumenical Call for Just Peace*, 3.

35. Ibid., 4.

36. Observing the latest developments in the research of Pauline literature, my impression is that Ahn would have enjoyed the sociohistorical reading of Paul and would have welcomed much of that outcome to be in line with his interpretation of Mark. Cf.

realized that the passion of Christ is described in a very realistic way. And he was sure that this was not done without purpose.[37] It is much more the suffering Jesus who provides hope for the suffering, not so much the risen and ruling Christ. It is most obvious that a theologian like Ahn, who has been put to prison like a criminal simply because he seemed to be a threat to the powers, who experienced the realities of imprisonment of a military regime, who suffered from health problems for the rest of his life, reads the passion narrative of Jesus from that perspective of those experiences. He points out that there is nothing heroic in Jesus' pain, fear, abandonment by all his friends (except for the women).[38] "My God, My God, why hast Thou forsaken me?" (Mk 15:34) are the final words of the dying Messiah according to Mark. This is the experience of the absence of God! "Jesus dies, powerless to do anything in the face of such injustice."[39]

Ahn argues that it is this very experience that allows the *ochlos* to identify with Jesus, as Jesus has identified himself with them, from the beginning to the end of his life span. This has become formative for minjung Christology. "We have discovered Jesus as minjung, and the Jesus event as minjung event."[40] Minjung in Mark can see their own death from Jesus' death, Ahn says. By dying this death, Jesus is minjung. *Han*, the experience of collective sorrow and anger, is portrayed in this death. It is the crucified minjung.

Ahn continues to explain, that "minjung-theologian Mark" interprets Jesus' death as "the end of the vicious cycle of reality which is from strength for strength and violence to violence."[41] Jesus' dying "for us" is to be interpreted first of all as a starting point of changing realities here and now, not as a saving act of paying tribute for the sins of human kind in order to satisfy God! "The sword of violence loses its grip because he did not respond to the sword with a sword but responded to it by dying by the

---

for example Gerber, *Paulus und seine "Kinder."*

37. Cf. Ahn, *Jesus of Galilee*, ch. 11.

38. Ahn offers a whole chapter on the special role of women in *Jesus of Galilee*, which would be yet another aspect to be taken into account here. Cf. Ahn, *Jesus of Galilee*, ch. 8. See also p. 232.

39. Ibid., 241.

40. The differentiation of *identification* and *identity* has helped the discussions on minjung theology at this crucial point: "we may identify Jesus as minjung, but we may not say that Jesus and minjung are the same (identity). Furthermore, we may say that Jesus is minjung, but we cannot say that minjung is Jesus." David Kwang-Sun Suh, foreword, xiv.

41. Ahn, "Minjung Theology from the Perspective of the Gospel of Mark."

enemy's sword. Such resistance exposes the ugly face of the people who were trying to kill him," Ahn reads in Mark.

To profit from these key insights of minjung Christology for the ongoing discussion on peace building in God's kingdom and overcoming injustices in the ecumenical realm, we need to revisit our interpretations of the passion of Christ. For minjung, it seems to be the key to understand how much they are part and taken into the God-Story: to the very end and even beyond ("And Jesus said to them, 'After I am risen, I will go before you into *Galilee*'" [Mark 14:28])! For the "principalities and powers" the cross is an act of unmasking the limits of their power. And for all of us it is the "once and for all" affirmation that those vicious cycles of violence and injustice are reversible. They are not eternal. To comply with such realities as if they were stronger than the love of Jesus for minjung is the same as betraying Jesus/minjung anew and crucify him/them again. To understand the truth of Jesus' passionate way of non-violent resistance is in fact the ultimate logic and promise of the coming Kingdom.

It is from this Kingdom-perspective that the churches need to explore their own role in the Jesus, Son of God, Son of Man, minjung—story. If this is missing in our ecumenical deliberations on Just Peace, we have nothing to add to the political discussions of our time. But if we re-discover the identification of the suffering Jesus and the suffering *ochlos*, we might be able to interpret our realities in a totally different way—to a degree that those realities might change, as we have seen in East-Germany, as we have seen in South Korea.

## Conclusion

It seems to be a fact that minjung theology has lost its influence and power in Korea (some say that this is the case since the minjung started to drive cars) and formerly influential institutions like the KTSI, which had become a truly ecumenical space for so many, are questioning their own future. But I believe that there are aspects in this contextual minjung approach to theology that the ecumenical family of churches cannot afford to overlook. This is especially true for the current deliberations on Just Peace as an emerging paradigm for a common, ecumenical theological ethics.

The minjung movement of the context I live in Germany has taught us that it is possible to change political realities against all odds. It has proven that the churches are in fact able to play a decisive role in the minjung struggle for freedom and democracy. One condition seems to be that the churches are minjung churches, as marginalized as the most powerless, yet ready to provide ecumenical spaces, embracing the struggle of the people. After political freedom is won, the challenge arises to use that freedom responsively: the freedom to build just and peaceful relationships across all borders. Together with Christians from around the globe we realize that this is a gift and a calling that needs to form the ecumenical communion. If the ones who have experienced liberation fail to use our freedom in that regard, we might as well question if we have simply replaced ideologies, causing new dependencies and marginalization.

To follow an ecumenical approach is to welcome and listen to all contextual theologies: in order to see the realities of today's minjung in every region as well as to learn from their theological insights *and* methodologies. Korean minjung theology in particular offers a richness of wisdom that was born in situations of struggle. Here I could only discuss a few, still key aspects. To allow such a theological approach to challenge some of the traditional dogmas as well as the self-understanding of the church is to take the New Testament accounts of the Jesus narratives seriously. It is through the eyes of minjung that the church and its theologies need to be reformed time and again, if the claim to be "Christian" shall have any credibility. Ecumenism implies to provoke each other to a courageous faith and to strengthen each other in following Jesus towards justice and peace. "In the end, ecumenism is the joint participation of the congregations of Christ in the suffering and liberation of ochlos," Jürgen Moltmann summarizes his introduction to minjung theology.[42] My hope and my prayer is that those of us who have experienced liberation—from what kind of oppression ever—continue to allow those who still suffer to teach us Christian theology—the way of Jesus of Galilee, the Christ.

---

42. Moltmann, Minjung, Vorwort, 11.

# 11

# Minjung Theology and Global Peacemaking
*From Galilee to the US Military Camptown (kijich'on) in South Korea*

—Keun-joo Christine Pae

## Introduction

THE MINJUNG REFERS TO the particular group of people who are oppressed by unjust social structures such as colonialism, poverty, military dictatorship, and more. Minjung theology was born out of the minjung's struggle for political, economic, and spiritual liberation fueled by their critical reflection on God's love and justice in the world of suffering. Although it is a Korean term (the minjung is associated with the particular history of the suffering mass of Korea), minjung theology has called all Christians to be in solidarity, especially with those who are alienated and marginalized by the dominant power structures. For this reason, minjung theology is not simply the Korean local theology of liberation, but also a matter of global discourse and practice.

In order for minjung theology to pursue meaningful solidarity with other liberation theologies, it is necessary to delineate whose experiences should be theologically meditated, how their experiences uncover unequally distributed power in global politics, and how minjung theology can be held accountable to these people. Among the various roots of oppression, this essay is particularly interested in the excessive militarization of the world through the Cold War and the current war on terrorism. Focusing on gender relations and sociopolitical power relations, this chapter will question how transnationalized militarism[1] has affected the lives of the female minjung. For the theologically robust contemplation on the relationship between transnationalized militarism and the minjung, this chapter takes the militarized sex-industry around U.S. military bases in South Korea as a case study, and compares the female sex-workers' experiences of oppression to those of Ahn Byung-Mu's *ochlos* in Galilee. This analytical comparison seems important for many reasons, of which three are of particular significance in this chapter.

First, the analysis of militarized prostitution can bring gender-specific knowledge into Ahn Byung-Mu's *ochlos*–minjung theology. Although Ahn Byung-Mu names women as important members of the *ochlos*, the crowd following Jesus, minjung theology has generally ignored gender differences among the minjung that affect their understandings of oppression and liberation. As a result, Korean women's particular experiences of state power, colonialism, poverty, and sexual oppression have been generally unnoticed among male minjung theologians. A critical analysis of and theological reflection on Korean women's experiences of war (e.g. militarized prostitution) would offer new perspectives on liberation.

Second, Ahn's geopolitical analysis of Galilee can be a useful tool in theologizing U.S. military camptowns (*kijich'on*)[2]—a modern day Galilee. Around US military bases exist camptowns, where American soldiers look for entertainment. These camptowns have played the roles of borderlands between the mainstream Korean society and the U.S. military. Just as Galilee was exploited by the colonial authorities of the Roman Empire and alienated by the Jerusalem-based religious authorities for the sake of religious purity, so too have U.S. military camptowns been exploited and alienated for the sake of peace and security in the Far East. As the providers of entertainment for American soldiers, local people often experience prejudice and alienation from the majority of society. The comparison between Ahn Byung-Mu's Galilee and camptowns will demonstrate why culturally, racially, and

---

1. Transnationalized militarism refers to one country's military power stationed beyond its own national boundaries. The best example is the US military. The United States has eight hundred military installations in one hundred thirty countries, and the US Special Forces operate in nearly one hundred seventy nations. See Maguire, *A Moral Creed for All Christians*, 14. To "transnationalize," emphasize the process of constructing the power structure crossing the national borders.

2. *Kiji* is a Korean word for "military base," and *ch'on* means "village."

Part III: Critical Responses to Ahn Byung-Mu's Minjung Theology

religiously hybridized borderlands are important to understand the minjung's struggle for liberation.

Third, in the twenty-first century minjung theology needs to work to accelerate global solidarity for peace and justice beyond the Korean Peninsula. Although minjung theologians, including Ahn Byung-Mu, have articulated the importance of global peace, justice, and security, their discourse often remains within the Korean Peninsula, rather than locating the peninsula in the global context. The primary goal of this chapter is to map out how minjung theology can further contribute to peace and justice on a global level when transnationalized U.S. militarism greatly affects the lives of many people—Americans, soldiers, civilians, women, men, children, people of color, and most of all, prostituted bodies of poor women.

## Ahn Byung-Mu's Minjung Theology

### The *Ochlos*–Minjung

Similar to C. S. Song, a Taiwanese liberation theologian who identifies Jesus as the collective story of suffering and crucified people,[3] Ahn Byung-Mu argues that Jesus is the collective identity of the minjung: "Where there is the Minjung, there is Jesus. And where there is Jesus, there is the Minjung."[4] Ahn's Jesus is elaborated based on his careful analysis of Jesus in the Gospel of Mark who belonged to and was always associated with the *ochlos*, "the crowd" in modern English. Making an analytic comparison between the *kerygmatic* Jesus of the Pauline doctrine whose individual heroic action of salvation becomes universalized and abstract, Ahn focuses on the Markan narrative of Jesus whose life of flesh and blood is historicized and concretized in first century Galilee.

Ahn's analysis of the *ochlos* through the eyes of the minjung, and vice versa, offers an alternative perspective on the crucifixion of Jesus as the liberationist event of the *ochlos*. Examining the audience of Jesus as well as the theo-political purposes of the Markan narrative, Ahn logically reconstructs the characteristics of Jesus' community and the *ochlos*—the particular followers and the crowd of Jesus who witnessed the death of Jesus, and secretly carried out the story of Jesus' resurrection.[5]

3. Song, *Jesus, the Crucified People*, 12–14.

4. Ahn, "Jesus and People (Minjung)," 167.

5. Ahn Byung-Mu names rumor as Minjung's subversive action to undermine colonial and political authorities. When social and political persecution was a reality,

According to Ahn, by repeating the *ochlos* thirty six times as compared with *laos* (the people of God) used three times, Mark attempted to highlight the special relationship between Jesus and the *ochlos*.[6] The *ochlos* were politically, religiously, culturally, socially, and economically alienated. Plausibly they might be excluded from leadership in the early church of whose interests laid on appeal to religious Jews and Gentiles.

Ahn Byung-Mu further argues that if Jesus unconditionally loved people, that sort of love would be applicable only to the *ochlos*; while the *ochlos* were condemned as the sinners by the religious and political authorities, Jesus never rebuked them or told them to repent in order to enter the kingdom of God.[7] Here, Ahn examines the religious and social structures that alienated the *ochlos* and further condemned them as sinners. Due to poverty, race/ethnicity, gender, profession, or physical and mental disability, these people could not fulfill their religious duty. The poor were condemned because they could not afford to offer tithes or animal offerings to God. The sick were alienated because they were not physically able to participate in the rituals. Women and children were considered insignificant because they were not allowed in the synagogue. Instead of changing the social structures or religious regulations that would enable them to fully participate in religious rituals, both political and religious authorities continued to ignore their living situations.

Tax collectors were also among the followers of Jesus cited as sinners.[8] Although the majority of tax collectors might not be poor, they were condemned by the nationalists who fought against the Roman Empire, and by the religious elites who denied their right to make offerings for the poor and to testify in the Judaic court.[9] Jesus' association with tax collectors demonstrates that he embraced anyone who was alienated and despised in the community.[10]

---

Minjung spread the story of the resurrected Jesus as if it were a rumor. By doing so, they avoided political persecution. Minjung's real intention was to reveal the truth about political and economic oppression and injustice. See Ahn Byung-Mu, "The Transmitters of Jesus-Event Tradition."

6. Ahn Byung-Mu, "Jesus and Minjung in the Gospel of Mark."

7. Ibid., 4.

8. According to Ahn Byung-Mu's historical analysis, there were two groups of tax collectors. One was contracted by the Roman Empire and often exploited people. The other was employed by the first group and often worked part time. As employees, the latter group might be exploited by the first group (ibid.).

9. Ibid.

10. Ibid.

# Part III: Critical Responses to Ahn Byung-Mu's Minjung Theology

## Galilee: The Alienated Land
## Yet the Birthplace of Political Revolution

The alienated *ochlos* who followed Jesus responded to the political contexts of Galilee under the rule of the Roman Empire. Jesus was a Galilean. So were his disciples such as Peter, John, and Andrew. Ahn argues that Galilee has minjung-like characteristics, for example, the resistance of the colonial powers based on the firm belief in the kingdom of God. The history of Galilee can be compared to that of the Korean Peninsula, which was invaded and occupied by foreign superpowers such as China, Russia, and imperial Japan.[11] Since Galilee had been conquered and subjugated by various foreign powers for more than six centuries, the region was pejoratively called the land of Gentiles by Jews and treated as the periphery of Judea. In other words, Galilee was the alienated land, and its people were treated as the second-class citizens. The sociopolitical situations in Galilee enabled the Roman colonizers and Jerusalem-based religious authorities to economically exploit Galileans.

In spite of political and religious oppression, the minjung of Galilee had risen up against foreign powers, including the Roman Empire. Their uprisings were often motivated by nationalism and solidarity with oppressed people in other regions. While political and religious elites in Jerusalem were adjusted to the colonial ruling of the empire, Galilee became the site for political and religious revolution. If based on the Davidic tradition, Jerusalem called Jews for the religious unity and purity, Galilee's religious and political movement was motivated by longing for the kingdom of God, accentuating respect for the poor. For Galileans, therefore, it was not strange to have a messiah born from a poor family. Differently from Matthew and Luke, whose emphasis lies on the Davidic lineage of Jesus, Mark highlights that Jesus arose among the *ochlos* in Galilee.[12]

Ahn further contrasts Galilee with Jerusalem. Jerusalem is the place "where Jesus was arrested and executed."[13] Differently from the minjung of Galilee, who consistently showed loyalty to Jesus, the minjung of Jerusalem had once greeted Jesus but deserted him when he was crucified. According to Ahn, the passion of Jesus in Jerusalem should not be interpreted as an individualized or isolated event but as the execution, unlawful judgment, and abandonment that the *ochlos*—minjung experienced in his time. Their

---

11. Ibid.
12. Ibid.
13. Ibid.

experience resonated with Jesus' last cry to God—"why have you forsaken me." What the minjung witnessed through the death of Jesus was the vicious cycle of violence to violence that they experienced every day.[14] However, through silence to the brutal reality of violence and oppression, Jesus revealed the ugly faces of religious and political authorities that killed him.[15]

Considering the political contexts of Galilee, Ahn argues that Jesus' last promise for his disciples to meet at Galilee has the theologically important meaning of hope, or a new beginning. When the Gospel of Mark was written, Jerusalem was destroyed, an event that caused psychological despair among people in Israel. After the fall of Jerusalem, Mark, acting as a minjung theologian, made the resurrection of Jesus be "the starting point of the new hope by suggesting the coming parousia or the kingdom of God" to his minjung in Galilee.[16]

## Western Princesses through the Lens of the *Ochlos*-Minjung

### Western Princesses' Location in Society and Minjung Theology

Ahn recognizes women as important members of the *ochlos*. They had followed Jesus to Golgotha, and first encountered the resurrected Jesus. Unfortunately, Ahn's *ochlos*–minjung theology does not give the robust picture of the female followers of Jesus. Since Ahn takes a gender neutral approach to the *ochlos*-minjung, beyond the simple recognition of women's presence in the Jesus' community, he hardly shows who these women were, what professions they took, which social class they belonged to, what sort of relationship they had with men in Jewish society, and more importantly, why they participated in the Jesus' community, and what visions they had.

Despite his analysis of why tax collectors became Jesus' associates, Ahn does not pay an equal attention to prostitutes whom Mark also named as the followers of Jesus. Ahn seems to conventionally understand prostitutes as sexually corrupt women without considering the political economy behind prostitution. If this were a case, that would need further investigation from minjung theologians, how can we disabuse Ahn's

---

14. Ibid., 15–16.
15. Ibid. 16.
16. Ibid.

## Part III: Critical Responses to Ahn Byung-Mu's Minjung Theology

minjung theology of intentionally or unintentionally judging prostitutes, or reproducing the moral value of female chastity? I contemplate this question by reexamining Ahn's minjung theology through the experiences of sex workers in the U.S. camptowns in South Korea.

"Western princess" (*yang-gong-ju*) is a derogatory term used to designate the Korean sex workers who cater to American soldiers stationed in South Korea. In spite of the more than sixty-year presence of the U.S. military and the sex industry around U.S. bases in South Korea, it was not until the early 1990s that Western princesses started refusing to remain silent about their experiences of sexual, physical, and psychological violence as well as various other forms of injustice. In the early 1990s, several important sociopolitical events occurred in South Korea. The victims of the imperial Japanese military 'comfort women' system publicly testified against military sexual slavery during World War II. The democratically elected nonmilitary president gave people hope to investigate military violence. Furthermore, the case of Yun Gum-Yi, a twenty-six-year-old sex worker whose body was mutilated after having been brutally murdered by Private Kenneth Markel brought the public attention to the lives of sex workers in U.S. camptowns. Anti-American sentiments among Koreans demanded that politicians renegotiate the status of the U.S. forces (SOFA) with the United States.

Scholarly articles and books, news reports, and documentary films concerning Western princesses would soon become available. At the turn of the twenty-first century, feminist global networking accentuated women's rights as human rights, denouncing any forms of violence against women. Gender-based militarized violence, including forced prostitution and sexual slavery, was especially repudiated. This global movement, however, has not necessarily brought liberation and justice into the lives of the Western princesses.

Mainstream Korean society is still silent about the historical presence of the camptown sex industry, as if Western princesses were "ghosts." Taking a sociological and psychoanalytic approach to the idea of a "ghost," Grace Cho insightfully argues that the Western princess is a ghost nurtured through "shame and secrecy" that Koreans consciously and unconsciously attempt to hide. Yet, this ghost has haunted Koreans and Korean Americans transgenerationally and transnationally.[17] Cho's notion of ghost alludes to the extreme form of alienation that one might experience. The Western princesses' existence is consistently erased, denied,

---

17. Cho, *Haunting the Korean Diaspora*, 3–5.

and intentionally forgotten by mainstream society. Let us consider what factors have rejected their humanness.

First of all, since Neo-Confucian morality and Koreanized Christianity still emphasize female chastity, it has been difficult to publicly talk about the sex industry. Where the image of a prostitute is consistently used as an example of a wanton woman with an uncontrollable sex drive, robust political, ethical, and theological discourse on human sexuality, sexual violence against women, and the sex industry has been nearly impossible.

Furthermore, as Grace Cho points out, the militarized sex industry around U.S. bases forces Koreans to reflect upon their traumatic memories of the Japanese military "comfort-women" system, the unfinished Korean War, and Korea's military, political, and economic dependency on the United States.[18] The division between North and South Korea and issues of national security also make it difficult to publicly and theologically discuss camptown prostitution.

Although minjung theologians often theologize the Korean Peninsula's tragic history marred with superpowers' invasions and colonization, they tend to homogenize the Korean minjung's identity, experiences, and political consciousness for liberation. Kwok Pui-Lan argues that, while laudably constructing Asian liberation theologies in the midst of the Asian revolutions, these male-dominated theologies fail to recognize their own homogeneous and patriarchal understanding of Asia's past, elitism, and sexist values.[19] Ahn Byung-Mu's minjung theology can hardly be excused from Kwok's critique. Although Ahn did not publish many writings in English available to criticize from a feminist perspective, as a New Testament theologian, Ahn is primarily interested in connecting Mark's *ochlos* to the Korean minjung, who were exemplified by Kim Chi-Ha's *The Golden Crowned Jesus*—beggars, specifically, male beggars.[20] To demonstrate the significance of understanding the feminist distinction, let us historically analyze the experiences of Western princesses that may be different from those of the minjung in *The Golden Crowned Jesus*.

---

18. Ibid., 5.
19. Kwok Pui-Lan, *Introducing Asian Feminist Theology*, 30.
20. See, Ahn, "Jesus and People (Minjung)."

## Part III: Critical Responses to Ahn Byung-Mu's Minjung Theology

### Reconstruction of the Intentionally Forgotten History of the Western Princesses

By the end of 1945, a few months after the arrival of the U.S. troops in newly independent South Korea from imperial Japan, Bu-Pyung, a small town between Seoul and Inchon, became the first camptown where American soldiers stationed at Inchon sought out liquor and women for recreation. Soon simple houses for bars, clubs, and brothels sprang up in a neighborhood, where around one thousand women served American soldiers.[21] Since then, camptown prostitution has evolved in different stages: the early stage (1945–49), the foundation of the Relaxation and Recreation (R&R) business (1950s), the golden days (1960s), the systematic corporation (1970s to mid-1980s), and declining period (mid-1980s to the present). These stages correspond to the number of American soldiers stationed in South Korea, the changes of American international policy, and the economic growth of South Korea.

During the Korean War (1950–53), some groups of women followed troops, making money from prostitution. These camp followers were called a "blanket unit," as they offered themselves to the U.S./U.N. soldiers for outdoor sex.[22] Between the beginning of the Korean truce talks in 1951 and the time when the U.N. troops started returning to their countries in 1956, the number of Western princesses had increased and military prostitution as the R&R business had become settled.

In 1957, in order to control venereal disease, the Korea Ministry of Public Health and the U.S. Eighth Army agreed to gather Western princesses within geographically marked places—U.N. bases, Korean military bases, and large cities, including Seoul, Busan, and Daegu. According to this agreement, the U.S. Eighth Army made official ten service places in Seoul, twelve dance halls in Inchon, and two dance halls in Busan.[23] While prostitution was illegal in South Korea, the Korean government regarded the U.S. military prostitution as an exceptional case, as sexual entertainment for American GIs was believed to be necessary for the national security and peace of South Korea.

Expansion of camptown prostitution, especially during the 1960s and '70s, correlated with the gaining of economic benefits from U.S. military bases. U.S. military bases offered great economic opportunities to Korean

---

21. Ji-Yeon Yuh, *Beyond the Shadow of Camptown*, 20.
22. Ibid., 233.
23. Yi Yim-Hwa, *Korean War and Gender*, 232–33.

women marked with poverty and lower-class status, even until the mid-1980s. According to Yi Yim-Hwa's analysis of the postwar Korean society through the lens of gender, a significant number of Western princesses were war widows, divorcees, and rape victims—especially domestic workers from rural areas who were raped by their employers.[24] Economically vulnerable women took prostitution as their last means to make money.

In the 1970s, camptowns experienced a new project called the "Camptown Cleanup Campaign," which was operated by the Park Jung Hee administration. The Nixon Doctrine of 1969 initiated the withdrawal of twenty thousand American soldiers from South Korea by March 1971.[25] The Park administration considered the reduction of the US forces in South Korea a risk for national security. In order to prevent the further reduction of American soldiers, the Korean government modernized camptowns, and effectively controlled Western princesses. The Campaign also corresponded with the US military's concerns about spreading venereal diseases among soldiers as well as escalated racial tension between black and white soldiers.

Through the campaign, better services for American GIs in camptowns were established, clubs and bars were redecorated, and new roads and streetlamps were put in place. The Korean authorities taught Western princesses not to discriminate between American GIs. They also commanded clubs and bars to play African American music.[26] The U.S. Eighth Army regularly made a visit to clubs and bars in order to check out the interaction between Western princesses and American soldiers.

In order to control venereal disease (VD), the Korean government established more VD clinics around camptowns, and ordered prostitutes to have mandatory weekly checkups. If medical checkups confirmed that they did not have VD, the prostitutes would obtain a VD card as an official sanction to sell their bodies to American soldiers.[27] If a U.S. soldier was found to have VD, he was required to point out the prostitute with whom he had slept.[28] In order to make this naming process easier, the U.S. military made sex workers register for their camptown businesses.

24. Ibid., 138.

25. Bae Geung-Chan, "Global Changes and North-South Korea Relations in the Early 1970s," 22. In 1969, 52,580 American military servicemen were stationed in Korea, but by 1971, the number was down to 33,250.

26. Moon, *Sex among Allies*, 75–77.

27. Mandatory medical checkups for prostitutes were later applied to all women in the sex industry in Korea.

28. Moon, *Sex among Allies*, 95.

Sex workers wore name tags on their chests or around their necks, "as if they were dogs to be picked up."²⁹

Both the US military and the Korean government justified the Cleanup Campaign in the name of patriotism. The American argument was that the American military presence was defending South Korea against communist North Korea. Therefore, if prostitutes pleased American GIs in a safe way, the GIs could do a better job of defending South Korea. The Korean government taught camptown prostitutes that to serve American GIs was to be loyal to their country because the presence of American troops in Korea was essential for national security.³⁰ Both the United States and South Korea believed that satiating the sexual desires of American GIs would strengthen the US-Korea relationship.

Camptown prostitution generated the so-called *ghisaeng* tourism (a Korean version of the sex tour, especially for the Japanese) in the 1970s. While South Korea had a curfew, camptowns as well as foreign recreational places could run any form of entertainment business with no regulation. Korean sex workers for foreign men, including Western princesses, were instructed by the government that their work was important for the national economy and security. In 1978, *ghisaeng* tourism contributed to bringing one million tourists into Korea.³¹

These days, entertaining camptowns import poor women from Third World countries. Korean sex workers left for better jobs, serving the domestic men or working in the red-light districts in Japan, North America, and Australia. Dark-skinned Southeast Asian women (mostly Filipinas) or white women from the former Soviet Union work in the militarized sex industry, filling out the places where Korean sex workers left. However, many Korean sex workers have not been able to leave camptowns since they entered the sex industry in the 1960s, '70s, and '80s. Former sex workers still live in camptowns in their old age, their bodies and minds painfully remembering the hidden history of modern Korea.

## Militarized Prostitution through the Lens of *Ochlos*-Minjung Theology: The Beginning of Liberation

Where can Western princesses meet the *ochlos* and become united in the liberationist struggle of the minjung? How can Ahn Byung-Mu's

29. Lee and Lee, *Camp Arirang*.
30. Moon, *Sex among Allies*, 101–3.
31. Kwon Insook, *The Republic of Korea Is the Military Troop*, 36.

*ochlos*–minjung theology be the message of liberation for Western princesses who have been oppressed by patriarchal nationalism, religion, and culture along with poverty and geopolitical situations?

I first consider theologically liberative resources from Ahn Byung-Mu's *ochlos*–minjung theology. Despite the lack of gender analysis in Ahn's *ochlos*–minjung theology, his emphasis on the historical and political Jesus over the kerygmatic Jesus enables the *ochlos* to embrace Western princesses. Ahn's historical and political Jesus can also be in a dialogue with feminist theologians who criticize body-mind dualism and Christian condemnation of female sexuality—the two main theological ideas that have denied humanness of Western princesses.

Criticizing the kerygmatic Jesus sophisticated in the writings of the early church fathers, Ahn argues that political and religious authorities tried to erase the presence of the minjung in Jesus' life.[32] Only a careful historical analysis can exhume Jesus so that he can still live and breathe among the minjung. Presumably, the kerygmatic Jesus was the theological product of the early church fathers' own dualistic understanding of the body-mind hierarchy. For the salvation of human souls, they treated the bodily reality of Jesus insignificantly. Jesus only had to do with the spiritual salvation of humans, rather than liberation from unjust social systems. Within this paradigm, it is nearly impossible to theologically consider the human dignity of Western princesses. In other words, Christian theology judgmentally points to Western princesses' sexual corruption, forcing them to repent rather than attempting to transform the patriarchal and the militarized social structures. Similar to Ahn's analysis of the social structures which alienated sinners and tax collectors in Jesus' time, therefore, we should analyze the concrete structures in which the prostitutes, the followers of Jesus, lived in order to map out minjung theology for and by Western princesses.

Asian and Asian American feminist theologians have critically analyzed the images of prostitutes used in the bible. Among them, Rita Nakashima Brock argues that "while Jesus of Nazareth declared that prostitutes were going to precede the publicly righteous into heaven," the doctrine of the early church fathers portrayed prostitutes as examples of female inferiority and sexual corruption.[33] Unfortunately, the early church fathers' condemnation of female sexuality is still alive in the church today. A possible way to disabuse Christianity of misusing the image of prostitutes is to reconstruct why Jesus was associated with them, similar

---

32. Ahn, "The Transmitters of Jesus-Event Tradition."
33. Brock and Thistlethwaite, *Casting Stones*, 229–33.

Part III: Critical Responses to Ahn Byung-Mu's Minjung Theology

to the way in which Ahn contemplated why Jesus shared his life with the socially and religiously condemned sinners. More specifically, what sort of righteousness did Jesus find among prostitutes?

Among the stories concerning Jesus' association with sexually suspicious women is found the encounter with the adulteress (John 8:1—11). When the adulteress is caught and about to be stoned by the mob, Jesus askes anyone without sin to throw the first stone at her. Reading this story from an Asian feminist perspective, Kwok Pui-Lan suspects that the scribes and the Pharisees at the scene were concerned about how to keep the law and tradition, while Jesus wondered what the use of the law was if it could not even protect a downtrodden woman.[34] Ahn would agree with Kwok's interpretation. Female sexuality in Jesus' time was judged and regulated according to rigid religious purity, while in a war-torn region such as Galilee, women might be forced to prostitute themselves or be raped, as Jean Kim, a Korean feminist biblical scholar, argues in her feminist postcolonial reading of Jesus of Nazareth.

According to Kim, Jesus' hometown of Nazareth in Galilee was a borderland where death, military violence, rape, and prostitution were familiar, as were resistance against imperialism and religious authorities.[35] His illegitimate birth might have led Jesus to proclaim the radical vision of the reign of God and to embrace the so-called unlawful women who were raped by or prostituted to Roman invaders.[36] Doesn't Nazareth sound strikingly similar to the U.S. camptowns in South Korea? If Jesus was associated with prostitutes and sinful women, it was not just because these women were alienated from society, but because Jesus, as the illegitimate child of Mary, was one of the children of these women. He understood how colonial wars invaded these women's bodies, while Jewish nationalism and the purity law of religion unjustly punished them. By declaring the righteousness of prostitutes, Jesus criticized the religious and political authorities for abandoning the most vulnerable. In other words, it is not prostitutes whose morality should be interrogated but the social systems that marginalize prostitutes. Righteousness as a moral value must be examined at a social level rather than an individual level.

The contextual similarities between Galilee and U.S. camptowns may open the second meeting point for Western princesses and the *ochlos* to be the minjung together. Mainstream Korean society has silenced Western

34. Kwok, *Discovering the Bible in the Non-biblical World*, xiii.
35. Kim, "Hybrids but Fatherless," 30–32.
36. Ibid., 42–43.

princesses behind its resentment of Korea's dependency on the U.S. military. U.S. military camptowns are where this resentment is most visible, and often creates a violent conflict between American servicemen and local Koreans. At the same time, camptowns are the arbitrary borderlands between South Korea and the United States. These borderlands create the third space, or the hybridized space, where the oppressive structures are maintained by both US military imperialism and Korean nationalism.

In Korea, there are two types of borders and borderlands in terms of the geographical demarcation: the Demilitarized Zone that crosses from the east to the west of the Korean peninsula and camptowns which have been the buffering zones between U.S. military camps and South Korea. If the DMZ signifies complete separation between Koreans who share the same language, culture, and history and between two different political-economic ideologies, camptowns refer to the hybridized third space where two different languages, multiple cultures, religions, masculinities, patriotisms, and races intermingle with each other. In the context of the U.S.-Mexican border, Gloria Anzaldua, a Chicana feminist says that the border is "a dividing line, a narrow strip along a steep edge" to define safe and unsafe and to distinguish "*us* from *them*."[37] As borderlands, camptowns have been considered unsafe, compared to larger Korean society. Western princesses, who live in the borderlands, have been consistently defined as them from us—Koreans or good women. An ex-Western princess addresses the beginning of camptown in her village:

> American soldiers always looked for women to sleep with. Many village girls and women were raped by them. So, the village leaders divided the village into uptown and downtown. Then, all women, who had been raped by American soldiers, were forced to live in downtown. They would later become Western princesses for survival. Men protected women in uptown from American soldiers every night, and told the soldiers to go to downtown. If a woman visited uptown from downtown, she was beaten by a village man because she would pollute other women."[38]

Her testimony shows that early Western princesses were the victims of Korean War, but they were violently alienated from society—villagers, good women, or us. So-called downtown (camptown) became the buffering zone between the unsafe and wild American world and the safe Korean world.

---

37. Anzaldula, *Borderlands: La Frontera; The New Mestiza*, 25.
38. *The Story of Yun Sun-Hwa*, 55–56.

## Part III: Critical Responses to Ahn Byung-Mu's Minjung Theology

Although death and violence are familiar in the camptown, its particular social structures enable the camptown residents to see injustice both in U.S. imperialism and in Korean nationalism, such as racism, classism, xenophobia, racial purity, patriarchal religion, and so forth. As a result, the camptown has been the site for local Koreans to resist US military violence and Korean authorities' discrimination. The camptown's third space-like characteristics—neither Korean nor American or both Korean and American—can be compared to Galilee in Jesus' time. Due to the third space-like characteristics in Galilee, Jesus and the *ochlos* could be keenly aware of the political and economic misery caused by Roman imperialism and Jewish nationalism. As it was mentioned earlier, Galileans often spoke up with their voice for the justice-oriented Kingdom of God. Western princesses know how American imperialism has added misery to the bodies of poor Korean women and how Korean nationalism has participated in that process. The stories of Western princesses collected by the Sunlit Center and My Sister's Place, two prominent advocacy centers for camptown sex workers, testify that Western princesses have often organized themselves in order to deliver their interests to bar owners, Korean authorities, and the US military. They also protect each other from violence and resist military violence and economic exploitation as much as they can.

Furthermore, the bodies of Western princesses are the borderlands caught between South Korea and the United States. Just as Cynthia Enloe argues, their bodies deal with multiple masculinities—blacks, Latinos, whites, Koreans, and others. Their survival depends on how skillfully they deal with these masculitinies.[39] These women's bodies have to be available to various American soldiers, disciplined by Korean bar owners and pimps, loyal to their families, and regulated by the Korean authorities. Their bodily experiences, therefore, demonstrate the intersection among the multiple layers of injustice, while their survival wisdom may suggest how to resist injustice. Theologically speaking, their bodies embody Galilee. If Jesus promised to meet his disciples at Galilee after his resurrection, he would meet them among the bodies of the *ochlos*—Western princesses.

Finally, it may not be an exaggeration to say that Western princesses are the core group of the *ochlos*–minjung. I argue for this not because Western princesses are the most oppressed, but because their experiences embody the multiple forms of oppression, whether they are cultural, religious, physical, economic, political, or psychological, to name only a few. At the same time, they articulate what justice means and find their own ways to pursue

39. Enloe, "It Takes Two," 22–24.

justice and more importantly, human life. A critical analysis of militarized prostitution can, in fact, make minjung theology prolific in the twenty-first century.

Ahn Byung Mu's minjung theology does an excellent job of historically analyzing and reconstructing the *ochlos,* but his minjung further needs a historical and contextual analysis aided by gender consciousness. In the twenty-first century, the minjung cannot be a monolithic group of genderless poor Koreans. The minjung must be considered as the multiple groups whose struggles for liberation also have multi-faces. Each group's experience of oppression needs a careful analysis with focus on how multiple groups' experiences of oppression intersect with each other. The lives of Western princesses can show this intersection.

Ahn Byung-Mu's analysis of the *ochlos* surely shows the existence of multiple groups in Jesus' community. These groups often experienced tension due to different strategies for political liberation. Nonetheless, they could be united under the vision of the kingdom of God, where justice and respect for the poor rule. Prostitutes existed among the *ochlos* not simply because of their experiences of oppression and alienation but because of their vision for God's justice. Presumably, Mark's own sexism and prejudice towards these women prevented him from properly addressing why they followed Jesus. By the same token, Ahn Byung-Mu may not be able to see Mark's sexism due to his lack of self-critical analysis of sexism in Korean society or even in the minjung. In spite of Mark's intentional or unintentional ignorance of the presence of prostitutes next to Jesus, like ghosts, they continue to haunt the Gospel.

According to Jane Schaberg's groundbreaking work on Mary Magdalene, the image of Mary Magdalene as a prostitute developed by the early church fathers had two purposes. First, they had to undermine women's leadership in Jesus' community and the early church community. Second, their Christology had to emphasize the explicitly male Jesus' unfathomable grace in his willingness to embrace the prostitute, the dirtiest woman.[40] The New Testament does not give any clear evidence concerning Mary Magdalene's prostitution, but in her hometown, Migdal, prostitution was a common method of survival taken by many local women. Since Migdal was a borderland where diverse cultures, religious practices, and ethnicities encountered each other; where bloody wars and revolts happened for independence, while the region would later become prosperous

---

40. Schaberg, *The Resurrection of Mary Magdalene,* 74–87.

through trade and tourism, the stigma of prostitution was given to Mary.[41] The story of Mary Magdalene suggests that all female *ochlos* were not free from the stigma of prostitution. By the same token, the female minjung have not been free from the patriarchal stigma of sexual corruption. If this stigma concerns minjung theology, what we need is not to claim Mary Magdalene's chastity or Western princesses' innocence, but to analyze how prejudice on borderlands, geopolitics in the Korean peninsula, U.S. militarism, Korean nationalism, patriarchal militarism, and national security and peace affect gender relations. The goal of minjung theology must also include how to transform unequal gender relations.

## Toward the Liberative Trajectory in the Militarized World

Western princesses' lives demonstrate that neither militarized American imperialism nor Korean nationalism will bring peace and justice into their lives. In addition, the withdrawal of the US forces from Korea or the reunification of the two Koreas may not fully liberate Western princesses from the past, present, and future stigma of corrupted women, just as Mary Magdalene has been remembered as the forgiven prostitute throughout the history of Christianity. True liberation of the downtrodden such as Western princesses in our militarized world can only be possible when the world arduously works toward global peace and demilitarization.

Concluding this chapter, I would like to consider how Ahn's suggestions for the church found in "Minjok, Minjung, and Church" can dismantle militarized US imperialism and Korean nationalism so that liberation for the minjung—Western princesses can be pursued. Although what sort of church Ahn speaks to is unclear, I consider the church as the imagined community where the members are in solidarity to realize the kingdom of God on earth through praxis. Just as Shawn Copeland, a womanist theologian, envisions, the church is the flesh of Christ and, "in solidarity and in love of others, we are (re)made and (re)marked as the flesh of Christ, and the flesh of his church."[42] This flesh of Christ bears the marks of Western princesses. The community built upon the flesh of Christ brings Western princesses and their allies together, and strives to embody God's peace and justice on earth. Here I make four suggestions for the church, the flesh of Christ.

---

41. Ibid., 352–53.
42. Copeland, *Enfleshing Freedom*, 83.

First, Ahn argues that the church must focus its energy on the minjung.[43] This argument needs a new interpretation in our contemporary world marked with ever-increasing interconnectedness among nations and people. Christianity is a globalized religion, and its institutional power is often exercised beyond national boundaries. If Christianity was the religion of the European empires and fed their imperial triumphalism before, the church of the twenty-first century should repent of its previous marriage to imperial power and pay attention to the lives of the minjung, including Western princesses, the victims of and the protesters against imperialism. As a globalized institution, the church can network the diverse minjung in different regions and create solidarity among these people for God's peace and justice. In the case of Western princesses, the church should offer a space for women, who are raped, sexually violated, and prostituted during war or under military occupation.

Most important, the church, especially the Korean church, needs to move toward global solidarity for justice against U.S. military expansion rather than evangelizing non-Christians in foreign countries. This argument is similar to the argument of Fr. Aloysius Pieris: true conversion is not conversion into institutionalized Christianity or the kerygmatic Jesus, but into spiritual and physical liberation from oppression.[44] What Korean Christians should spread in the world is the message of liberation from oppression such as militarized prostitution.

Second, Ahn suggests that the church needs to develop a new value system of love grounded in the concrete life of the minjung.[45] The essence of Christianity is love, a love that was once concretely expressed though the body of Jesus and his compassion towards the *ochlos*. Love requires compassion, and vice versa. Compassion arises when one is truly empathetic to others' suffering. Love becomes concrete when one puts compassion into real action to end this suffering. The crucifixion of Jesus is the event in which the *ochlos* and Jesus became compassionate with each other, and felt as if the world were abandoned by God. Now, the church's role is to become a voice of the minjung such as Western princesses so that the world can hear their suffering and stand up together for justice. One may argue that Western princesses as part of the minjung should publicly speak up with their experience of injustice and work for justice. Although they want to deliver their voices into the mainstream society and the

---

43. Ahn Byung-Mu, "Nation, Minjung, and Church."
44. Pieris, *An Asian Theology of Liberation*, 124–26.
45. Ahn, "Minjok, Minjung, and Church."

global community, these women may not be able to do that without empathetic support of the community. The church should be this community first before telling them what to do.

Therefore, in order to be a robust voice for justice, the church should attentively listen to Western princesses as well as militarized sex workers beyond its national territory. Namely, U.S. military prostitution in South Korea should be considered on a global level. For example, after the closure of the US navy base at Subic Bay in the Philippines, Filipina sex workers migrated into the camptowns in Korea. These sex workers are now joining the Korean minjung. Especially in the Asia-Pacific region, many people's lives are affected by the U.S. military. The church needs to continue to compassionately listen to those whose lives are threatened by militarized US imperialism. Minjung theology should not prioritize the Korean minjung's liberation, but focus on liberation of the global minjung by examining the Korean minjung's political location within global liberation from military violence.

Third, Ahn suggests that any Christian movement should "nonviolently" resist violence.[46] If the root cause of injustice in camptown prostitution is transnationalized U.S. militarism, the form of resistance against militarism should be nonviolence moving toward global peacebuilding. Nonviolence is especially needed in Korea, where only the military power is believed to keep peace and security in the country. According to Kwon Insook, a Korean feminist scholar, since the institutionalized military system is ingrained in Korean society, even democratic protesters against military dictatorship in the 1980s actively sought excessive violence, just like military police used in hunting down protesters.[47] In spite of the experience of the bloody Korean War and the hostile confrontation against North Korea, in South Korea, where men over eighteen years old must serve the military, it has been difficulty to properly develop the theory and practice of nonviolent peacemaking. Minjung theology now needs to map out nonviolent peacemaking grown out of the minjung's survival wisdom. In other words, we need strategies to spread praxis of peace without depending on military power, and to denounce masculinized practice of militarism as a way to peace.

Finally, peacemaking theory and practice must incorporate a gender impact analysis. Before proposing any political decision or theological ideas, the minjung-oriented church should consider how these ideas

---

46. Ibid.
47. Kwon, *The Republic of Korea Is the Military Troop*, 213–15.

impact gender relations and whether they will bring just relations among human beings. Korea's historical events, which have been the resource for minjung theology, also need to be reanalyzed through the lens of gender. Through a gender impact analysis, the minjung theology will be able to produce more gender-specific knowledge and concrete ideas for bringing about God's justice on earth. Gender-specific knowledge and concrete ideas are especially important for the strategy to build global solidarity beyond national territories. For instance, during the Koza Uprising by Okinawans on the night of December 20, 1970, Okinawans intentionally refrained from harming African American soldiers, saying that they were "the same as us."[48] Then Okinawan minjung's uprising exemplifies that when historically and racially conscious knowledge is produced, minjung can refrain from doing injustice to the marginalized in the dominant group, just as Jesus embraced tax collectors, who were viewed on the side of the powerful. Based on historically, racially, and sexually specific knowledge and ideas, minjung theology should continue to practice solidarity with the marginalized beyond the Korean national territory. The ultimate aim of the minjung theology must be the attainment of global peace.

Before putting the above four suggestions into action, one must remember that Western princesses must be provided an adequate shelter; enough food; health care; and legal protection from sexual, physical, and psychological violence, and economic exploitation. Instead of being curious about and condemning their past or current involvement in militarized prostitution, society must first consider them humans like anyone else and that human values cannot be reduced to their occupation. What they need is not moral correction but healing from violence and alienation. In solidarity for healing and God's peace and justice, the minjung will embody the flesh of Christ and become the strong community of us where Western princesses fully enjoy their humanness created in image of God.

---

48. Wesley Iwao Ueunten, "Rising Up from a Sea of Discontent: The 1970 Koza Uprising in U.S.-Occupied Okinawa," 96.

# 12

## "If They Send Me to Hell, Jesus Will Rescue Me"
### Minjung Theology and the Iban Movement

—Min-Ah Cho

WE DO NOT KNOW his name, but his pseudonym, "Yookwoodang"—meaning "a person who has only six friends." His "six friends" were alcohol, cigarettes, sleeping pills, makeup foundation, green tea, and a rosary. He was a nineteen-year-old Korean gay activist and poet. On April 26, 2003, he took his own life. His body was found by his fellow gay activists after he hanged himself on the door of their small office. In his will he wrote, "I haven't achieved anything in all my life but suffered depression all the way through. After death, I want to go to heaven where I can proudly say I am gay, with no need to suffer, no need to hide myself anymore."[1] He was a devout Christian. He dreamed of the boundless love of Jesus that would heal the wound he had received from "the ministers and priests." He said, "If they send me to hell, Jesus will rescue me."[2]

At the time of his death, Yookwoodang had been campaigning against the Youth Protection Committee's classification of homosexuality as a "sexual perversion" and an "obscenity."[3] One Korean newspaper run by a fundamentalist Protestant church promoted homophobia, pushing

---

1. International Gay & Lesbian Human Rights Commission, "South Korea: Solidarity Messages Requested in wake of Suicide of Gay Youth Activist."

2. Yookwoodang, from his posthumous poem collection, *My Soul Becoming Flower Rain,* Solidarity for LGBT Human Rights of Korea, 2003.

3. A four-year campaign against classifying homosexuality as sexual perversion was successful in April 2004.

the Youth Protection Committee to adopt this classification. This was a fundamentalist Christian backlash against the latest decision of the Korean National Human Rights Protection Committee, which had requested the removal of statements reflecting misconceptions of sexual minorities from textbooks as well as the removal of homosexuality from the list of sexual perversions. Yookwoodang was one of the activists fighting against the Youth Protection Committee and the church-run newspaper.

The four-year battle between Korean Christian fundamentalists and GLBTQ communities regarding the law of Youth Protection ended in 2004, as the Committee finally decided to get rid of homosexuality from the list of sexual perversions. However, the event was just the beginning of fundamentalists' crusade against Korean GLBTQ people, now termed *Iban*.[4] The battle served as a means through which fundamentalists formed the basic features of their antigay rhetoric. Public sexual harassment against *Iban* commonly occurred in both online and offline contexts without any restriction. The Christian Council of Korea (CCK), the representative fundamentalist organization in Korea, took a leading role in promoting the antigay movement.[5] The outspoken antigay statement promoted by the CCK provided the anonymous abusers with spiritual credentials. Yookwoodang's suicide is only one example that shows how badly *Iban* Christians have been hurt and wounded by the fundamentalists, and how

---

4. *Iban* is an inclusive term for sexual minorities in Korea. Its English equivalent is "queer." The debate over the origin of the term still continues since its emergence in the Korean language in the 1990s. Some claim that it means "second-class people," contrasting with *Ilban*, which means people in general or a default first class; others claim that it indicates those people who are "different"(異般人) or "out of alignment" from the "normal," "standard," and "usual" people. Just like its English equivalent "queer," *iban* has sociopolitical connotations. It is often used by those who reject traditional gender identities, those who overcome self-depreciation, and those who view themselves as oppressed by the heterosexual normativity of the larger culture. See the website of Solidarity for LGBT Human Rights of Korea at http://www.lgbtpride.or.kr/lgbtpridexe/?mid=english/.

5. Established in 1989, the Christian Council of Korea (CCK) is an umbrella organization of Christian fundamentalist churches and individuals across South Korea that has represented Korean Christian fundamentalism since the 1990s. According to its own statistics, the CCK is the largest alliance of churches in the nation, which comprises sixty-one denominations and twenty Christian organizations, and includes over twelve million members. The CCK identifies itself as "a cooperative organization of Christian denominations that follow the teaching of the Old and New Testament. The organization's purpose is to study, confer, and work together for the accomplishment of the Church's earthly mission, while maintaining the individuality of its members (Constitution Chap. 1, Art. 3)." See the website of the CCK at http://www.cck.or.kr/eng/html/about01.htm/.

harshly the fundamentalist antigay rhetoric trampled upon the spirituality and faith of *Iban* Christians.

While homophobia in Korea has been specified and nurtured by Christian fundamentalists, theologians have not significantly mobilized responses to counter the Christian fundamentalists' antigay movement. Compared to fundamentalist Christians' overwhelming commitment to attack *Ibans*, the inclusion and development of an *Iban* perspective in the field of theology have not shown remarkable progress. Progressive and liberationist theologians' voices regarding the *Iban* movement are rare and reluctant, except for some feminist theologians who have addressed the issue of homosexuality along with the issue of women.

What is at stake for the theologians concerned with homosexuality in the battle with the fundamentalist antigay movement is, I believe, not simply a humanistic gesture to embrace *Iban* Christians, or to produce an apologetic statement for *Iban* Christians by rehashing the same studies on the same Bible verses. More analytic approaches to the relation between the *Iban* movement and the antigay movement are required because, first, gay rights is involved with the unjust social and political conditions of fellow human beings to which Christianity has greatly contributed; and, second, the conflict between the *Iban* communities and Christian fundamentalists suggests the current trajectory of liberationist theologies in Korea regarding the margins of Christianity. A theological analysis of the issues around the *Iban* movement suggests one way to add vigor to liberationist theologians' reflections on the bitter and painful reality of church and society in Korea.

The following essay proposes minjung theology as a methodology to advance an *Iban* perspective in the field of theology and also as a competent partner to work with the *Iban* movement to challenge antigay Christian fundamentalists. As I assess the possibility of the dialogue between minjung theology and the *Iban* movement, I avoid demonstrating a simple parallel or confirming an empathic comradeship between them. Although minjung theology and the *Iban* movement share liberationist strands with each other, affirming the *Iban* movement as part of the minjung theological agenda or stressing minjung theology as an ally of the *Iban* Christians is not the main concern I deal with in this essay. Instead, I look at a discursive strategy of Ahn Byung-Mu's minjung theology, the language of "rumor" in particular, and demonstrate it as a critical tool that helps us deconstruct the fundamentalist antigay agenda and thus create a dialogue between minjung theology and the *Iban* movement.

## Min-Ah Cho—"If They Send Me to Hell, Jesus Will Rescue Me"

I begin this essay by discussing the implication of rumors of the minjung in Ahn's reading of the Gospel of Mark. Then, I argue that rumor has been ubiquitously present in queer discourses and thus that there is ample room for discussion as to what minjung theology and the *Iban* movement can share with each other in dealing with rumors. My suggestion of a particular rumor about *Ibans* will serve as a case study to demonstrate how to utilize rumors as a resource to subvert the fundamentalist antigay ideology. By examining a discursive space created by rumors about *Ibans*, I suggest how false rumors, even though they could jeopardize the lives of Iban minjung, reveal the cracks and gaps hidden in fundamentalist rhetoric and thus enable us otherwise to create a counter-discourse.

## Rumor in Minjung Theology

"Rumor" is a unique discursive strategy of the minjung about which Ahn develops a fresh insight in his writing. Ahn explains that rumor is a critical tool for the minjung to be aware of their political status in society and to shape their identity in relation to others. If we first look at the term minjung, we learn that it is a fluid and inconclusive term used across various disciplinary fields in Korea. Once employed for theology, minjung has more complex characteristics than other fields.[6] Minjung in Ahn's theology is not a prescriptive word or even a descriptive word, since it always demands one's participation in and reflection on minjung events after the model of Jesus described in the Gospels. To participate in minjung events as a theologian means more than to speak of a political event on behalf of the collective mass or speak for them. Precisely because Jesus was not a simple deliverer of a stifled truth expressed by the collectivity, minjung theologians do not merely place themselves ahead or to the side of the oppressed in order to affirm the determined truth of the collectiv-

---

6. While minjung is used to denote grassroots people who are economically poor, politically deprived, and socially marginalized, it is more than a term describing one's social status. Hee Ahn Choi suggests that minjung refers to any people caught "in the middle of war, poverty, the desert, and any other form of suffering. See Choi, *Korean Women and God*, 200. However, it is also more than a generic term indicating the oppressed. Ahn Byung-Mu writes that minjung is to be defined only within the relations of people who interact with a present power configuration. Ahn Byung-Mu, "Jesus and the Minjung in the Gospel of Mark." Multiple factors, including class, gender, sexual orientation, physical disability, and age differences, influence the defining and redefining of minjung. Today, the breadth of minjung identity surpasses ethnicity and nationality as well, since the scope of a power configuration is increasingly determined by the global political economy.

ity. Instead, minjung theologians struggle against the forms of power that alter people into its object and instrument through their participation in minjung events.[7] In other words, the bearing of witness to minjung events and reflecting on them according to the teaching of Jesus are the primary tasks of minjung theology.

In the Gospel of Mark, minjung events are mostly delivered through stories. Story is the most distinctive characteristic of the language of minjung. Unlike proclamation or apologetic arguments, story does not claim authenticity or authority. Stories must hide the author or obscure authenticity and rather invite a wide mass to be part of creating and revising the original source, because minjung events take place under the censorship of a dominant political body. The transmission of stories is therefore critically challenging and important in the process of composing minjung narratives. Ahn suggests that for the minjung of Jesus, the particular method of transmitting the story is "rumor."

Ahn pays close attention to the ambivalent nature of rumor in the Gospel of Mark. According to Ahn, rumor is employed by both the oppressive class and the minjung of Jesus. While the oppressive class uses rumor in order to carry its unreasonable policies that delude the oppressed, minjung wield rumor to make a collective effort to disclose the fabricated facts and discern the hidden truth. Rumors disguise and misrepresent truth, but they also are used to examine and reconstruct truth. In the Gospel, once the rumors of Jesus slide into the lives of the minjung, the minjung do not simply share the information. They interpret the rumor from their location and recognize the significance of the event of Jesus. The collection, analysis, and reconstruction of rumors are important processes through which the minjung recognize their political condition and gather their voices, which would otherwise remain scattered and silent. For the minjung, employing rumor does not only risk their exposure to an equivocal and even dangerous situation, but also facilitates their recognition of their agency, which is capable of indulging in deviancy and thus arising as a bearer of alternative possibilities. As Ahn rightly puts it, the rumor for the minjung of Jesus in the Gospel of Mark is an "effort to ascertain their position" by acknowledging and reshaping the historicity of Jesus into their own life context.[8]

---

7. Ahn seems to suggest that such minjung events include not only a certain political event, but also the everyday lives of the minjung.

8. Ahn Byung-Mu, "Transmitters of Jesus Event."

Fabricated by different groups and individuals, rumor constructs a discursive space in which diverse social locations, ideas, and languages interact with one another and challenge determinative categories between and among social groups. One could argue that rumor contradicts the essential point of the "truth" of minjung. Rumor does not guarantee an authentic status to the truth of minjung. Rumor is a "weak narrative," something like a "fable," in the words of the French philosopher Michel de Certeau, which is set aside by both authorized regimes of truth and the official rhetoric of delivered truth.[9] However, different from a lie or untruth, rumor contains truth or at least cracks and gaps that may reveal truth. It is therefore a truth fragmented, deviated, dispersed, ruptured and reshaped by the minjung. The attempt of rumor to abolish the center of dominant discourses and fixed truth does not mean that it makes the desire to express the truth void. Nor does it expunge all the given and established truths accumulated in the lives of the minjung. Instead of affirming and proclaiming the legality of truths, rumors lead us to see the process of deconstructing and reconstructing truth wherein multiple perspectives and experiences gather together and assimilate with one another. Through countering and forwarding rumors, one learns that truth is not so much about the accuracy and validity of the sign as about the desire of the minjung to express the reality of their lives through a medium celebrated in community.[10] What gets counted as truth within rumor depends on the persistent efforts of the minjung to see rumors in the broader picture and deconstruct the fallacy of rumors on the one hand, and to bear, reconstruct, and deliver the truth for which they strive, on the other hand.

The discursive space created by rumor draws my attention, particularly for a discussion of minjung theology's compatibility with the *Iban* movement. Ahn's analysis of the rumor of minjung suggests its ambivalent and indeterminative nature as a kind of discourse. Rumor occurs, as in the Gospel of Mark, at the time of social and political persecution, when a certain group's or individual's claim is "banned or restricted by the authorities or were falsely accused."[11] Yet, the discursive space in which rumor grows is shared by both the oppressive and the persecuted, but it is not dominated by either. The discursive space is a contact zone where the oppressive and the persecuted compete with each other. The space thus allows one to observe the process of shaping and reshaping of power

---

9. Certeau, *Mystic Fable*, 1:290.
10. McBriaen, *The HarperCollins Encyclopedia of Catholicism*, 1148.
11. Lee, "The Ecology of the Rumor."

and further utilize rumors in both an oppressive and liberating way. The location of *Iban* discourse in relation to Korean Christian fundamentalism precisely points toward this ambivalent discursive space where rumors operate. Like queer people in any other society, Korean *Iban* groups and individuals have been harassed by rumors and scandals. False perceptions about homosexuality and irrational accusations have been manufactured and circulated by abusers across the society, and Christian fundamentalists have unreservedly sanctioned these rumors with biblical literalism and rigid dogmatism. However, the *Iban* movement, through confronting the rumors about homosexuality, has revealed the facts about the persecuted existence of *Ibans* in Korean society and ascertained the necessity of resistance. The *Iban* movement exemplifies the way in which rumors can contrapuntally serve to disclose the fallacy of Christian fundamentalism. A deliberate minjung theological reflection on the *Iban* movement and the rumors around *Iban* minjung is therefore called forth.

## Analyzing a Homophobic Rumor from a Minjung Theological Perspective in a Korean Context: Fundamentalist Antigay Rhetoric, Anticommunism, and Minjung

Let me adapt Ahn's minjung theological method and examine the possibility of using rumors as a resource to analyze Christian fundamentalism. In what follows, I mostly focus on the deconstruction of rumor by demonstrating how false rumors can be useful to read the political motivation behind the fundamentalist antigay movement. As mentioned above, *Iban* individuals and groups have long suffered from rumors. Particularly since the 1990s, when the tension between the *Iban* movement and Christian fundamentalism burst out, fundamentalist Christians have been manufacturing and spreading nasty rumors targeting *Ibans*. The 1990s marks the emergence of the gay rights movement in Korea. With the release of gay-themed films and shows in mass media, the coming-out of recognizable figures and celebrities, and the growth of interest in sexuality among intellectuals, homosexuality became a hot topic in public.[12] AIDS myths and misunderstandings also contributed to the increase of public awareness of homosexuality, though negatively.[13] The antigay movement followed soon

---

12. See the website of Solidarity for LGBT Human Rights of Korea at http://www.lgbtpride.or.kr/.

13. Partly in reaction to the increasing negative perception of sodomy due to AIDS

after the rise of gay rights activism, and Christianity became the majority leader of the antigay groups. The 1990s was a remarkable decade for Christian fundamentalism in Korea, too. Although the fundamentalist traits of Korean Christianity, particularly of Protestantism, have a longer history, Christian fundamentalism as an influential political movement was shaped in the 1990s, as a result of conservative Christian groups' reaction to both the declining situation of the Protestant Christians in Korea in the 1980s and the growth of progressive groups within Korean Protestantism, represented by the National Council of the Churches in Korea (KNCC).[14] The initiative of establishing fundamentalist groups, including the Christian Council of Korea (CCK) was, according to the leaders, to "evangelize society" and "teach the 'pure' gospel." Recruiting a great number of conservative Christians, fundamentalism has rapidly grown as a visible movement in Korea.[15] As fundamentalists encountered the growing *Iban* movement, they took antigay propaganda as one of their signature agendas. The two movements clashed, and predictably, it resulted in the fundamentalists' verbal abuse, spiritual condemnation, and social exclusion against *Iban* groups and individuals.

---

threats, many *iban* groups and organizations emerged and came out, including, but not limited to, the Solidarity for LGBT Human Rights for South Korea, Korean Sexual-Minority Culture and Rights Center, the Korean Gay Men's Human Rights Group (Chingusai), the Lesbian and Gay Alliance against Discrimination in Korea, and the Lesbian Counseling Center in South Korea.

14. Korean Protestant Christianity is well known for its extraordinary "success" in the 1970s to 1980s. However, the dramatic growth rates of the two decades proved impossible to sustain. Since the 1990s Korean Protestantism has faced challenges. While the Catholic Church increased its membership by 74 percent between 1995 and 2005, Protestant membership decreased by 16 percent. There is much discussion about the reasons for the decline, but one undeniable fact is that Korean Protestantism has failed to respond to social changes that have required participation in constructive and cooperative dialogue with other religions and ideologies. In addition, a series of scandals—having to do with sex, embezzlement, cultic practices, and various forms of betrayal—have besmirched the reputations of famous church leaders and further shaken the credibility of the church. The overall situation has consequently allowed believers to skirt responsibility for making changes. See Kim, "Korean Protestant Christianity in the Midst of Globalization."

15. Recently, the moral authority of the CCK has been challenged due to its leaders' involvement with sex scandals, financial deceptions, power struggles, and church splits. However, the influence of the CCK upon Korean society is still remarkable. It appears to unite all conservative Protestant Christian voices in Korea and to impose significant demands on Korean politics and culture. The CCK also extends its boundaries to global society, as it officially joined the World Evangelical Alliance in June 2009. Eric Young, "World Evangelical Alliance welcomes South Korea's largest church body."

Part III: Critical Responses to Ahn Byung-Mu's Minjung Theology

## The Emergence of a Rumor: Are Ibans Threatening the National Security?

The fundamentalists' typical misrepresentation of biblical verses regarding same-sex relationships, their irrelevant dogmatism, and particularly the myths around AIDS can be types of "rumor" themselves and have been countered by a number of scholars.[16] Limiting the scope of this essay and also locating the relationship between minjung theology and the *Iban* movement, I concentrate on one particular rumor that bespeaks the alliance between religion and politics around the *Iban* issues. This rumor began as absurd statements of fundamentalist leaders, and gradually spread into conservative Christians by leading them to believe that homosexuality is a destructive force against national security.

Recently, Korean fundamentalists began to portray the connection between communism and the *Iban* movement. In the statement released on November 16, 2010, the CCK defended Article 92 of the Military Law stipulating the punishment of homosexual soldiers. The CCK's campaign for keeping the law banning homosexuality in the military has signaled that the fundamentalists found combining antigay ideology with anticommunism useful. While *Iban* activists and civil rights groups called for the abolishment of the law, the CCK claimed, "If we open up the military to homosexuals, it will trigger conflict, endanger the *esprit d'corps*, and bring down overall military discipline."[17] Whereas the fundamentalist leaders' of-

---

16. Common threads that run through Korean Christian fundamentalists' antigay rhetoric are biblical literalism and the dogmatic assertions that homosexuality is an "incontrovertible sin," that the Bible "unambiguously condemns all homosexual acts," and that anyone who holds a "contrary view to the Bible" is also a sinner. Fundamentalists also insist on the idea that homosexuality is a "chosen behavior, and not an immutable genetic or psychological trait. Fundamentalists say that if gay men and lesbians are to be truly saved, God will remove their homosexual tendencies and convert them into exgays. Otherwise, they are all destined for hell after death. The religious implications of their antigay rhetoric extend to social and political implications, as they consider the same-sex physical relationships a symptom of a sick and decaying society. The AIDS myth is adapted to articulate homosexuality as a threat to society. Fundamentalists argue that AIDS proves that God classifies "homo sex" among "the gravest sins of humankind and deals with it firmly." The removal of homosexuality is one of the priorities for the restoration of society. Cited from a statement of the Christian Council of Korea: "The Christian Position responding to the Korean National Human Rights Protection Committee and the Youth Committee regarding homosexuality," released on April 7, 2003.

17. Military service is mandatory for all male citizens in South Korea. Enlistees are drafted through the Military Manpower Administration and required to take a psychology test that includes several questions regarding the enlistee's sexual preferences.

ficial statements do not explicitly link antigay ideology to anticommunism, the leading members of the CCK commented on the reason, stating that to keep the law is "to preserve military effectiveness" and "ultimately to protect the country from the threats of the communist North Korea." In their sermons and speeches, they ridiculously say that "homo sex will weaken the *esprit d'corps*, and it will give the North Korean communists 'a good chance to invade South Korea." The presence of homosexuals in the armed forces, they assert, would very likely create "an unacceptable risk to those high standards. Antigay is anticommunism."[18] They also highly criticize the politicians who support gay rights, accusing them of being communists for the same reason. The fundamentalists claim that if left wing politicians take power, they will "debacle the military in order to pave a way for North Korea to invade South Korea." In an online news article, a CCK member writes:

> The allowance of homosexuality in the military will demotivate and disempower the young soldiers. Because of homosexuals, young people may even grow to hate to serve in the military and try every means to avoid the draft. If so, the conscription system, which had secured the country for sixty years from the threats of North Korea, will be challenged too. The allowance of homosexuals in the military may look like a minor thing now, but it could create a butterfly effect that would result in the destruction of South Korea. It is not surprising that left-wing politicians consistently supported the allowance of homosexuality in the military. These politicians have persistently argued for the diminution of the number of military personnel. What do you think is their intention?[19]

The fundamentalist claim is becoming more and more preposterous. In a recent remark on the pass of the draft bill of the Students Rights Ordinance that includes non-discrimination protection for gay and lesbian

---

Homosexual military members in active duty are categorized as having a "personality disorder" or "behavioral disability." They can either be institutionalized or dishonorably discharged, although this was recently ruled illegal by a military court. The issue has been appealed to Korea's constitutional court. Dishonorable discharges for gay soldiers are a problem since South Korea does not allow for conscientious objection, and a dishonorable discharge bears with it significant social stigma, as many South Korean companies will request a complete military service profile at the time of a job application. Bae, "Will homosexuality be accepted in barracks?"

18. Quoted from Tori's article "Are *Ibans* and Communists the Axis of Evil for the Christian fundamentalists?"; online: http://www.pressian.com/.

19. The CCK News, "Will Human Rights Committee Abolish the Military?" at the CCK website: http://ccnkorea.com/news/articleView.html?idxno=840/.

youths, a fundamentalist pastor said that "to protect homo students is to disempower the teachers. The ultimate goal of this left wing policy is to provoke a communist revolution from the public schools, from the very bottom of South Korea."[20] According to their logic, allowing homosexuality in the military and in school is a first step to the communization of South Korea. Without any legitimate sources, antigay ideology becomes resonate with anticommunist ideology. The rumor began, and it slid into individual churches through sermons and prayer meetings.

While this rumor is evidently insipid, in practice it can be dangerous and threatens to politically spin out of control. Homosexuality is now described as not only a sin, but also a tangible destructive force to society. In spite of its ludicrousness, the rumor can be effective and damaging, particularly hindering the abolishment of the discriminative military law, because anticommunism is always potent in Korean society. The illegitimate rumors could fabricate public sentiment and shape public discourse unfairly for *Ibans*. However, I also see that the rumor is revealing the fallacy of fundamentalism. I consider it rather as a call for a careful examination to disclose the fundamentalists' motivation behind their rhetoric and to discern a role of minjung theology in relation to the *Iban* movement. The illegitimate and illogical claim discloses cracks and gaps through which minjung theologians and *Iban* minjung must collaborate in order to construct a counter-discourse. If so, how can minjung theology and the *Iban* movement work together in that space to reveal the truth out of the flux of words and further reconstruct truth from minjung and *Iban* perspectives?

### Unraveling the Rumor

Dealing with the fundamentalist rumor, I first invite both minjung theologians and *Iban* Christians to a discussion of analyzing the fabricated information of the rumor. To understand the dynamics of this rumor is important in order to unravel it and recover the truth it has distorted. I suggest two assumptions as the primary step to circumvent the rumor. First, I assume that Korean Christian fundamentalism, like any other religious fundamentalism, is not a purely evangelical movement. Instead, it is a considerably contemporary social and political movement with a traceable historical root. Second, fundamentalists' antigay rhetoric thus must be understood in a broader social and political context rather than

---

20. The CCK News at the CCK website: http://ccnkorea.com/news/articleView.html?idxno=1097/.

in a "religious" context. In other words, I believe that the major impetus that led Korean Christian fundamentalists was their aspiration to enforce their hegemony in Korean society, which pervasively affects the lives of the minjung in various places, not only *Iban* minjung. The rumor about *Ibans* plays a unique role in mitigating the persuasive power of the fundamentalist in conjunction with conservative domestic and global politics.

Based on these assumptions, let me begin my examination by looking at the social function of anticommunism in Korea. Anticommunism has been an invincible ideology that has always generated overwhelming social impacts on Korean society since the Korean War.[21] It has been pervasive in South Korea in general, but the anticommunism of Christian fundamentalists has been the most extreme, since the combinations of anticommunism, the capitalist spirit, and governmental support were the main vehicles that enabled the rapid growth of Protestantism in South Korea.[22] It also shaped the major characteristic of the majority of Korean Protestantism, which was socially quiescent and loyal to both the right-wing government and to the American alliance.[23]

The political and spiritual privileges of Korean Protestantism had not been challenged until the late 1980s and early 1990s. The event that

---

21. The division of Korea and the Korean War (1950–53) solidified the alliance between Korean nationalism and the Christian West. At the end of World War II in 1945, the Korean peninsula was divided along the 38th parallel by two great foreign powers: the Soviet Union took leadership in the North, and the United States installed leadership in the South. The Korean War left the two Koreas separated by the Korean Demilitarized Zone (DMZ) through the cold war to the present day.

22. The relationship between Protestantism and anticommunism is rooted in modern Korean history. The Korean War (1950–1953) left not only several million victims but also deep scars of division. The atrocious antagonism between the capitalist South and communist North—even though the state ideology of North Korean is *Juche*, which is rather closer to the Stalinist totalitarian dictatorship—was intensified during the cold war. Exclusivity and dogmatism were the principles of the cold war, not only for political ideologies but also for religions. During the Korean War, Christian churches experienced severe oppression by the North Korean regime. The cold war that came with the end of the Korean War was a time for the churches to arm themselves with an anticommunist spirit. This ideological and religious anticommunism of the church was well matched with the capitalist spirit of the South Korean political regimes in the 1970s and 1980s. As the South, confronting the North, necessarily set anticommunism as its national ideology, the South Korean authoritarian government after the war encouraged Christianity as it found the synergistic blend of Protestant ethics and the capitalist spirit useful for the restoration of the war-torn country.

23. There were exceptions among Protestant Christians like minjung theologians and the Urban Industrial Mission members who stood for the poor and marginalized, criticizing the dehumanizing aspects of capitalism.

Part III: Critical Responses to Ahn Byung-Mu's Minjung Theology

vigorously challenged the conservative traits of Korean Protestantism was the push for democracy in Korea and reconciliation between the two Koreas that gradually has emerged since the late 1980s. The former president Kim Dae Jung's adoption of the Sunshine Policy in 1998 stands as an example of the reflections of this social change in Korea. The principle of the Sunshine Policy was to pursue a peaceful coexistence between the two Koreas rather than absorbing the North or undermining its regime. As the Policy brought a greater political contact between the two Koreas and shaped a mood of reconciliation, anticommunism lost its appeal over society. The fundamentalists' anticommunist rhetoric, too, was confronted by a number of Christian churches and organizations summoned with the KNCC that agreed with and supported the Sunshine Policy. All these phenomena seem to have triggered anxiety in fundamentalist leaders. They were fearful of losing their privileged position that had guaranteed their spiritual leadership and material success. Breaking through this crisis, the CCK and other fundamentalist groups decided to go in the opposite direction of the mood of reconciliation. The fundamentalists never gave up anticommunism, but rather strengthened it. In addition, they needed to beg for support from a greater power, which was their American ally.

The facts about the relationship between Korean fundamentalism and American fundamentalism explain the reason why fundamentalists targeted *Ibans* and accused them of communism. While the alliance between Korean fundamentalists and American fundamentalists has a long history reaching back to the early missionary period in nineteenth-century Korea,[24] the influence of American Christian fundamentalism has become more extensive since the US fought on its United Nations' (1950–1953) sponsored side in the Korean War and helped build capitalism in South Korea. Ultimately, the political alliance between the two countries has firmed up the religious alliance between the two fundamentalist movements. Ardently and persistently, Korean fundamentalists have expressed their solidarity with the American Christian fundamentalists. Antigay propaganda is a significant example evincing the sticky relationship between Korean fundamentalism and American fundamentalism. Through sermons, speeches, and writings, fundamentalists effectively implant American antigay rhetoric into Korean soil by simply switching the

---

24. Numerous early missionaries to Korea were from American fundamentalist evangelical churches that were deeply influenced by the evangelical milieu of late nineteenth and early twentieth-century America. Those early missionaries were known for "notably conservative" theology and "puritan-type" behavior. See Dae Young Ryu's essay, "Understanding Early American Missionaries in Korea (1884–1910)."

subject. Korean Christian fundamentalists faithfully follow the footsteps of American Christian fundamentalists, not only in their antigay theology but also in the manner in which they prioritize opposing the social and political demands of *Ibans* as their most important objectives. Like their American allies, Korean Christian fundamentalists target gay men and lesbians as one of the most dangerous threats to building the nation's future according to God's purpose. Like American fundamentalists, they make a connection between the increasing social acceptance of homosexuality and the "various signs" that "God is removing His protection from Korea."

Although the association between anticommunism and antigay ideology is more expertly utilized by Korean Christian fundamentalists on behalf of the geopolitical particularities of the Korean Peninsula, the combination of homophobia and anticommunism is not new for American fundamentalist culture, too. A precedent is found in the postwar U.S. During the mid-twentieth century when the US was swept by McCarthyism, the fear of communist subversion was often accompanied by other ideologies. Homophobia was counted as one of the companions of anticommunism, along with the fears of "juvenile delinquency" and "of invaders from outer space."[25] In her essay "Anti-Communism, Homophobia, and the Construction of Masculinity in the Postwar U.S," Barbara Epstein suggests that there were elements of reason in the combination of anticommunism and homophobia in the postwar US According to Epstein, "the fact of Soviet power and the claim of widespread homosexual experience among American men provided grounds for fears about Communists and homosexuals."[26] For postwar Americans who wanted the security of social order, both were threats because "communism meant to challenge the prevailing social order and homosexuality presented an alternative to the prevailing sexual order."[27] This postwar irrationality seems to be continued by today's homophobic Christians in the US. Didi Herman accurately points out that there was a "fairly predictable relationship between the Cold War construction of 'the communist' and 1980s' representations of 'the homosexual'" in American Christian fundamentalist movements.[28]

The American brand of antigay rhetoric, particularly the precedent of an antigay and anticommunist amalgam, might be a timely instrument

---

25. See Epstein, "Anti-Communism, Homophobia, and the Construction of Masculinity in the Postwar U.S," 73.

26. Ibid., 75.

27. Ibid.

28. Herman, *The Antigay Agenda*, 26.

## Part III: Critical Responses to Ahn Byung-Mu's Minjung Theology

for Korean fundamentalists to break through current crises. Agitated by the fear of losing their privileged status, Korean Christian fundamentalists seem to have determined to take lessons from their suzerain state. Korean fundamentalists have incorporated their American partners' strategy to create a threat to secular democratic government and to the political rights of minorities, particularly sexual minorities. They have also learned how their American partners grew to control the levers of government in order to demand social and political changes beneficial to them. In addition, for these ardent resident ministers of US right-wing politics, to express solidarity and faithfulness to their American allies was one of their most important "missionary" agendas. They occasionally organized nationwide prayer meetings in order to beg the enhancement of diplomatic relations between the two countries, the strengthening of US military power within South Korea, and, most of all, the removal of the North Korean regime from the Korean peninsula.[29] Propaganda against the *Iban* movement was another way for Korean Christian fundamentalists to aggrandize their mission. For the fundamentalist mind, making *Iban* groups and individuals scapegoats was a useful incentive both to cause a backlash against progressive voices and to express their desire to remain aligned with American Christian fundamentalism. The CCK and Christian fundamentalist leaders began to associate homosexuality with communism. The amalgam of homophobia and anticommunism unwittingly reveals Korean Christian fundamentalists' defensive mechanism to cope with reality and to maintain their political identity rather than their evangelical identity.

The examination of the rumor against *Iban* minjung suggests that a careful analysis of rumor can be an effective mean to challenge Christian fundamentalism. The rumor demands that minjung theology and the *Iban* movement look at the larger mechanism of fundamentalist ideology and confront it together. While the rumor reveals some of the salient features of the fundamentalists' political intention in facing current crises, it also generates a good opportunity that turns to be beneficial for both the *Iban* movement and minjung theology in countering the fundamentalist ideology. The historical background and circumstantial facts around the rumor disclose the political motivation of Korean Christian fundamentalism,

---

29. While the tension between the George W. Bush administration and the North Korean government was rising, Korean Christian fundamentalists served to promote South Korea's dependence on US world leadership and economic aid. The CCK also represents one of the pro-base movement groups insisting US military bases stay in Korea. They occasionally organize counterdemonstrations in front of the Yongsan US army garrison in downtown Seoul and at Seoul's city hall. See Calder, *Embattled Garrisons*, 95.

which produces effects in the lives not only of *Iban* individuals and groups, but also all the minjung who are excluded from the privileged hegemony. That will suggest to the *Iban* movement and minjung theology not merely a possibility of collaboration but an imperative necessity to realize the dangers of Christian fundamentalism.

## Suggestion for Further Discussion between Minjung Theology and the *Iban* Movement

The application of Ahn's minjung theological method to analyze the rumor against *Ibans* highlights the strength of minjung theology in the twenty-first-century context. From its beginning, minjung theology has worked to collect and to give light to the ignored and unheard stories of people at the margins of society. It has reshaped theological discourses based on the experiences of minjung and reconstructed traditional theological resources from a minjung perspective. Raising the silenced voices of *Ibans* and revealing their hidden reality, the *Iban* movement points towards the subject where Ahn's minjung theology has been unearthed. Also, the *Iban* movement may help minjung theology see even more intensely the margins of society and enrich its critical function to bring up the stories of the "wretched" and the "miserable." Working with the *Iban* movement further challenges minjung theology to invite more strangers into theological discussions and access the truth in new and diverse manners.

My proposal about the rumor of minjung theology as a discursive strategy can suggestively encompass the discussions about the future of minjung theology and the *Iban* movement. The strategic use of rumor can also be considered an effective tool for both minjung theology and *Iban* movement not only to counter rumors, but also to create rumors.[30] Minjung theology suggests more than a humanistic gesture in its approach to the issues of *Ibans*. Above all, minjung theology must be one of the voices that can dare to say *yes* to our fellow Christians like Yookwoodang when they cry, "If [the ministers and priests] send me to hell, Jesus will rescue me."

---

30. Even though the positive use of rumors has not been significantly explored in the *Iban* movement in Korea yet, the contemporary queer movements in North America and Europe suggest ways of creating rumors through their aesthetic tactics of parodying, mimicking, and satirizing Christian symbols and signs. A suggestive and controversial example of a queer group creating rumors is the Sisters of Perpetual Indulgence (SPI). The SPI is a protest, charity, and performance organization that utilizes drag and religious imagery to bring attention to sexual intolerance.

# 13

# *Ochlos* and the Phenomenology of Wretchedness

—Jin-ho Kim

### The Beginning: Understanding Ahn's Minjung

THERE ARE TWO DIFFERENT ways of understanding Ahn's minjung: national minjung and *ochlos*–minjung. The former is an understanding of a majority of minjung scholars; however, the latter is Ahn's unique concept that includes all aspects of alienation, which is different from the national or class minjung. These views do not consider the Teacher's perspective as being different from their own. As we have seen in my introductory article about Ahn Byung-Mu, Ahn's *ochlos* theory starts from the question of *ochlos* in Mark, which is distinguished from *laos* (as people). In other words, Ahn's *ochlos* theory is trying to understand the misery of the marginalized Korean minjung. The Greek word *laos* refers to Israelites who gathered together by commandments of Yahweh, according to the Septuagint. This expression connotes that they are people of Yahweh's law, assigned to the kingdom of Yahweh. The meaning of *laos* is similar to the modern concept of "people" who benefit from the protection of the law. In his famous essay, "Searching for a Model of Korean Christianity," Ahn sees minjung (*ochlos*) in modern society are laborers and peasants. In other words, the minjung are the most marginalized people.[1] Here, his understanding of minjung,

---

1. Ahn, "Searching for Model of Korean Christianity," 31.

who have suffered historical contradictions, can be defined as a "being that has sense of class attribution."

*Ochlos*–minjung theology not only represents a unique perspective among minjung theories in Korea, but also still sheds new light on our understanding of global minjung. To understand Ahn's *ochlos*–minjung theology we need examine other scholars' understanding of minjung theology. In particular, Suh Nam-Dong's *han* theology helped Ahn's theory of *ochlos* to deepen. The concept of *ochlos*–minjung was an innovative and brilliant insight; however, it did not receive the proper attention as compared with the national and class concepts of minjung during the 1970s and '80s in Korean society. However, given various aspects of suffering or marginalization at a local and global level, the concept of *ochlos*–minjung is much more important today than before.[2] In the following, we will examine Ahn's theory of *ochlos*.

## The Logical Structure of *Ochlos* Theory: The Concept of the Teacher's *Ochlos* and Suh Nam-Dong's *Han* as the Center

The term *nation* often defines an imaginary single-ethnic community, and the idea formed during the colonial modern period, and it is the keyword for unifying all members of the community. The narrative of unity mediated by this word has become a central discourse taking all issues under this idea of nation or Korea. Minjung theorists from the 1970s and '80s contend that dictatorship exploited and trampled on the sovereignty and human rights of the people. Korean people as a whole are the minjung who are marginalized and excluded from human rights. So the goal is they ("national people") must achieve their subjectivity through minjung-like class-consciousness. There is virtually no difference between the national minjung and minjung because, at least ideally, the two will be in deep solidarity.[3]

---

2. See Kim Jin-Ho, "Until Someone Called Them by Name."

3. About minjung theories of 1970s, refer to Minjung *and Korean Theology*. The nationalistic minjung was the main work of the democratic movement in Korea. However, in the mid-1990s, historians suggested some problems about democracy, and it led to a fierce dispute among scholars in early 2000. Im Ji Hyun's "A Critical Study on the Understanding of 'Minjok'" was the starting point of the real dispute about nationalism. His book, *Nationalism Is Treason*, compiled critical assessment of nationalism, showing the peak of this dispute.

## Part III: Critical Responses to Ahn Byung-Mu's Minjung Theology

However, to understand *ochlos*–minjung is to deny this continuity between nation and minjung. As we have seen *ochlos* in Mark, *ochlos* refers to the "public who are involuntarily deprived of their life."[4] They are therefore not members of the nation, or members of family, or members of any other group. They are invisible outsiders—perpetual nonbeings. Not only that, but many are denied existence even among the *ochlos*. This is a clear example of a phenomenon of collapse of language. In the narrative of the man with the evil spirit in Gerasene (Mark 5), *ochlos* run around the tomb and squawk horrible shrieks. He lives in the space of death and not of the living, and is described as a person who howls horrible sounds. He fails to express himself. Even in the only verse in which he speaks with the language of the people, when Jesus asks, "What is your name?," he answers, "My name is Legion" (5:9). The evil spirit is speaking. He has lost his words.

In the narrative of "the man blind from birth" in John 9, the disciples ask Jesus who has sinned that he was born blind (verse 2). Jesus' disciples think of *ochlos* as people under "sin." This is why Ahn interprets "sin" as the language of the ruling system.[5] He points out that the system of cleanliness and uncleanliness works as an apparatus of exclusion. The apparatus of exclusion shows that the *ochlos* is excluded from society. As we see in the depiction of the madman in Mark 5, many *ochlos* lose their capacity to use language because of social alienation and oppression. They are seen as possessed by evil spirits.[6]

On this point of sin, Suh Nam-Dong's study is helpful. Suh relates the concept of sin with *han*,[7] which Kim Ji-ha theologically develops. Kim Ji-ha resists the interpretation of *han*, which is continually interpreted as self-surpassing emotion about the hopeless situation. Suh abstracts this as the concept of sin. Sin, therefore, is not the result of minjung's guilt, but the result of exclusion and discrimination. In this sense, *han* is a lens through which to examine domination. Therefore Suh says, "Sin is the name that the powerful gave to the powerless."[8] Those who dominate the

---

4. Kim, "Until Someone Called Them by Name," 99. In the book, I used the expression of "expelled people to the outside of territories involuntarily."

5. Ahn, "Sin and the System."

6. About social aphasia refer to Jin-Ho Kim, "Theological Phenomenology of Wretchedness," 236–38.

7. Suh Nam-Dong's discussion about *han* ("Priest of *Han*" and "Embodiment of *Han* and Its Theological Introspection") if found in his book *Research of Minjung Theology*.

8. Kim Jin-Ho, "Hope and Philosophical Interpretation of *Han*," 78. For Suh's

language are the ones in power. Therefore sin has the effect of depriving language from the powerless. In other words, *han* is the phenomenon of disability (psychological and physical) on those who suffer exclusion and discrimination and cannot express their sadness properly. The language of minjung is stolen by the dominant system, which accumulates the wretchedness of *han*. So the minjung cannot help but express their emotion through other people's language, the language of the dominant system, because their language is already stolen. However, the body resists this phenomenon of deprived language. Aphasia, dysmnesia, and every other illness of the mind and body represent this.[9] That is why they often speak a language that is hard to understand. These are symptoms of *han*. According to Suh, *han* is the "sound of depression which appeals to the heavens, the sound of the nameless and the helpless."[10]

This nonverbal language, therefore, is not the national language. In other words, even in language, the relationship between the nation and minjung are severed. Minjung theologians are asked to mediate on this severed relationship. According to Ahn, minjung theologians are to recover this severed relationship between the nation and minjung through "testimony." They are people who hear the voice of the *ochlos* (*han*-ridden nonverbal sound) and try to break up the system of exclusion so that the life of the minjung can be restored. This is the role of "priests of *han*," according to Suh.

## Historical and Social Context of Minjung Theology: From National Minjung to *Ochlos*-Minjung

### The Age of Military Authorities, National Community, and Minjung

The military authoritarian regime pursued a mobilization system to garner all available resources for development.[11] So they applied military binding slogan "total unity" as the logic of social solidarity. Here *kukmin* ("national people") is interpreted as a single congregative body that refers to the national community. The nation tried to control the actions

---

concept of sin, see Suh, "Biblical Authority of Minjung Theology," 243.

9. See Kim, "Psychoanalysis of *Han*"; Min, "Psychopathology of *Han*."

10. Suh, "Priest of *Han*," 44.

11. It was the social mobilization for development led by the nation (1961–87), which combined the ideology of "anticommunism disciplinarity" with that of "developmental diciplinarity." See Cho, "The Development of Korean Democracy."

## Part III: Critical Responses to Ahn Byung-Mu's Minjung Theology

of the people and the content and methods of remembering. During this period, there were two main systems of control: anticommunism ideology and economic-development ideology. The former was a system to manage the anger[12] of the people and the latter was a system to manage the desires[13] of the people. They became the framework of social memory that adapted people's anger and desire into an official and collective form. Therefore, *kukmin* were birthed through the rapid developmental system and lived in slavish subjectivity.

Although *kukmin* is the concept of the undivided people like national minjung, in reality, there is an internal division between the normative good people and second-class people. The latter is the marginalized people in the rapidly urbanized and industrialized society: the urban poor who exist as "surplus persons," and laborers who work for the sake of success of the national community. These people were victims of a system of developmental mobilization, and whose existence is socially excluded.[14]

Ahn and Suh reveal the system of domination and expose the misery of the minjung who are deprived of their language. They try to hear the genuine voice of the minjung,[15] interpreting the biography of sound, not merely words of them.[16] They also pay attention to exclusionary mechanisms within the discourse of national community development. Just like the question that disciples ask Jesus, "Who sinned, this man or his parents, that he was born blind?" Suh Nam-Dong and Ahn Byung-Mu see the misfortunes of the minjung were used as a device of exclusion.[17]

---

12. Anger about Communism was not only about government in North Korea but also about people in South Korea who took sides with the Communist ideal. Anger was used to control people's ideas and acts.

13. *Desire* here means economic aspiration to be well and rich. A device of discourse identifies the individual desire with national development, which is the ideology of development.

14. The uprising of the *Gwangju* Complex in 1971 was a symbolic event that demonstrated how desperate the reality of the poor people in the city was: victims of compulsory migration policy by the national ideology of developmental mobilization. Awful rumors went about: "Pregnant women who suffered from hunger ate their babies." See Kim, "Modern History of August: The Event of *Gwangju* Complex in 1971."

15. Uninterpreted "sound" of a cry, shout, or sigh.

16. See Suh Nam-Dong's important works: "Priest of *Han*," "Embodiment of *Han* and Its Theological Introspection," "The Hidden Stories," "Transmitter and Interpreter"; and Ahn, "Christianity and Minjung Language."

17. See Ahn, "System of Sin"; and Ahn, "The Story of Minjung Theology," 192–94; Suh Nam-Dong, "The Basis of Biblical Minjung Theology" and "Study of Minjung Theology," 243.

Facing this situation, Ahn develops the imagination about the minjung who are exiled outside the national community: the *ochlos*–minjung. Suh, on the other hand, explores the *han* of minjung.[18]

## Democratization: Consumer Society, Division of National Community and Minjung

After the late 1980s, the political atmosphere shifted to democratic institutionalization, which is a political and social experiment that tries to institutionalize the will of the people. I distinguish between state and people or citizens (national people). Whereas the former claims national security and success of its own, the latter interact and negotiate with the nation. Democratization is the "social process of the people."[19] However, *kukmin* (people) are not well taken care of due to the exploitation of corrupt powers and large private companies. In fact, social class division was deepened during the period of democratization.[20]

Meanwhile, during the same period the industry of durable consumer goods rapidly expanded.[21] In a consumer society, desire to consume plays a decisive role in the formation of subjectivity. I would call this phenomenon "marketization of citizenry."[22] Marketized citizens dominate those who are outside of the market. In sum, during this period of democratization, the internal division of the national community increased swiftly. The civil subjects who follow the rhetoric of "the age of everyday life as war" have become addicted to the game of individual authority and desire. This context robs the civil society's ability to think of the other.

These changes brought changes to the concept of minjung theology. In the past, minjung theology raised questions about national monopoly of power, which deprived rights of the minjung. However, the current discourse of minjung theology covers the mechanism of exclusion that subtly divides between the two unintended subjects—nation and citizen.

18. Ahn, "Jesus and Minjung in the Gospel of Mark."
19. Kim Jin-Ho, "Glorified Christianity and Korean Conservatism."
20. Myong-Ho Shin, "How and Why is Korean Society Being Polarized?" About concentration of capital, see Jong-bo Lee, "Research on "Rule over Nation by Capital."
21. Wook-in Paik, "The Formation of the Consumer Society and the Information Society in Korea."
22. About democratization of everyday life, see Giddens, *Modernity and Self-Identity: Self and Society in the Late Modern Age* (Korean translation). About the democratization of everyday life, see Tae-Suhk Jeong, "Reading about the Symptom of Social Structural Change in the Candlelight Protests against U.S. Beef Import."

Part III: Critical Responses to Ahn Byung-Mu's Minjung Theology

So far I complemented Ahn's *ochlos*–minjung theology with a focus on different kinds of the minjung in the age of democracy.[23] Choi Hyung-Muk also points out that today's minjung and minjung theology are very different from the perspective of Christian ethics.[24] On a microscopic level, he argues that the Reformed church and democracy embody daily lifestyle.[25] I have emphasized including the periphery outside the church as the subject of minjung theology,[26] and I've also suggested that *ochlos*–minjung theology must acknowledge various social exclusions as the context of minjung theology.[27]

## The Age of Globalization: Massive Mobility and Devices of Exclusion

In 1994, the Korean government moved toward to embrace globalization and opened the financial market too early, which resulted in the fatal foreign exchange crisis in 1997. This change brought many disasters to Korean society, including economic hardships and personal psychological sufferings. People are filled with anxiety, emptiness, and fear of irrevocably large-scale changes. People desire intimacy and tend to be hostile towards the unfamiliar. Ultimately, the entire globe is bound by countless cords of hostility, macroscopically or microscopically.[28] It means that life itself becomes a state of war. Therefore, we have to examine all aspects of suffering or pain in our lives. The point is that we have to see the problem of the minjung through the lens of pain.[29]

The idea of international economic community as an alternative to national or ethnic community has collapsed; for example, three East Asian countries (Korea, Japan, and Taiwan) have now lost their power.[30] As a re-

23. Lee, *Looking at the Teacher Again in the Age of Dead* Minjung.
24. Choi, *A Study on Economic Development and Democracy in Korea.*
25. Choi, *Korean Christianity and the Way of Power.*
26. Kim, *Radical Liberalists.*
27. See Kim Jin-Ho's articles: "Age of War Like Game"; "The Second Religious Reformation and Minjung Theology."
28. About globalization and institutionalization of exclusiveness, see Kim, "The Faith as 'the Desire for Unfamiliarity.'"
29. See Cho, "Politics of Memory and the Routinization of War and Division," 77; Jin-Ho Kim, "The Age of War Like Game."
30. During the early 1990s the Korean government activated a globalization policy and emphasized "business welfare" instead of "national welfare." Conglomerates limited welfare to their own employees and spread the discourse of a "lifelong job." See Song,

sult, many jobs have been lost. Then the once permanent workforce tends to be replaced by temporary workers, including non-Korean people who come to work in Korea.[31] Among the countries in the Organization for Economic Cooperation and Development (OECD), Korea has the highest percentage of low-income workers and the greatest income disparity among different classes. Today temporary workers make up over 50 percent of the workforce, and permanent workers do not feel job security. The workplace no longer is the place of belonging.

In addition, the ideal of "nuclear family" as resting place has collapsed. In a way, home is an extended place of work since workers bring their concerns home. Family members who do not contribute to the domestic economy will be forced from home. In extreme cases, they become homeless.[32] In a workaholic society,[33] excessive stress and anxiety bring domestic violence. Due to women's awareness of their equal rights, women are no longer submissive to men. This partly contributes to the high rate of divorce.[34] The rate of family breakup in Korea is the highest among the OECD nations. What were once traditional families in Korea now become more fragmented and broken down.

Also, young people find their sense of belonging in other communities such as cyberspace.[35] These alternative communities do not require conformity to rules; typical of this kind of community is myriad cyberspace users, called "netizens."[36] Young people are becoming endlessly floating subjects.[37]

Minjung theology has argued that the "floating subjectivity" of young people has to do with harmful violence such as cyberterrorism or group

---

"Structural Change of Organizational System and Hiring System"; Jung, "A Comparison of the Characteristics of Non-Standard Workers in Korea and Japan."

31. About polarization of Korea, see Park, "From Democratization to Humanization." Regarding the labor issue, see Eun-Jeong, "The Determinants of Working Poor's Poverty-Exit Possibility."

32. Kang, *Quality of Life and the Relations between Labor and Capital*.

33. Kim, "Workaholism: A Psycho-Social Approach Focusing on Work Attitude and Organizational Structure."

34. Jae-yop Kim et al. "Impact of Work-Family Conflict and Stress on Husband-to-Wife Violence."

35. Jang-young Lee et al., "A Study of Influential Factors on Friendship Forming Behaviors through Individual Web pages."

36. "Netizens" are Internet users who are actively involved in online communities.

37. About identity confusion of youth, see Chung, "Identity Crisis in the Cyber Space."

## Part III: Critical Responses to Ahn Byung-Mu's Minjung Theology

bullying in schools.[38] For example, short-term mission trips by the young people can be seen as an attempt to resubjectify their floating subjectivity.[39] Often young people who run away from their homes become victims of capitalistic marketplace.[40]

On the other hand, the "credit default" has emerged as a new form of exclusion.[41] Delinquent borrowers have increased rapidly since 1997, and by December 2004, they made up 16 percent of the total workforce. Over 70 percent of them held unstable jobs and could not cover all living expenses. There is a vicious cycle: They borrow money from private money markets to pay the credit-card debts. But their debts are bigger, and their interest rates are going higher. They end up in bankruptcy and come up with severe stress or depression. In many cases, they end up with family violence, divorce, family breakup, or suicide. Minjung theology takes serious all these issues related to credit default in a globalized society, and examines the social and cultural background of this new exclusion done by credit default and related issues.[42]

One more thing I want to comment here is the problem of marriage and immigration of foreign "guest workers" in Korea. According to government statistics, 70 percent of foreign sojourners in Korea are foreign guest workers. The number of them reaches about seven hundred thousand.[43] Marriage-related immigration has also increased, and the number in 2010 was one hundred thirty-six thousand.[44] These people are the most vulnerable and poor in Korean society. Most of them are illegal immigrants, who do not have regular lodging places, wandering from here and there. They go through social and cultural exclusions and many unimaginable hardships. Some of them are involved with notorious crimes and

---

38. Jin-Ho Kim, "Cyber Terror of Anti-Christianity versus Aggressive Overseas Christian Mission."

39. Yu and Kyung, "Subjectification Program of Christianity in Globalized Age and Experience of Community of Youth."

40. Jun, "Empirical Examination and Research on the Labor Condition of the 'Drop-Out Teens.'"

41. "Delinquent borrower," defined by the Bank Federation, are people who have more than three hundred thousand *won* in loans and credit card debt, and are more than three months behind in their payments. Being a delinquent borrower limits all kinds of bank services, and even after paying back all the loans and card debt, they still suffer financial disadvantages. See Kim, "Betrayal of Democratization."

42. Kim, "Discourse of Incompetence and Delinquent Borrower."

43. http://www.kosis.kr/learning/learning_002007.jsp.

44. Byun et al., "Commercialized Women."

their hardships are doubled because of that.⁴⁵ Many of foreign women who come to marry Korean men are reported to have serious cases of mental illness that may lead to suicide.⁴⁶

In this age of globalization, we have looked into the minjung's experience of privation of belonging. In this sense, Ahn's focus of *ochlos* is very pertinent to our understanding of the minjung today because their existence is in peril at many levels. The concept of social exclusion is an important topic of study for minjung theology in a globalized age; it is more than the exclusion of economic or political level. The mechanisms of exclusion work variously in global, capitalistic society today, even in a civil society. Even beneficial systems such as social welfare are becoming a mechanism of exclusion.⁴⁷ According to research about the underclasses, members of the lower class have a greater tendency toward criminal behavior, having extremely low levels of self-respect.⁴⁸ The process of self-destruction of minjung is much like this. Many people cannot portray their situation properly, and they babble and repeat themselves. A good number of people have lost their labor capacity.⁴⁹ Some of them are violent to their families, friends, colleagues, or even to anonymous others.⁵⁰ Civil society is not prepared to deal with the language of minjung. The experience of minjung is not properly expressed, and their language has collapsed, as Suh's *han* suggests.

At the same time, the minjung is isolated from the space of other citizens because of the market economy. There is no adequate space for the minjung in downtown because it is too expensive for them to live.⁵¹ The only way that they can live with other citizens is to live as their servants,⁵² and most of them are immigrants. There are also sanitary problems. Since they have no money to take care of their health, the rate of various illnesses

---

45. Suk Won Jung, "Guest Workers."

46. Kwon and Chung, "The Effects of Group Art Therapy on Acculturative Stress and Self-Esteem of Married Migrant Women."

47. See Choi, "To Make a Culture of Poverty."

48. Park and Choi, "The Concept of Social Exclusion and Underclass and Their Implication for the Poverty Policy in Korea."

49. Jung, "Research on the Critical Factor of Escaping Poverty of the Poor Worker Class."

50. Kim and Lee, "The Type of Communication between Husband and Wife and Family Violence."

51. Kim, "Lost Labor Community?"

52. Lee, "Emigrant Filipinas in Rome, LA, and Suhul—A Book Review. *Servants of Globalization* by Parrenas."

is very high.[53] Since they are thought of as unclean, they are not welcome to live with other citizens. These various people of *ochlos* are considered unclean and therefore seen as degrading factors to a civil society. This kind of social exclusion or prejudice is a serious problem in Korea today. Although this phenomenon is the same throughout history, the intensity of pain and techniques of exclusion is much larger and complex than ever. In a globalized society the tightly knit power net of social exclusion brings about endless deprivations of belonging and sense of self-respect. Therefore, as Ahn's minjung theology implies, it is very important to understand the minjung's pain or suffering from many different perspectives.

## *Ochlos* Theology and Its Task

I argued elsewhere in my article that the task of minjung theology is phenomenology of pain or suffering.[54] The reason for using the expression "phenomenology" was to defer theories about the essence of suffering and to focus on the experiences from the site of pain. For this I employ theological anthropology as a tool for the study of phenomenological theology of pain. Anthropology emphasizes the task of looking at multilayered causality, entangled synchronically and diachronically in the experience of people who are suffering.[55] Meanwhile, "theological" emphasizes liberation and salvation of people who are suffering.

In the story of Syrophoenician woman in Mark 7, the relationship between this woman and Jesus cannot be explained by the mere fact that her daughter is suffering from possession by the evil spirit. We need to understand why Jesus is so mean to this woman. According to Gerd Theissen, Palestine was flooded with Israelite migrants, who made up the lower classes in that society.[56] If these people's lives were sustained by picking up food off the table of noble women like this woman, then they should "let the children be fed first." The comment "it is not fair to take the children's food and throw it to the dogs" (v. 27) suggests that Jesus was connect-

---

53. The prevalence rate refers to the rate of people who have certain illnesses within a specific group at a specific time. For an empirical study of inequity of health, see Lee, *Chase Iniquity of Health in Korea*.

54. Kim, "Theological Phenomenology of Wretchedness and Violence."

55. It is the expression that takes into account Geertz's "thick description." See Geertz, *The Interpretation of Cultures*.

56. Gerd Theissen infers that drifting Jews in this area come from socially backward classes. Gerd Theissen, "The Story of the Syrophoenician Woman and the Border Region between Tyre and Galilee."

## Jin-ho Kim—*Ochlos and the Phenomenology of Wretchedness*

ing two related sufferings: her suffering caused by her daughter and the suffering of the poor who were exploited by the rich. Moreover, there is hierarchical relationship of the rich and the poor between the natives and migrants. By considering the situation from complex and multilayered perspective, we can now understand this text.

From her comment in verse 28 ("Sir, even the dogs under the table eat the children's crumbs."), we can read between the lines. If the social suffering resulting from asymmetrical relationships between the rich and the poor and between natives and immigrants is implied in the text, it is possible to relate the interpretation of the conversation between Jesus and the woman to social suffering. The implication is that the salvation of this woman does not stop with her personal liberation from suffering, but that salvation must be social, spreading to her surroundings.

I have a story to share. There was a homeless person who was in his mid-forties and had lived miserable life.[57] He kept failing in his life until he became destitute and eventually became homeless. When I saw him for the first time, he was drunk. When he became sober, he wanted to take a bath. Maybe he regretted his drunken life and wanted to be purified. When he talked with me, his language was fragmented. He spoke bluntly, regardless of his context, and often repeated what he had already said. I rarely understood his words. I went to his house. There were three persons, including his wife, an elderly mother, and his son who was in elementary school. Far from waiting for him to come home, they hated him and were afraid of him. He was a drunkard and a violent tyrant. This is how they remembered him. He broke furniture, asking for money and shouting that he would take away the rental agreement. A social worker labeled him as a quasi-incompetent person.[58] He was limited as to his legal possibilities. In other words, he exists but does not exist legally.

Neighbors remembered him as a violent person. According to one neighbor's testimony, he had several part-time jobs after he was thrown out from his previous work; however, he quit each job after a few days. He was a person who could not hold a normal job. Other neighbors had a similar view about him: he brought his own misfortunes upon himself. When he became sober, he felt ashamed of what he said, of what he did, and of his powerlessness. His family, his neighbors, and the nation, assessed him negatively, as he himself did. The result was that there was no

---

57. Kim, "Discourse of Incompetence and Delinquent Borrower."

58. A quasi-incompetent person is someone who has been determined to have a weak mental capacity and is one whose juridical possibilities are limited by the law. Therefore such a one exists but legally is not a person.

possibility of reassessment. He further demonstrated his incompetence through his contemptible acts. From this I saw the phenomenon of *naked incompetence*.

So I began my interest in "powerlessness." I could not find any possibility of salvation for him in his circumstance. He was like a victim who had no right to plead for his case, and he lived his life to prove his guilt. He was a perpetrator of domestic violence. When he was sober, he was in pain of humiliation; when he was drunk, his humiliation turned into hostility towards others. And this hostility was directed violently towards the weak. Is it possible for minjung theologians to testify on behalf of perpetrators of domestic violence? Not finding answers, I struggled to interpret the problem of exclusion in a globalized society.

Suffering or pain comes to everyone without exception, and everyone has a coping mechanism. Some sufferings are uttered while others are not. Some responses, such as shouting, are uttered. But some others cannot be uttered and expressed through substitution. Substitution happens when one is faced with overwhelming events or when one cannot handle repetitive pain.[59] The most representative substitution is hatred. Hatred towards the self is expressed with self-destructive behaviors, and the most extreme case is suicide. Sometimes, the hatred of the other can be substituted for pain. In many cases, domestic violence or group exclusion are results of transferring pain to others. Sometimes the other to whom pain is transferred is a group, as we see in the Holocaust.

## Summary

In this article I focused on the suffering of the *ochlos* (the minjung). I attempted to show the minjung failed to express their misery and often expressed it symptomatically. I also pointed out that we should consider matters of social space, divided into inside and outside of space. Outside means "outside of the inside." That is, the minjung are not living an integrated existence "inside" the society, but they exist within the *rupture* from that space.

Jacques Rancière argues that the social process of integration, that is, the process of organizing participation and distribution, is not politics but police, which is "a symbolic constitution of the social." Often politics exposes ruptures in integration and perpetuates the state of social

---

59. See Kim, "Substitution of Suffering, Concerning Grounds of the Brutality."

exclusion.⁶⁰ Therefore, the testimony of minjung theologians is not to simply plead for this man who is homeless, a perpetrator of domestic violence and someone without the ability of self-narration, but to describe how the system of suffering affects him. He is not merely a perpetrator of violence but also a victim of social suffering. Furthermore, testimony is the action of creating a rupture by exposing how the social suffering system is realizing its integration by activating the mechanism of exclusion.

In this article I used the phenomenology of wretchedness instead of the phenomenology of suffering. This is to emphasize the lowest point of suffering and the experience of it. Sometimes, it cannot be expressed in language because this kind of suffering is unspeakable and fatal. Therefore, it can be expressed through the sound of *han*, which according to Suh is a non-linguistic language. The meaning of the term phenomenology of wretchedness emphasizes that we have to strive for decoding the phenomenon of sounds of the minjung.

We have seen *ochlos*–minjung in Ahn's theology. *Ochlos*–minjung is a term to refer to persons who have experienced exclusion in various ways. So the phenomenon wretchedness of the *ochlos*–minjung can be best understood when the multilayered reality of their site of suffering is examined. In this sense, *ochlos*–minjung and phenomenology of wretchedness go side by side. Therefore, asking about *ochlos*–minjung theologically is like setting up a monument for those who are forgotten, or hidden, from the gaze of those who are dominant in our age. To borrow from Hardt and Negri's *Empire*, it's like setting up a monument for fugitive persons.⁶¹

Testifying to the stories of the fugitives who are deprived of belonging also means a fight with dominant theology and faith narratives. For example, the traditional relationship model of theology and church is based on unilateral relationship between God, believers, and the other, which is analogous to the relationship between a king or dictator, people, and foreigners. The discourse of reformation of the church aims for collapsing the division between the clergy and believers and emphasizes bilateral communication. This goes hand in hand with bilateral communication between nation and citizen within the discourse of democracy. However, even at this point, the dichotomy between the inside and the outside of the church remains strong. In this sense, the theological movement to set up

---

60. Rancière and Jin Tae Won, "Jacques Ranciere 'Labor Movement of Temporary Position is the Hope of the New Politic.'"

61. Kim, *Monument of Fugitive People: The Myth of Main Stream in the Fruit of Korean Society*.

the "monument for fugitive people" includes the dissolution of doctrinal, fundamental Christian practice, which claims the outside of the church is sinful, and which ignores nonprivileged others as mere objects of charity. This mirrors the mechanism of social exclusion that labels the brand of "collective guilt" on the minjung. Also minjung theology also has to examine the idea of canon[62]—the key factor of church-centrism and the basis of Christian superiority towards other religions and non-religious people. The testimony of *ochlos*–minjung theology aims at dissolution of all kinds of centrism in all areas of traditional theology. Indeed, all space is God's where all people are part of. The minjung cannot be put outside of the established space.

---

62. Kim Jin-Ho, *A Subversive Reading of the Bible*.

# 14

## "The Person Attacked by the Robbers Is Christ"

*An Exploration of Subjectivity*
*from the perspective of Minjung Theology*

—Yong-Yeon Hwang

## Introduction

SUH NAM-DONG, ONE OF the pioneers of Korean minjung theology, shows a unique understanding of the "Good Samaritan" parable (Luke 10:25~37), and asks, "Who plays the role of Christ among the characters in the parable?"[1] In the traditional understanding of the parable, the Samaritan plays the role of Christ, but in Suh's view the one who plays the role of Christ is "the person attacked by the robbers."[2] How can "the person attacked by robbers" play the role of Christ? Suh explains,

> The moaning (Han) of the person, who was attacked, deprived of his money, beaten by the robbers, and almost dead, is the calling of Christ to passers-by. One's attitude to the moaning person is exactly his or her attitude to Christ. On the response and action to the moaning, a latent humanity within a human being either awakens or disappears. Therefore, on this moaning, the crossroads between Salvation and Damnation exists.[3]

1. Suh Nam-Dong, *Exploring Minjung Theology*, 107.
2. Ibid.
3. Ibid.

Part III: Critical Responses to Ahn Byung-Mu's Minjung Theology

Ahn Byung-Mu, another pioneer of minjung theology, takes a similar position in this regard,

> I think that Christ is not an almighty being who can provide an easy solution to complicated problems but a screaming person whose scream touches our heart and deconstructs our routine life and the conventional logic in it.[4]

"The person attacked by the robbers" is an example of the concept of the minjung in minjung theology. For both Suh and Ahn, minjung plays the role of the agent of salvation that occurs in marginalized places in society. In this essay, therefore, I will examine the history of minjung theology and explore the subjectivity of minjung as the agent of salvation.

## Minjung in Early Minjung Theology

### The Event of Jeon Tae-Il: Minjung Came as a Shock to Minjung Theologians

Minjung theologians say that minjung theology cannot but arise when considering the tragedy of Jeon Tae-Il, a textile worker, who set himself on fire in 1970.[5] He tried to improve the extremely poor working conditions and low wages for himself and fellow workers. For this purpose, he tried to organize fellow workers but found no help from the outside. His lack of education due to poverty, his lack of education, and his influential friends created barriers to finding a solution. Nevertheless, he verified the poor working conditions and sent petitions for the improvement of the working conditions to the government. However, the government ignored his petitions, and the owner of his workplace fired him. No one helped him during this process. Consequently, he chose self-immolation as the last means of appeal. As he set fire to himself on November 13, 1970, he yelled, "We are not machines!" Since his death, he has been remembered as the symbol of Korean labor movement.[6]

The event of Jeon's suicide had two implications to the minjung theologians. At first, it came as a big shock to them because they realized Jeon could not get any help even from those who were engaging in the protests

4. Ahn Byung-Mu, *Telling Minjung Theology*, 117–18.
5. Ibid., 257.
6. Young-Rae Cho, *Jeon Tae-Il's Biography*.

resisting the military dictatorship. For example, when he read a book about labor law and had difficulty understanding many of the Chinese characters and the legal language, he hoped to find "a friend attending the university," who could help him understand the text better. Yet, he could find no "friend attending the university" to help him though students were participating in antigovernment strikes. The fact that no one showed solidarity with Jeon in his suffering and struggle for liberation before his suicide meant that even those engaging in the democratic movement, including minjung theologians, did not recognize the widespread yet concealed social suffering of the marginalized in Korean society. They also realized that their "doing theology" had gone in the wrong direction because Western theologies were of no use in recognizing the suffering of the marginalized in Korean society.

On the other hand, in the view of minjung theologians, Jeon's actions showed the power of marginalized suffering people though they are not recognized. For example, even without "a friend attending the university," Jeon read difficult books about labor law. He touched the hearts of fellow workers with his passion and established a workers' union. His suicide became a critical point for reactivating the labor movement in Korea. According to Ahn Byung-Mu, though the dictatorial government banned mentioning Jeon's suicide, it was still the subject of discussion among people.[7] The theologians who received this shock and recognized the power of marginalized suffering people from Jeon's event could not but coin a new word to refer to these people. The new word was minjung.

## Phenomenology on Minjung: Powerless, Therefore, Powerful

Ahn Byung-Mu says he does not explain who the minjung are.[8] In other words, he rejects defining minjung and establishing academic concepts about it. According to Ahn, when concepts about something are established, the concepts are dislocated from the reality of the thing, and enter into the struggles among concepts separated from reality.[9] The rejection of defining Minjung is understood to result from the shock of Jeon's suicide, on the one hand, and to be an attempt to explore a new way to overcome the influence of Western academic discourses heavily dependent on establishing academic concepts and theory, on the other. Therefore, in the works of

7. Ahn, Ibid., 258.
8. Ibid., 284.
9. Ibid., 27.

Part III: Critical Responses to Ahn Byung-Mu's Minjung Theology

minjung theologians, especially of early minjung theologians, the meaning of minjung is understood as subjects who can be revealed not by knowledge but only by experience. In other words, Minjung is not so much explained through establishing theory as described through exposing their traces.

Due to this attitude of describing minjung, various images coexist in the works of minjung theologians. Among the images, one of most common images is that of "the lowest class." In this case, "the lowest class" sometimes means the ruled, such as the working class, but often means people who have no power or even any access to a way of appealing their suffering. Ahn Byung-Mu raises one illustration from his lecture in Germany.[10] An audience member asked Ahn, "Who are the minjung in Germany?" At first, he could not answer because there were no slums in Germany and German workers had strong labor unions. Then he thought of the migrant workers, including Turkish workers, and answered, "Can I say the minjung in Germany are the migrant workers? Of course, this may not be the answer but another question." The reason why migrant workers were considered as minjung but German workers were not is that German workers had the power to appeal their rights through labor unions, but immigrant workers did not.

This image of Minjung as "the lowest class" also appears in Ahn's discussion on *ochlos* in the Gospel of Mark. He focuses on the fact that the author of the Gospel of Mark uses not the Greek word *laos* but the Greek word *ochlos* to express the crowd following Jesus.[11] In his view, *laos* means people belonging somewhere and is understood as referring to a kind of "national people."[12] On the contrary, *ochlos* means people who do not belong anywhere and hence have no duty or rights within the social structure.[13] According to Ahn, those from "the lowest class" in the Gospel, such as tax collectors, sinners, invalids, and women are none other than *ochlos*.[14] These people appear as the objects of social discrimination in the context of Gospels and Jesus supports them and breaks such discrimination. Therefore, when Jesus meets these people, there are often conflicts between him and the Pharisees and Sadducees. After all, in Ahn's discussion, *ochlos* who appear as people who have no power and access to appeal their suffering are today's Minjung.

10. Ibid., 285–86.
11. Ahn, *Jesus of Galilee*, 137.
12. Ibid., 136.
13. Ibid., 137.
14. Ibid., 138.

## Yong-Yeon Hwang—"The Person Attacked by the Robbers is Christ"

However, besides the image of Minjung as those from "the lowest class," there appears another important image of "Minjung" in the discussions of Minjung theologians, that is, "the subjects who change society and history". One of the most impressive examples of such an image of Minjung is "Chang Il-Dam", created by Kim Chi-Ha and introduced by Suh Nam-Dong in the 1970s.[15] According to Suh, Chang Il-Dam was born from an untouchable man and a prostitute who had continued their business through three generations. This means Chang was born from "the lowest class" of Korean society. While he was wandering the bottom of Korean society, he came across a scene of childbirth where a prostitute suffering from a severe venereal disease and a mental disease was bearing a child. He was struck with wonder at the unusual scene saying, "Ah! A new life is born from the severely damaged body. It is the birth of God. God is in the wombs of such women." This observation awakened him to the realization that Messiah was born from the bottom of society. Based on this awakening, he taught people saying, "Bread is Heaven. Thus, whenever you eat bread, you bring God into your body. Therefore, bread should be equally shared." Gathering people with this teaching, he marched with them to Seoul to rebel against the unjust regime and to build a new world. However, Chang was captured because of the betrayal of one of his followers, and beheaded, but resurrected on the third day after his death. Here, it is worthwhile to note the unique method of Chang's resurrection. He separated the head of the betrayer from his body and connected his own head to the body of the betrayer. This implies that Chang is the savior of even the betrayer.

In Chang's story, the image of minjung appears as those from "the lowest class" at the beginning. The prostitute's giving birth is revealed to Chang as the birth of the Messiah and becomes the starting point of his new social movement. In other words, the image of "the lowest class" as the starting point is transformed into the image of "the subjects who change society and history." If Chang had not come across the prostitute giving birth, he would not be awakened. Therefore, in Chang's story, minjung are powerless, but also powerful, because of the very fact that they are powerless. This "powerless, therefore, powerful" image is the essential feature of Minjung theology.

The "powerless, therefore, powerful" image also appears in the concept of "Han," one of the most famous concepts of minjung theology. According to Suh Nam-Dong, *han* is generated when people are oppressed but no one hears the appeal of their suffering, or there is no access to a solution for the

---

15. Suh, 79–82.

injustice acted upon them.[16] In other words, the essential feature or characteristic of Han is the impossibility of appealing one's suffering.

This impossibility is often deepened through the word 'sin.' Minjung theologians expose how the Christian concept of 'sin' functioned as an oppressive mechanism against Minjung. Kim Jin-Ho, for instance, points out that the structure of discourses about sin in Christianity establishes the identity of Christians under the gaze of God. This structure inevitably identifies God's gaze with power, and internalizes necessary obedience to that power. According to Kim, such dangerous power hierarchy has been realized ceaselessly in the history of Christianity.[17] Likewise, as Suh articulates, *sin* is usually a label that rulers apply to their opponents and the powerless to exclude them.[18] *Sin* as a label prevents people from helping the powerless by depriving them of the justification for help. Hence, the powerless experience more difficulty in appealing their suffering and that deepens their Han. In this sense, Han is regarded as a prime example of the powerlessness of Minjung who have no power to appeal.

In this way, *sin* and *han* are essentially intertwined as Suh clarifies it, "'Sin' is a language of rulers and 'Han' is a language of minjung."[19] In other words, minjung's reality, which is labeled as sin by rulers, is in fact the reality of minjung's *han*. It is worthwhile to compare Suh's discussion of *han* with that of Andrew Sung Park. Park insists that while sin is of the oppressor, *han* is of the oppressed. We can understand Park's assertion in relative terms: when the oppressor commits sin, the oppressed are harmed by the sin of the oppressor, and come to have and deepen their *han*.[20] In Park's view, sin and *han* are essentially related but the subjects of sin and *han* are separated. On the contrary, In Suh's view, both sin and *han* are words defining the same reality of Minjung. The difference between the two terms lies mostly in the perspectives on the same reality of minjung: sin labeled by the rulers and *han* expressed by the minjung. This dichotomy of perspectives exposes the conflict between minjung and the oppressors.

One of the essential points of minjung theology is that when minjung's *han* is accumulated, it is transformed into minjung power to change society and history. For instance, in the Chang Il-Dam story, Kim Chi-Ha insists that to transform Han into Minjung power the oppressed should

16. Ibid., 44.
17. Kim, "The Discourses of 'Sin' and the Power of Gaze of Church," 250~69.
18. Suh, Ibid., 106.
19. Ibid.
20. Park, *The Wounded Heart of God*, 69.

practice the dialectic between *han* and *dan* (cutting). This means that the oppressed should be angry about oppression, and accumulate their own *han*, not exploding it immediately. Then, they should transform their accumulated *han* into higher mental power to overcome their oppression. Kim Chi-Ha calls this process as the dialectic of *han-dan* (cutting).[21]

Suh also talks about a redeeming aspect of minjung's *han*.[22] According to Suh, minjung's *han*, once generated and accumulated, finds a voice to expose their oppressive situation in the efforts to resolve it and thus compels other people to join in solidarity the movement for liberation from the oppression.[23] In this way, *han* has a transforming power to redeem not only the *han*-ridden minjung but also those who join the liberation movement in solidarity with them. Here, solidarity has significance in relation to the transformation of *han*. A good example can be found in Ahn's experience of his interaction with the families of the victims of the military dictatorship, many of whom were executed or imprisoned for a long term in 1970s.[24] When Ahn met with them he faced the question, "how can I introduce Jesus to these *han*-ridden families?" Ahn found an answer for the question from Jesus in the Gospel of Mark. In Ahn's view, Jesus in the Gospel of Mark is a man who suffered abandonment not only by his followers but even seemingly by God at the time of his unjust execution. He shouted, "My God, my God, why have you deserted me?" but there was no answer from God. For Ahn, this desperate exclamation by Jesus represents minjung's *han*. Through this reading of Jesus' crucifixion as an unjust execution of minjung, Ahn shared his insight with the families—that, like Jesus, they had also suffered injustice in the absence of God. According to Ahn, this sharing provided them with great comfort and strength to survive and fight. In other words, finding solidarity with powerless Jesus empowers the powerless people. The process of transformation shows that Han results from powerless situations and can result in powerful changes, that is to say, powerless, therefore, powerful.

In relation to this point of "powerless, therefore, powerful," it is worth discussing Ahn Byung-Mu's emphasis on the necessity of minjung's self-transcendence. According to Ahn, the minjung are not only powerless but selfish. In other words, they get crooked due to their suffering, and hence sometimes betray other people. For this reason, Ahn does not

---

21. Suh, Ibid., 81.
22. Ibid., 108.
23. Ibid.
24. Ahn, *Telling Minjung Theology*, 300–303

## Part III: Critical Responses to Ahn Byung-Mu's Minjung Theology

romanticize the minjung.[25] Nevertheless, he asserts that the minjung can transcend themselves. Though minjung's self-transcendence cannot be directly derived from their reality, the events always happen.[26] In other words, minjung can overcome his or her powerlessness and selfishness in reality and win his or her own salvation. This means that minjung are awakened to all other minjung's suffering through the experience of his or her own suffering, and struggle not only for her- or himself but also for all other Minjung.[27] Jeon's event is a good example of such transcending.[28] In this context, both minjung's powerless and humble images and minjung's self-transcendence coexist in the minjung reality. This reality of minjung is not so much explained as revealed and witnessed by Ahn. This witness is made possible by minjung theologians' recognition of their own limitation as intellectuals. Therefore, this witness becomes a kind of phenomenology on minjung. Engaging with this phenomenology, the question of minjung theology becomes, "how, when, and where do minjung appear?" rather than, "who are the minjung?"

For minjung theologians, minjung's self-transcendence appears at special moments and takes the form of liberation events, such as events in Jesus' life and Jeon Tae-Il's actions. Minjung theologians call these liberation events, "Minjung events." However, the potential for minjung events already exists in minjung's reality. Thus, liberation events take place like volcanic eruptions in a 'volcanic chain' as Ahn uses the metaphor.[29] To minjung theologians, today's minjung events are re-occurrences of such liberating events of salvation as occurred in Jesus' life.

In minjung events, the participants influence and change each other and Jesus or God, is no exception. For example, Ahn Byung-Mu interprets the story of the unnamed woman pouring the perfume on Jesus' head (Mark 14:3–9) as follows: Jesus' reaction to her action, "She prepares my burial"(v. 8), means he understood her action as her suggestion that he should go through the crucifixion, which he had not decided on yet.[30] This means the unnamed woman changed Jesus. It is noteworthy that women are regarded as a kind of *ochlos* in Ahn's interpretation. In this context, Minjung and Jesus or God participate in the Minjung events together and

25. Ibid., 103.
26. Ibid., 27.
27. Ibid., 116.
28. Ibid., 103.
29. Ibid., 26.
30. Ahn, *Jesus of Galilee*, 195.

equally. Here, the question of minjung theology is not, "who is the subject of salvation?, but how, when, and where do the events of salvation occur (whether or not these events occur in the Christian tradition)?"

## *Minjung* in Current Minjung Theology

### After South Korean Democratization: The Appearance of "Citizens" and "Noncitizens"

The early minjung theology discussed above developed in the 1970s and early 1980s. In those times, violence committed by the state power was regarded as the most important social problem in South Korea. Therefore, democratization, which was understood as preventing the state power from committing violence, was thought to be the most urgent social issue for the resolution of this main problem. At that time, minjung were usually understood as the victims of violence committed by the state power, and hence the people supporting the democratic movement struggled to help Minjung and partially identified themselves with minjung. "To provide solutions to the problems that inflict suffering on Minjung" was one of the most justifiable causes of the democratic movement.

Along with the democratization of South Korea after the South Korean social movement partially defeated the violent government in 1987, the word "citizens" has generally been used to indicate the subjects of civil rights establishing and maintaining (liberal) democratic society. Therefore, instead of "providing solutions to the problems that inflict suffering on the minjung," "obeying the will of citizens" has been one of the most justifiable causes of social movements since 1987. Here we should not miss the point that the image of citizens is that of the powerful, unlike that of minjung, that is, of the powerless. For in democratized South Korea the power to govern comes from "citizens."

In South Korean society, which has been maintained by these 'citizens' since Korean democratization, success and failure coexist in two aspects of politics and economics. In regard to the political aspect, the liberals supporting democratization think that they achieved success because they overcame the violent state power and established a democratic government. On the other hand, they think that they have experienced failure because the democratic government lost the people's support and the violence of the state power has been partly revived by the present conservative government since the presidential election of 2007. Conversely, ,

## Part III: Critical Responses to Ahn Byung-Mu's Minjung Theology

the conservatives think that they achieved success because they overcame the threat from North Korean communism and established a successful country based on liberal democracy and capitalism. On the other hand, they think that they have experienced failure because their counterparts, the liberals, damaged liberal democracy and capitalism especially during the presidency of Kim Dae-Jung and Roh Moo-Hyun (1998–2007). However, in regard to the economic aspect, these two counterparts share the same thought about success and failure. For both of the parties, success means achieving per capita income of $20,000 and establishing multinational corporations, such as Samsung Electronics. Failure means economic disparity and the loss of decent jobs.

Current minjung theologians concentrate on explaining the subjects of sociopolitical activities in South Korea by focusing on the phenomenon of "the appearance of citizens" after democratization. Kim Jin-Ho, who is currently one of the more important minjung theologians, focuses on the transformation of the subjects of sociopolitical activities from "national people" before democratization to "citizens" after democratization.[31] Kim defines "national people" as those who passively internalize national aspiration, and "citizens" as those who actively negotiate with the state power to realize their own aspiration.[32]

Of course, the fact that citizens can negotiate with the state power to realize their own aspiration is an important example of democratization. However, the aspiration of "citizens" is exposed in the "struggle to be acknowledged" which pursues the justification of their own sociopolitical and cultural views with no concern for sacrificing other citizens' justification.[33] The conflict between liberal citizens and conservative citizens is one of the main "struggles to be acknowledged" in South Korea. On the other hand, another aspiration of citizens is expressed in their active internalization of capitalist aspirations under the current globalization of consumer society in South Korea.[34] Therefore, Kim calls the appearance of the citizens' aspiration in these two directions as "self-division between the aspiration for democracy and that for capitalism."[35]

---

31. Kim, "The Citizen is self-divided between aspiration for democracy and that for capitalism." Accessed, Apr. 14, 2010: http://www.hani.co.kr/arti/society/society_general/416128.html.

32. Ibid.

33. Ibid.

34. Ibid.

35. Ibid.

## Yong-Yeon Hwang—"The Person Attacked by the Robbers is Christ"

Due to this self-division, mania and melancholia are crisscrossing the present Korean society and the "citizens" are ill with "manic-depressive disorder," as I already mentioned in a Korean article.[36] In my view, mania happens due to political and economic success, which seems to be followed naturally by cultural success[37] and self-confidence corresponding to such success. On the other hand, melancholia happens when one encounters the political opponents who damage this self-confidence.[38] By extension, I would say mania corresponds to the citizens' aspiration for capitalism, and melancholia to the citizens' struggle to be acknowledged (aspiration for democracy).

Now, in order to minimize the damage from the manic-depressive disorder resulting from citizens' aspirations moving in two directions, there must be a mechanism to deal with the disorder of 'mania' and 'melancholia.' The mechanism is found in the system of exclusion, which the citizens establish to remove the obstacles to their manic pleasure as well as the problems causing depression. The system of exclusion also has two directions. In the direction of the "struggle to be acknowledged" (aspiration for democracy) to minimize depressive damage actions, "citizens" exclude those who seem to damage the self-esteem of "citizens" by threatening their sociopolitical and cultural views and aspirations. On the other hand, in the direction of the internalization of capitalist aspirations to minimize mania damage actions, "citizens" exclude those deemed incompetent who appear to have no ability for the competition inevitable in capitalist aspiration.[39] Citizens themselves have intensified this exclusion because Korean society after democratization has become a society in which no one can be free from the panic of economic failure. In other words, while the shadow side of modernization mainly resulted from the violence of the state power before democratization, after democratization it has resulted from the collaboration between the still-remaining violence of the state power and the citizens' aspirations in the two directions.[40] Therefore,

---

36. Hwang, "Manic-Depressive Disorder," 38.

37. This cultural success is achieved mainly in the sports area and expressed with the shouting of "Daehanminkook." *Daehanminkook* is formally translated as the "Republic of Korea" but can be translated literally as "Great Democratic Republic of Korea." The examples of the cultural success are Korea's hosting of 2002 FIFA World Cup and Yu-Na Kim, who was the gold medalist of women's figure skating in the 2010 Olympic Winter Games.

38. Hwang, "Manic-Depressive Disorder," 39.

39. Kim, Ibid.

40. Kim, "'Death of Minjung' and Re-viewing Ahn Byung-Mu," 26.

noncitizens, those who are excluded by the collaboration, began to appear after Korean democratization.⁴¹

## Minorities as Noncitizens and Minjung: Those Recognized but Simultaneously Rejected

At the time of military dictatorship, the existence of minjung was prevented from being exposed in public spaces and discourses such as mass media and academic discourses because such exposure could threaten the justification of the regime. As state control has weakened since Korean democratization, various minorities have been recognized by "citizens," for example, workers lacking job security, people with disabilities LGBTQ people, immigrant workers, homeless people, and so on. As minorities often appear as "miserable people" in public discourses and mass media, they have come to be an object of pity among "citizens" and play the role as grounds for a social welfare system. At the same time, however, these minorities often become the object of social blame, prejudice, or indifference, particularly when they appear as a threat to the citizens' status quo rather than just miserable.⁴²

In the case of immigrant workers, for example, the mass media have often reported on their poor working conditions and their vulnerable status to the violation of human rights. However, such exposure of their condition through mass media is often used to strengthen the grounds for their exclusion: the employers of immigrant workers say to their immigrant employees, "Did you watch the broadcast? Your working condition is better than the broadcast, so you should not complain."⁴³ In addition, many Korean people support the crackdown on "illegal" immigrant workers for the reason that most of immigrant workers are undocumented. Moreover, the areas where many immigrant workers live are often assumed to be dangerous places with a high probability of crime. Some Korean people have already started a social movement against immigrant workers beginning at the turn of the twenty-first century. They established a nongovernment organization for the movement, titled "Association of Citizens for the Counter Plan against Immigrant Workers."

In the case of homeless people, providing them food and shelter has been one of the most popular social welfare activities in South Korea.

41. Ibid.
42. Hwang, "Typology of Theology and Theological Typology," 217.
43. Myeong-Gi Yoo, "Immigrant Workers," 322.

However, providing sleeping areas for the homeless in public buildings, such as railroad stations, is very controversial and has been met with opposition on the grounds that homeless people may cause discomfort and do damage to "common people" because of their unhealthy lifestyle, such as drunkenness.

The issue of workers lacking job security has been regarded as one of the most important social issues. Some people have only part time jobs with low-income, or are forced to work as a freelancer though they are actually employed at a particular workplace, and others are threatened by losing the means of their living by their company's downsizing. People want to avoid such unstable employment status rather than to overcome it. Most Korean people think, "To avoid unstable employment, I should improve my job skills by having good English skills, technical licenses, and a diploma from one of the top universities." This kind of attitude strengthens the exclusion of those deemed incompetent, such as workers lacking job security.

These circumstances of exclusion share several common characteristics:

- The suffering of minorities is recognized as a social problem.
- This recognition does not exclude the justifications for the exclusion of the minorities on the grounds that they are illegal, dangerous, incompetent, and so on.
- Such justifications are taken for granted by some citizens, including even those who support democratization.
- Therefore, the justifications for the exclusion of minorities are established not only by the state power but also by "citizens."

Justifying the social exclusion of minorities with plausible excuses is one of the important features of citizens' social actions. For example, in expressing their anger toward the criminals who commit extreme sexual violence, many citizens object to the protection of human rights of such criminals. Thus, when the police without his consent show a criminal's face to the public, many citizens support the action, saying, "Such a criminal has no human right to be protected because he already gave up living as a human being." To take another example, when some workers whose wages are relatively high go on strike, even the citizens supporting democratization often condemn their strike as the "avarice of labor aristocrats." These cases imply that anyone can be excluded by the standard of citizens' justification though s/he doesn't belong to commonly recognized minorities, such as workers lacking job security, the disabled, LGBTQ people, immigrant workers, and homeless people. In this way, anyone can be a minority at any time. With this state of affairs, the word *minorities* goes beyond the reference of certain groups of people and comes to refer to a kind of dangerous condition to which anyone can be exposed. I call this phenomenon "the universalizing of minorities," and suggest this phenomenon of the universalizing of minorities as one answer to one of the essential questions of minjung theology: how, when, and where do minjung appear?

In this regard, I find Kim Jin-Ho's discussion of "the phenomenology of suffering" provides useful insights for overcoming the universalizing of minorities. Kim insists that current minjung theology should pursue a "phenomenology of suffering" to expose the concealment of 'non-citizens.'[44] Here, "phenomenology on suffering" concentrates on exposing one's suffering as it is, rather than applying a certain social justification or theory to the suffering, no matter how noble the purpose for imposing the justification, such as the dynamics of democracy.[45] In my view, this "phenomenology of suffering" can be understood as a clue to the rejection of the citizens' justifications of their exclusion of others, that is, "non-citizens."

### The Cases of Minorities' Struggles for Salvation

How is salvation possible in the situation of the universalizing of minorities? In this regard, I will introduce a couple cases of minorities' struggles for salvation. First, Mincheol's story[46] provides a clue for one way of salvation for minorities. Mincheol's father ran a medium-sized business, but his company failed at the time of the Korean financial crisis of 1997–1998. He tried other businesses, but failed in all of them. As a result, his wife went out to work for a living. The fact that he failed and his wife earned money to make a living seriously damaged his self-esteem. He often quarrelled with his wife, and divorced her. After his parents' divorce, Mincheol left home to be independent from his parents and had various part-time jobs whereas his younger brother became a gangster. After his father remarried, Mincheol came back home and found that his grandmother who always missed Mincheol's mother and the family's past success did not accept his stepmother. His father blamed himself for what happened and not being able to take care of his family. His stepmother also blamed herself for the

---

44. Kim, "Theological Phenomenology of Suffering and Violence."
45. Kim, "*Ochlos* and Phenomenology on Misery."
46. Uhm Ki-Ho, *No one should care for other people*, 100–103; 114–15.

situation as she thought that she did not do a good job as stepmother and wife.

Struggling to comfort his father and stepmother, Mincheol sometimes held drinking parties for them. However, while his father and stepmother thanked him, they were becoming more apologetic to him. This made him somewhat annoyed. One night, Mincheol said to his father and stepmother, "This is not our fault. No one among us is to blame." His comment helped his father and stepmother to stop blaming themselves for the situation and to overcome their despair.

In Mincheol's story, a clue to overcome the despair is found in Mincheol's comment that provided a turning point: "This is not our fault." The comment does not point to an adaptation to an existing social system as an effort for survival. Rather, it points to the rejection of any justification for the social exclusion they experience, such as the citizens' insistence that minorities themselves are in part to blame for their miserable conditions. In other words, those who experience social exclusion can find the grounds for their very existence from the rejection of the social structure that excludes them. To speak from the perspective of Minjung theology, the starting point of their salvation is not by accepting their 'sins' as labeled, but instead, by rejecting them. Of course, it is only a starting point, and not a completion of salvation. However, for minorities, salvation can be experienced mainly through surviving with the self-esteem as minorities. To keep this crucial self-esteem, it is significant for minjung to reject sins as labeled by the surrounding mainstream society.

Another example of the rejection of the social system that excludes minorities is found in the struggle for the Students' Human Rights Ordinance, which was initiated by youth activists and approved by the Seoul Metropolitan Council in 2011. At first, the ordinance for elementary and secondary school students in Seoul faced a serious objection by conservative civic organizations because it includes clauses prohibiting discrimination based on the students' sexual orientation and/or pregnancy. Facing such objection, the major party of the Seoul Metropolitan Council, though it is the liberal party of South Korea, planned to delete from the ordinance the clauses describing the cases of concrete discrimination to be prohibited, such as discrimination against LGBTQ students or pregnant students.

Knowing this plan, LGBTQ activists and youth activists occupied the assembly hall of the Seoul Metropolitan Council. This was the first occupation struggle for South Korean LGBTQ activists. They also asked for solidarity to carry the ordinance with no amendment, and successfully gained strong support through internet mobilization. After six days of occupation, the Council carried the ordinance with no amendment. In this way, LGBTQ youth in Seoul won the right not to be discriminated against for their sexual orientation.

This case shows how minorities reject social exclusion and win their rights. In the process of the rejection, they expose themselves as resisting minorities. Such rejection threatens majorities and that is why they strongly oppose minorities' rejection of exclusion. Consequently, the exclusion of minorities can be overcome not by the tolerance of the majorities, but by the struggles of the minorities. In the process of these struggles for salvation, the very existence of the minorities exposes the social exclusion and such exposure becomes a starting point for liberation through which Minjung can achieve their salvation. .

## Conclusion—How Is Witness Possible?

In the 1960s, radicals who liked to quote poetry favored Bertolt Brecht's "To Posterity,"[47] which includes these lines):

> Ah, what an age it is
> when to speak of trees is almost a crime
> for it is a kind of silence about injustice!

Brecht's poem stimulates one's will to expose injustice unsaid and unrecognized. Such a will is an essential point for the witness of Minjung theology. Minjung theologians have defined their own theology as a "theology of witness," and have made efforts to expose the sufferings of Minjung that have been concealed by the state power.

However, Paul Celan's poem, "A Leaf, treeless—for Bertolt Brecht,"[48] stimulates one's thought in a different direction. In his poem, he implies that the crime is to make things too explicit, rather than not saying anything about them. Then, what does that imply in terms of the witness of injustice as an essential task of minjung theology?

The South Korean social situation since democratization as I described above can suggest one answer to this question. After winning democracy, citizens have been able to negotiate with the state power to realize their

---

47. This poem of Brecht (as translated by H.R. Hays), written in response to the Nazi book burnings in 1933, expresses a lament during World War II for not being able to write about the good and the beautiful.

48. Celan, Paul, trans. by Hamburger, Michael, *Paul Celan: Poems*, 287.

aspirations. In addition, they have recognized minority issues and insisted on the necessity of a social welfare system for minorities. This means that suffering of minorities have been vocalized and made explicit as problems in public discourses. However, it is necessary to admit the limitation of such discourses that "includes so much made explicit," to borrow Celan's expression, because such discourses provide an excuse to "citizens" that they already know the issues of minorities (as made explicit from their views) and hence have the right to blame the minorities when they believe minorities' voices become unreasonable regarding their circumstances.

As a result, even the nation's democratization, the citizens' recognition of minorities, and their efforts for building social welfare system cannot provide solutions to the problem of the exclusion of minorities. Rather, in many cases, citizens have participated in the exclusion actively by insisting that minorities themselves are in part to blame for their miserable condition. To return to the parable of "the person attacked by the robbers," now "the person attacked," who is identified with Jesus in Minjung theology, is cared for by the citizens, but they tell her/him why s/he deserves to be attacked.

Now and in the future, many minorities will appear. They will be concealed, and recognized, and be cared for. However, as long as this recognition and the actions to take care of them serve to justify and strengthen their exclusion, such public discourses and actions should be witnessed as a crime. Therefore, true witness is possible only when social suffering is exposed by a continuous deconstruction of the structure of such justifications for exclusion. Of course, the deconstructing power comes from the people who suffer. To witness to these people is the goal at which minjung theology still aims.

# Bibliography

Allport, G. W., and Leo Postman. "The Basic Psychology of Rumor." *Transactions of the New York Academy of Sciences* Series 11/8 (1945) 61–81.
Ahn, Byung-Mu.
———. "The Meaning of Sufferings." *A Voice from the Wilderness* 1. Nov. 1951.
———. "Theory of Pastorate—If I Serve as a Pastor." *A Voice from the Wilderness* 3. Feb. 1952.
———. "Lay Ministry." *A Voice from the Wilderness* 7/1(1953) 6–24.
———. "What Is Sin?" *Existence* 1 (July 1969).
———. "The Image of Korean Christians." *Existence* 31 (May–June 1972).
———. "In What Sense Are You Christian?" *Existence* 27 (January 1972).
———. "To the Outside of the Castle Gate." *Existence* 54 (September 1974).
———. "Chosen Minjung." *Existence* 104 (1979) 3–14.
———. "Transmitter and Interpreter." *Existence* 101(May 1979) 48–56.
———. "Christianity and Minjung Language." *Existence* 108/1 (1980) 8–20.
———. "The Subject of History of the Gospel of Mark." In *Minjung and Korean Theology*, edited by the National Council of Churches in Korea. Seoul, 1981.
———. "Searching for Model of Korean Christianity." In *With Minjung in Front of History*, 13–34. Seoul: Hangil, 1986.
———. *Draussen vor dem Tor: Kirche und Minjung in Korea*. Theologie der Ökumene 20. Göttingen: Vandenhoeck & Ruprecht, 1986.
———. "Korean Democratization and the Responsibility of Intellectuals." *New East-Asia* 333 (June 1987).
———. "The Matrix in Which the Jesus Events Were Transmitted." In *The Development of Korean Minjung Theology in the 1980s*. Seoul: Korea Theological Study Institute, 1990.
———. *Talking about Minjung Theology*. Seoul: Korea Theological Study Institute, 1990.
———. "Sin and the System." In *Talking about Minjung Theology*, 186–208. Seoul: Korea Theological Study Institute, 1990.
———. *Jesus of Galilee*. Cheonan: Korean Theology Study Institute, 1993.
———. "Come and See." In *Nevertheless, God Didn't Return Them to Eden*, 131–43. Seoul: Korea Theological Study Institute, 1995.
———. "Jesus and the Minjung in the Gospel of Mark." In *Voices from the Margin*, edited by R. S. Sugirtharajah, 85–104. Maryknoll, NY: Orbis, 1997.

# Bibliography

———. "Jesus and People (Minjung)." In *Asian Faces of Jesus*, edited by R. S. Sugirtharajah, 136–72. Maryknoll, NY: Orbis, 2005.

———. "The Transmitter of Jesus-Event Tradition." In *Reading Minjung Theology in the Twenty-First Century*, edited by Yung Suk Kim and Jin-Ho Kim, 27–48. Eugene, OR: Pickwick Publications, 2013.

———. "Jesus and Minjung in the Gospel of Mark." In *Reading Minjung Theology in the Twenty-First Century*, edited by Yung Suk Kim and Jin-Ho Kim, 49–64. Eugene, OR: Pickwick Publications, 2013.

———. "Minjung Theology from the Perspective of the Gospel of Mark." In *Reading Minjung Theology in the Twenty-First Century*, edited by Yung Suk Kim and Jin-ho Kim, 65–90. Eugene, OR: Pickwick Publications, 2013.

———. "Minjok, Minjung, and Church." In *Reading Minjung Theology in the Twenty-First Century*, edited by Yung Suk Kim and Jin-Ho Kim, 91–97. Eugene, OR: Pickwick Publications, 2013.

———. "Mark's Theology Considered from His Passion." *Sinhaksasang* 3.

———. "The Theology of Mark in the Passion History." In *Theological Thought* 3.

Anzaldula, Gloria. *Borderlands: La Frontera; The New Mestiza*. 4th ed. San Francisco: Aunt Lute Books, 2012.

Ashcroft, Bill et al. *Post-Colonial Studies: The Key Concepts*. Routledge Key Guides. New York: Routledge, 2000.

Bae, Geung-Chan. "Global Changes and North-South Korea Relations in the Early 1970s." In *The Socio-Political Change of Republic of Korea in the Early 1970s*, edited by Academy of Korean Studies, 11–66. Seoul: Baiksan-Seodang Publishing, 1999.

Bae, Ji-Sook. "Will Homosexuality Be Accepted in Barracks?" *Korea Times*. National section. June 6, 2010. Online: http://www.koreatimes.co.kr/www/news/nation/2010/06/117_67179.html/.

Baek, Gunne. *Geschichte Israels bis Bar Kochba*. Translated by Moon Hui suk. Seoul: Korea Theological Study Institute, 1982.

Baker-Fletcher, Karen. *Sisters of Dust, Sisters of Spirit. Womanist Words on God and Creation*. Translated by Moon Hui suk. Minneapolis: Fortress, 1998.

Baron, S. W. *A Social and Religious History of the Jews*. Vol. 1. Philadelphia: Jewish Publication Society, 1952.

Barth, Karl. *Die Auferstehung der Toten*. Munich: Kaiser, 1926.

Barrett, C. K. *A Commentary on the First Epistle to the Corinthians*. Harper's New Testament Commentaries. New York: Harper & Row, 1968.

Baur, Walter. *A Greek-English Lexicon of the New Testament and Other Early Christian Literature*. 2nd ed., revised and augmented by F. Wilbur Gingrich and Frederick W. Danker. Chicago: University of Chicago Press, 1979.

Bhabha, Homi. *The Location of Culture*. New York: Routledge, 1994.

Billerbeck, P. *Kommentar zum Neuen Testament aus Talmud und Midrasch*. Vol. 1. 6 vols. Munich: Beck, 1922.

Bornkamm, Günther. *Jesus von Nazareth*. Urban Bücher 19. Stuttgart: Kohlhammer, 1959.

Brock, Rita Nakashima, and Susan Thistlethwaite. *Casting Stones: Prostitution and Liberation in Asia and the United States*. Minneapolis: Fortress, 1996.

Brown, Stephen. *Von der Unzufriedenheit zum Widerspruch*. Frankfurt: Lembeck 2010.

Brueggemann, Walter. "Trajectories in Old Testament Literature and the Sociology of Ancient Israel." *Journal of Biblical Literature* 98 (1979) 161–85.

# Bibliography

Bruce, F. F. *Zeitgeschiehte des Neuen Testaments: Von Babylon bis Golgotha*. Wuppertal: Brockhaus, 1975.

Bultmann, Rudolf. *The Theology of the New Testament*. 2 vols. Translated by Kendrick Grobel. New York: Scribner, 1951–55.

———. *Theologie des Neuen Testaments*. 3rd ed. Tübingen: Mohr/Siebeck, 1958.

———. *Die Geschichte der Synoptischen Tradition*. FRLANT 12/29. Göttingen: Vanden-hoeck & Ruprecht, 1958.

———. "Die Erfoschung der synoptischen Evangelien." In *Glauben und Verstehen*, Vol. 4. Tübingen: Mohr/Siebeck, 1965.

———. *Die Geschichte der Synoptischen Tradition*. Translated by Huh Hyuk. Seoul: Daehan Kidokgyoseohwe, 1970.

Byun, Woo-eyul et al. "Commercialized Women Reality of Shameful International Marriage." *Dong A Daily*, July 10, 2010. Online: happylog.naver.com/omcckr/post/123460939124/.

Carey, Greg. *Elusive Apocalypse: Reading Authority in the Revelation to John*. Studies in American Biblical Hermeneutics 15. Macon, GA: Mercer University Press, 1999.

———. *Ultimate Things: An Introduction to Jewish and Christian Apocalyptic Literature*. St. Louis: Chalice, 2005.

———. "Symptoms of Resistance in the Book of Revelation." In *The Reality of Apocalypse: Rhetoric and Politics in the Book of Revelation*, edited by David L. Barr, 169–80. Society of Biblical Literature Symposium Series 39. Atlanta: Society of Biblical Literature, 2006.

———. "The Book of Revelation as Counter-Imperial Script." In *In the Shadow of Empire: Reclaiming the Bible as a History of Faithful Resistance*, edited by Richard A. Horsley, 157–76. Louisville: Westminster John Knox, 2008.

Calder, Kent E. *Embattled Garrisons: Comparative Base Politics and American Globalism*. Princeton: Princeton University Press, 2007.

Celan, Paul. *Poems*. New York: Persea, 1980.

Certeau, Michel de. *Mystic Fable*. Vol. 1, *The Sixteenth and Seventeenth Centuries*. Translated by Michael B. Smith. Religion and Postmodernism. Chicago: University of Chicago Press, 1995.

Chisholm, Shirley. *Unbought and Unbossed*. New York: Avon Books, 1970.

———. "The Relationship between Religion and Today's Social Issues." In *Can I Get A Witness?: Prophetic Religious Voices of African American Women*, edited by Marcia Y. Riggs, 183–88. Maryknoll, NY: Orbis, 1997.

Cho, Hee-yeon, "The Development of Korean Democracy and the Civil Movement." In *Resistance, Solidarity and Politics of Memory 2*, edited by Jin-Kyun Kim, 141–74. Seoul: Cultural Science Press, 2003.

Cho, Uhn. "Re-membering the Korean War and Politics of Memory." *Society and History* 77 (Spring 2008) 191–229.

Cho, Grace. *Haunting the Korean Diaspora: Shame, Secrecy, and the Forgotten War*. Minneapolis: University of Minnesota Press, 2008.

Cho, Young-Rae. *Jeon Tae-Il's Biography*. Seoul: Dolbaegae, 1990.

Choi, Hee Ahn. *Korean Women and God: Experiencing God in a Multi-Religious Colonial Context*. Maryknoll, NY: Orbis, 2005.

Choi, Hyung-Muk. *Korean Christianity and the Way of Power*. Seoul: Minyechong, 2009.

*Bibliography*

———. "A Study on Economic Development and Democracy in Korea from Christian-Ethical Perspective." PhD diss., Hanshin University, 2011.

Choi, Mun-young. "To Make a Culture of Poverty: The Study of the Relationship between Poverty and Welfare in Slums." Master's thesis, Seoul National University, 2001.

Chung, Hyun Kyung. "'Han-pu-ri': Doing Theology from Korean Women's Perspective." In *Frontiers in Asian Christian Theology*, edited by R. S. Sugirtharajah, 52–62. Maryknoll, NY: Orbis, 1994.

Chung, Won-sup. "Identity Crisis in the Cyber Space." *Eastern Western Thought* 9 (Summer 2010) 207–30.

Comission on Theological Concerns of the Christian Conference of Asia. *Minjung Theology: People as the Subjects of History*. 2nd rev. ed. London: Zed Press, 1983.

Cone, James H. *God of the Oppressed*. San Francisco: Harper & Row, 1975.

Conzelmann, Hans. *Der erste Brief an die Korinther*. Meyers Kommentar 5. Göttingen: Vanderhoeck & Ruprecht, 1969.

Copeland, M. Shawn. *Enfleshing Freedom: Body, Race, and Being*. Innovations. Minneapolis: Fortress, 2010.

Dalman, Gustaf. *Arbeit und Sitte in Palästina*. 7 vols. in 8 bks. Gütersloh: Bertelsmann, 1928–1939.

Dibelius, Martin. *Die Formeschichte des Evangelisiums*. Tübingen: Mohr/Siebeck, 1919.

———. *Botschaft und Geschichte*. Tübingen: Mohr/Siebeck, 1953.

———. *Die Formgeschichte des Evangeliums*. Tübingen: Mohr/Siebeck, 1961.

Douglas, Kelly Delaine. "Womanist Theology: What Is Its Relationship to Black Theology?" In *Black Theology: A Documentary History*, edited by James H. Cone and Gayraud S. Wilmore, 2:290–99. 2 vols. Maryknoll, NY: Orbis, 1993.

Deichgräber, Reinhard. *Gotteshymnus und Christushymnus in der frühen Christenheit*. Studien zur Umwelt des Neuen Testament 5. Göttingen: Vandenhoek & Ruprecht, 1967.

Dodd, C. H. *According to the Scriptures*. London: Nisbet, 1952.

Du Bois, W. E. B. "The Talented Tenth." In *The Negro Problem: A Series of Articles by Representative American Negroes of To-Day*, edited by Booker T. Washington, 31–75. New York: Pott, 1903.

Duff, Paul B. *Who Rides the Beast?: Prophetic Rivalry and the Rhetoric of Crisis in the Churches of the Apocalypse*. Oxford: Oxford University Press, 2001.

Enloe, Cynthia. "It Takes Two." In *Let the Good Times Roll: Prostitution and the U.S. Military in Asia*, by Saundra Pollack Sturdevant and Breanda Stoltzfus, 22–29. New York: New Press, 1992.

Enns, Fernando. "Breaking the Cycle of Violence: Building Community—Mechanisms for Overcoming Violence and Some Suggestions for Theological Reflection" *Ecumenical Review* 53/2 (2001) 180–89.

———. *Ökumene und Frieden*. Theologische Anstösse 4. Neukirchen-Vluyn: Neukirch-ener 2012.

Epstein, Barbara. "Anti-Communism, Homophobia, and the Construction of Masculinity in the Postwar U.S." *Critical Sociology* 20 (1994) 21–44.

Eun-Jeong, Ji. "The Determinants of Working Poor's Poverty-Exit Possibility : Path Dependency of Working Poor Labor Market." *Korean Journal of Social Welfare* 59/3 (2007) 147–74.

# Bibliography

Falcke, Heino. *Wo bleibt die Freiheit? Christ sein in Zeiten der Wende.* Freiburg: Kreuz 2009.

Farmer, W. R. "Judas, Simon and Anthronges." *New Testament Studies* 4 (1957/58) 147–55.

Foakes-Jackson, F. J., and Kirsopp Lake, editors. *The Beginnings of Christianity.* Vol. 1, *Prolegomena I: The Jewish, Gentile and Christian Backgrounds.* London: Macmillan, 1920.

Foerster, Werner. "The History of the Inter-Testament Period." In *From the Exile to Christ: A Historical Introduction to Palestinian Judaism.* Translated by Gordon E. Harris. Philadelphia: Fortress, 1964.

Foreman, James, Jr. "Why Care about Mass Incarceration?" *Michigan Law Review* 108 (2010) 993–1010.

Friesen, Steven J. *Imperial Cults and the Apocalypse of John: Reading Revelation in the Ruins.* Oxford: Oxford University Press, 2001.

Gauck, Joachim. *Freiheit: Ein Plädoyer.* Munich: Kösel, 2012.

Geertz, Clifford. *The Interpretation of Cultures.* New York: Basic Books, 2008.

Genzo, Tagawa. *The Gospel of Mark and Liberation of the People—A Study on the Early Christianity.* Translated by Kim Myoung-Shik. Four Seasons Press, 1983.

Gerber, Christine. *Paulus und seine "Kinder": Studien zur Beziehungsmetaphorik der paulinischen Briefe.* Beihefte zur Zeitschrift für die neutestamentliche Wissenschaft und die Kunde der älteren Kirche 136. Berlin: de Gruyter 2005.

Giddens, Anthony. *Modernity and Self-Identity: Self and Society in the Late Modern Age.* Stanford: Stanford University Press, 1991. Korean Translation, Seoul: Saemulgyul, 1997.

Giddings, Paula. *When and Where I Enter: The Impact of Black Women on Race and Sex in America.* New York: Morrow, 1984.

Gnilka, Joachim. *Das Evangelium nach Markus.* 2 vols. Evangelisch-Katholischer Kommentar zum Neuen Testament 2. Zürich: Benziger, 1978–1979.

Goppelt, Leonhard. *Christentum und Judentum im ersten und zweiten Jahrhundert.* Beiträge zur Förderung christlicher Theologie 2/55. Gütersloh: Bertelsmann, 1954.

Gottwald, Norman K. *The Tribes of Yahweh: A Sociology of the Religion of Liberated Israel, 1250–1050 BCE.* Maryknoll, NY: Orbis, 1979.

Grant, Jacquelyn. "Black Theology and the Black Woman." In *Black Theology: A Documentary History, 1966–1979,* edited by Gayraud Wilmore and James H. Cone, 2: 418–33. Maryknoll, NY: Orbis, 1979.

———. *White Women's Christ and Black Women's Jesus.* American Academy of Religion Academy Series 64. Atlanta: Scholars, 1989.

———. "Civil Rights Women: A Source for Doing Womanist Theology." In *Women in the Civil Rights Movement: Trailblazers and Torchbearers, 1941–1965,* edited by Vicki L. Crawford et al., 39–50. Blacks in the Diaspora. Bloomington: Indiana University Press, 1993.

Haenchen, Ernst. *Der Weg Jesu: Eine Erklärung des Markus-Evangeliums und der kanonischen Parallelen.* Sammlung Töpelmann 2/6. Berlin: Töpelmann, 1966.

———. *Die Apostelgeschichte.* Kritisch-exegetischer Kommentar über das Neue Testament 3. Göttingen: Vandenhoeck & Ruprecht, 1957.

Hardt, Michael, and Antonio Negri. *Empire.* Cambridge: Harvard University Press, 2000.

# Bibliography

Hengel, Martin. *Judentum und Hellenismus*. Wissenschaftliche Untersuchungen zum Neuen Testament 10. Tübingen: Mohr/Siebeck, 1969.

Heidegger, Martin. *Being and Time*. Translated by John Macquarrie and Edward Robinson. New York: Harper & Row, 1962.

Herman, Didi. *The Antigay Agenda: Orthodox Vision and the Christian Right*. Chicago: University of Chicago Press, 1988.

Herz, J. "Großgrundbesitz in Palaestina im Zeitalter Jesu." *Palastina Jaahrbuch* 24 (1928) 98-113.

Hoffman, Paul. *Studien zur Theologie der Logienquelle*. Neutestamentliche Abhandlungen 8. Münster, Aschendorff, 1972.

Hoffmann-Richter, Andreas. *Ahn Byung-mu als Minjung-Theologe*. Missionswissenschaftliche Forschungen 24. Gütersloh: Mohn, 1990.

Hwang, Yong-Yeon. "Typology of Theology and Theological Typology: What Is the Possibility of Theological Thought in Korean Society?" *Christian Thought* 585 (September 2007).

———. "Manic-Depressive Disorder: The Location in Which Establishing Fan-Club of 'Daehanminkuk' Becomes Im/Possible." In *Contemporariness and Minjung theology*, edited by Jin-Ho Kim. The Christian Institute for the 3rd Era, vol. 11. Seoul: DongYeon, 2009.

Hyun, Young-hak. "Attempt to Interpret Korean Masque-Theological Interpretation." *Eehwa Nonchong*, 1979.

———. "Minjung as the Servant of Suffering and His Hope." *Theological Thought* 51 (1985) 863–74.

International Ecumenical Peace Convocation. "Living Letters: Ecumenical Team Visits." Online: http://www.overcomingviolence.org/en/peace-convocation/preparatory-process/living-letters-visits.html/.

———. "Past Expert Consultations and Events in Relation to the IEPC." Online: http://www.overcomingviolence.org/en/peace-convocation/preparatory-process/expert-consultations/past-events.html/.

Im, Ji Hyun. "A Critical Study on the Understanding of 'Minjok' among Korean History Scholars." *Critical Review of History* 28 (Summer 1994) 114–37.

———. *Nationalism Is Treason*. Seoul: Sanamoobook, 1999.

International Gay & Lesbian Human Rights Commission, "South Korea: Solidarity Messages Requested in wake of Suicide of Gay Youth Activist." Online: http://www.iglhrc.org/content/south-korea-solidarity-messages-requested-wake-suicide-gay-youth-activist/.

Jeong, Tae-seok, "Reading about the Symptom of Social Structural Change in the Candlelight Protests against U.S. Beef Import." *Economy and Society* 81 (2009) 251–72.

Jeremias, Joachim. *Jerusalem zur Zeit Jesu*. Göttingen: Vandenhoeck & Ruprecht, 1962.

———. *The Eucharistic Words of Jesus*. London: SCM, 1964.

Jervell, Jacob. *Imago Dei*. Forschungen zur Religion und Literatur des Alten und Neuen Testaments 76. Goettingen: Vandenhoeck & Ruprecht, 1960.

Jun, Kyungsuk. "Empirical Examination and Research on the Labor Condition of the 'Drop-Out Teens.'" *The Korea Journal of Youth Counseling* 14/1 (2006) 3–21.

Jung, E-hwan. "A Comparison of the Characteristics of Non-Standard Workers in Korea and Japan." *Korean Journal of Sociology* 36/1 (2002).

Kang, Su-dol. *Quality of Life and the Relations between Labor and Capital*. Seoul: Hanul Publishing Group, 2001.

Kim, Jae-youp, and Lee Suh-won. "The Type of Communication between Husband and Wife and Family Violence." Korean Academy of Social Welfare Symposium, Fall 2001.

Kim, Jae-yop et al. "Impact of Work-Family Conflict and Stress on Husband-to-Wife Violence: Focus on Male Violence Offenders." *Journal of Korean Home Management Association* 26.1 (2008).

Kim, Jean K. "Hybrids but Fatherless." In *Ewha Journal of Feminist Theology: Doing Theology from Korean* 3 (2005) 30–60.

Kim, Jin-Ho. "The Discourses of 'Sin' and the Power of the Gaze of the Church." In *A Smile of Counter-Theology*, edited by Jin-ho Kim, 250–60. Seoul: Samin, 2001.

———. "The Faith as 'the Desire for Unfamiliarity.'" In *A Smile of Counter-Theology*, edited by Jin-Ho Kim, 39–57. Seoul: Samin, 2001.

———. "Preface: For Monument of Fugitive People." In *Monument of Fugitive People: The Myth of Main Stream in the Fruit of Korean Society*. edited by Jin-ho Kim, 4–9. N.p.: Itreebook. 2003.

———. "Understanding 'Han' from the Perspective of Philosophy of Hope." *Philosophy* 78 (2004) 319–45.

———. "Discourse of Incompetence and Delinquent Borrower—Civil Desire and Obsolescence of Evil." *Advocacy for a Democratic Society* 59 (July-August 2004).

———. "Substitution of Suffering, Concerning Grounds of the Brutality." In *In the Middle of Suffering in the Age of Anxiety*. Seoul: Thinking Tree, 2005.

———. "Until Someone Called Them by Name, They Were Not 'Flowers!'" In *Re-Reading Ahn Byung-Mu's Theory of Ochlos*. Seoul: Saminbooks, 2006.

———. "Two Kinds of Gospel—Jesus behind Whom Minjung Is Concealed and Jesus Transmitted by Minjung." In *In An Era of Minjung's Death, We Re-view Ahn Byung-Mu*, edited by Jin-Ho Kim, 133–46. Seoul: Samin, 2006.

———, editor. *In an Era of Minjung's Death, We re-view Ahn Byung-Mu*. Seoul: Seoul: Samin, 2006.

———. "The Death of Minjung and Re-reading Ahn Byung-Mu." In *In An Era of Minjung's Death, We Re-view Ahn Byung-Mu*, edited by Jin-Ho Kim. Seoul: Samin, 2006.

———. "Theological Phenomenology on Suffering and Violence." In *Memorial Society for Ahn Byung-Mu: The Vein of Ahn Byung-Mu's Theological Thought* vol. 2. Seoul: Korean Theological Study Institute, 2006.

———. "The Theological Phenomenology of Pain and Violence: About the Contemporariness of Minjung Theology." In *The Pulse of Ahn Byung-Mu's Theological Thought*. edited by Son Ku-Tae, 229–65. Seoul: Korea Theological Study Institute, 2006.

———. "Cyber Terror of Anti-Christianity versus Aggressive Overseas Christian Mission." In *Rude Christianity, Examining Problems and Alternatives to Korean Christianity's Mission Work*. Seoul: Sanchaeja, 2007.

———. "Glorified Christianity and Korean Conservatism." In *Contemporary Criticism*. Seoul: Woongjin Think Big, 2007.

———. "The Age When War Is Like a Game: Others' Sufferings Which Are Consumed." In *Essays in Celebration of HanByul Prof. Im Tae Soo After Teaching*, edited by Jin-Ho Kim, 603–20. Seoul: Handeul, 2007.

## Bibliography

———. "The Citizen Is Self-Divided between Aspiration for Democracy and for Capitalism." Online: http://www.hani.co.kr/arti/society/society_general/416128.html/.

———. *Radical Liberalists: Unfamiliar Travels with Four Gospels.* Seoul: Dongyeon Books, 2009.

———. *A Subversive Reading the Bible: Seeing by People.* Seoul: Samin, 2010.

Kim, Jong-ju, "Psychoanalysis of *Han.*" *Korean Imago* 2. July 1998.

Kim, Jun. "Lost Labor Community? The Formation and Dismantling of Shipbuilding Workers Community at the East District of Ulsan." *Economy and Society* 68 (2005).

Kim, Kyun-jin. *Resistance, Solidarity, and Politics of Memory* 2. Seoul: Cultural Science Press, 2003.

Kim, Myung-Su. *Ahn Byung-Mu: The Witness of the Era and Minjung.* The Series of Modern Theologians 11. Seoul: Sallim, 2006.

Kim, Sebastian C. H. "The Problem of Poverty in Post-War Korean Christianity: Kibock Sinang or Minjung Theology?" *Transformation* 24/1 (2007) 43–50.

Kim, Soon-young. "Betrayal of Democratization: The Structure and Characteristic of the Problem of Credit Defaulters." *Asian Studies Review* 48/4 (2005).

Kim, Sung Gun. "Korean Protestant Christianity in the Midst of Globalization: Neoliberalism and the Pentecostalization of Korean Churches." *International Review of Mission* 100/101 (2011).

Kim, Wang-Bae. "Workaholism: A Psycho-Social Approach Focusing on Work Attitude and Organizational Structure." *Korean Journal of Sociology* 41/2 (2007).

Kim, Won. "The Event of Gwangju Complex in 1971." *Komun.Net.* September 2008. 48–53.

Kim, Yong-bok. "Social Biography of Minjung and Theology." *Theological Thought* 24 (1979) 58–77.

King, Martin Luther, Jr. *Why We Can't Wait.* New York: New American Library, 1964.

Kingdon, H. P. "Who Were the Zealots and Their Leaders in AD 66?" *New Testament Studies* 17 (1970/71) 68–72.

Klausner, Joseph. *Jesus of Nazareth: His Life, Times and Teaching.* Translated by Herbert Danby. New York: Macmillan, 1953.

Klostermann, Erich. *Das Markusevangelium.* Handbuch zum Neuen Testament 3. Tübingen: Mohr/Siebeck, 1950.

Koester, Craig. *Revelation and the End of All Things.* Grand Rapids: Eerdmans, 2001.

Kreissig, Heinz. *Die sozialen Zusammenhänge des Judäischen Krieges.* Schriften zur Geschichte und Kultur der Antike 1. Berlin: Akademie, 1970.

Kümmel, W. G. *Einleitung in das Neue Testament.* Heidelberg: Quelle & Meyer, 1963.

Kwok, Pui-Lan. *Discovering the Bible in the Non-biblical World.* Bible & Liberation Series. Maryknoll, NY: Orbis, 1995.

———. *Introducing Asian Feminist Theology.* Cleveland: Pilgrim, 2000.

Kwon, Insook. *The Republic of Korea Is the Military Troop: Peace, Militarism, and Masculinity from a Feminist Perspective.* Seoul: Ch'oeng Nyun Sa, 2003.

Kwon, Jinkwan. "Minjung (the Multitude), Historical Symbol of Jesus Christ." *Asian Journal of Theology* 24 (2010) 153–71.

Kwon, Yu-kyoung, and Yeo-ju Chung. "The Effects of Group Art Therapy on Acculturative Stress and Self-Esteem of Married Migrant Women." *Journal of Rehabilitation Psychology* 16/2 (2009) 173–91.

# Bibliography

Küster, Volker. *The Many Faces of Jesus Christ: Intercultural Cristology*. Maryknoll, NY: Orbis, 2001.

———. *A Protestant Theology of Passion: Korean Minjung Theology Revisited*. Studies in Systematic Theology 4. Leiden: Brill 2010.

Lee, Chang-gon. *Chase Iniquity of Health in Korea*. Seoul: Mimbooks, 2007.

Lee, Diana S., and Grace Yoonkyung Lee, producers and directors. *Camp Arirang*. San Francisco: National Asian American Telecommunications Association, 1996. VHS videotape.

Lee, Jang-young et al. "A Study of Influential Factors on Friendship Forming Behaviors through Individual Webpages." *The Journal of Information and Society* 9 (2006) 1–33.

Lee, Jong-bo. *Research on Rule over Nation by Capital Under Democracy: Focus on Samsung*. Seoul: Hanul, 2010.

Lee, Jung-Hui. *Looking at The Teacher Again in the Age of Dead Minjung*. Seoul: Samin, 2006.

Lee, Jung Young. "Minjung Theology: A Critical Introduction." In *An Emerging Theology in World Perspective Commentary on Korean Minjung Theology*, 3–34. Mystic, CT: Twenty-Third Publications, 1988.

Lee, Sang-Hee. "The Ecology of the Rumor." In *On Rumor*, edited by Won Woo-Hyeun, 215–33. Seoul: n.p., 1982.

Lee, Sun-young. "Emigrant Filipinas in Rome, LA, and Suhul—A Book Review. Servants of Globalization by Parrenas." *Theoria: A Journal of Feminist Theories and Practices* 20 (2009) 251–61.

Lee, Yeong Mee. "A Political Reception of the Bible: Korean Minjung Theological Interpretation of the Bible." Online: http://sbl-site.org/Article.aspx?ArticleID=457/.

Lohmeyer, Ernst. *Soziale fragen im urchristentum*. Wissenschaft und Bildung 172. Leipzig: Quelle & Meyer, 1921.

———. *Das Urchristentum*. Göttingen : Vandenhoeck & Ruprecht, 1932.

———. *Galiläa und Jerusalem*. FRLANT 52. Göttingen: Vandenhoeck & Ruprecht, 1936.

———. *Kyrios Jesus: eine Untersuchung zur Phil. 2:5–11*. 1928. Darmstadt: Wissenschaftliche Buchgesellschaft, 1961.

Maass, Fritz. "Jerusalem." In *Religion in Geschichte und Gegenwart*. Vol. 3. Tübingen: Mohr/Siebeck, 1959.

Maguire, Daniel. *A Moral Creed for All Christians*. Minneapolis: Fortress, 2006.

Mangina, Joseph. *Revelation*. Brazos Theological Commenary on the Bible. Grand Rapids: Brazos, 2010.

Mantyla, Kyle. "Why the Religious Right Opposes Government Assistance for the Poor." Blog. *Right Wing Wach*. Posted September 19, 2011. Online: http://www.rightwingwatch.org/content/why-religious-right-opposes-government-assistance-poor/.

Marshall, John. *Parables of War: Reading John's Jewish Apocalypse*. Studies in Christianity and Judaism 10. Waterloo, Ontario: Wilfrid Laurier University Press, 2001.

Marxsen, Willi. *Mark the Evangelist: Studies on the Redaction History of the Gospel*. Translated by James Boyce et al. Nashville: Abingdon, 1969.

———. "Die urchristlichen Kerygmata und das Ereignis Jesus von Nazareth." *Zeitschrift für Theologie und Kirche* 73 (1976) 42–64.

# Bibliography

———. *Einleitung in das Neue Testaments: Eine Einführung in ihre Probleme.* 4th ed. Gütersloh: Mohn, 1978.
McBrien, Richard et al., editors. *The HarperCollins Encyclopedia of Catholicism.* San Francisco: HarperSanFrancisco, 1995.
Mendenhall, George. "The Hebrew Conquest of Palestine." *Biblical Archaeologist* 25/3 (1962) 66–87.
Meyer, Eduard. *Ursprung und Anfänge des Mormonen: mit Exkursen über die Anfänge des Islâms und des Christentums.* Vol. 2. 3 vols. Halle: Niemeyer, 1912.
Moltmann, Jürgen, editor. *Minjung: Theologie des Volkes Gottes in Südkorea.* Neukirchen-Vluyn: Neukirchener 1984.
———. "Politische Theologie in ökumenischen Kontexten." In *Politische Theologie: Neuere Geschichte und Potenziale,* edited by Francis Schüssler Fiorenza et al., 1–12. Theologische Anstösse 1. Neukirchen-Vluyn: Neukirchener 2011.
Montefiole, C. G. *The Synoptic Gospels.* Vol. 1. London: Macmillan, 1927.
Moon, Cyris H. S. "A Korean Minjung Perspective: The Hebrews and the Exodus." In *Voices from the Margin: Interpreting the Bible in the Third World,* edited by R. S. Sugirtharajah, 228–43. Maryknoll, NY: Orbis, 1995.
Moon, Katherine H. S. *Sex among Allies: Military Prostitution in U.S.-Korea Relations.* New York: Columbia University Press, 1997.
Mühlmann, W. E. *Chiliasmus und Nativismus.* Studien zur Soziologie der Revolution 1. Berlin: Reimer, 1961.
Niles, D. Preman, compiler. *Between the Flood and the Rainbow: Interpreting the Conciliar Process of Mutual Commitment (Covenant) to Justice, Peace, and the Integrity of Creation.* Geneva: WCC Publications, 1992.
Noth, M. "Heiligen des Höchsten." In *Gesammelte Studien des Alten Testament,* 1:274–90. 2 vols. Munich: Kaiser, 1957–1969.
Obama, Barack. *The Audacity of Hope.* New York: Three Rivers, 2006.
Otfried, Hofius. *Der Christushymnus Philipper 2:6–11.* Wissenschaftliche Untersuchungen zum Neuen Testament 17. Tübingen: Mohr/Siebeck, 1976.
Otto, W. F. *Herodes: Beiträge zur Geschichte des letzten jüdischen Königshauses.* Stuttgart: Metzler, 1913.
Paik, Wook-inn. "The Formation of the Consumption Society and the Information Society in Korea." *Economy and Society* 77 (Spring 2008) 199–225.
Park, Andrew Sung. *The Wounded Heart of God.* Nashville: Abingdon, 1993.
Park, Byung-hyun and Sun-mi Choi. "The Concept of Social Exclusion and Underclass and Their Implication for the Poverty Policy in Korea." *The Korean Journal of Social Welfare* 45 (2001) 185219.
Park, Myung-lim. "From Democratization to Humanization." In *A Source Book on 'Yeohae' Peace Forum (21. October 2010)* 10–31.
Phillips, Layli. "Introduction—Womanism: On Its Own." In *The Womanist Reader,* edited by Layli Phillips, xix–lv. New York: Routledge, 2006.
Pieris, Aloysius. *An Asian Theology of Liberation.* Edinburgh: T. & T. Clark, 1988.
Porteous, N. W. *Das Danielbuch.* Alte Testament Deutsch 23. Göttingen: Vandenhoeck & Ruprecht, 1962.
Rancière, Jacques, and Jin Tae Won, "Jacques Ranciere 'Labor Movement of Temporary Position is the Hope of the New Politic.'" *Hankyoreh,* February 12, 2008.
Reicke, Bo. *Neutestamentliche Zeitgeschichte.* Sammlung Töpelmann 2/2. Berlin: de Gruyter, 1968.

# Bibliography

Roberts, J. Deotis. "Black Theology and Minjung Theology: Exploring Common Themes." In *An Emerging Theology in World Perspective Commentary on Korean Minjung Theology*, edited by Jung Young Lee, 99–108. Mystic, CT: Twenty-Third Publications, 1988.

Rosnow, Ralph L. "Lives of a Rumor." *Psychology Today* (June 1979) 88–92. Translated by Won Woo-hyun, 1979.

Rowley, H. H. *The Relevance of Apocalyptic*. London: Lutterworth, 1944.

Ruiz, Jean-Pierre. "Taking a Stand on the Sand of the Seashore: A Postcolonial Exploration of Revelation 13." In *Reading the Book of Revelation: A Resource for Students*, edited by David L. Barr. Society of Biblical Literature: Resources for Biblical Study 44. Atlanta: Society of Biblical Literature, 2003.

Ryu, Dae Young. "Understanding Early American Missionaries in Korea (1884–1910): Capitalist Middle-Class Values and the Weber Thesis." *Archives de sciences socials des religions* 46/113 (January 2001) 93–117.

Said, Edward. *Culture and Imperialism*. New York: Knopf, 1994.

Schaberg, Jane. *The Resurrection of Mary Magdalene: Legends, Apocrypha, and the Christian Testament*. New York: Continuum, 2002.

Schmidt, Karl Ludwig. *Der Rahmen der Geschichte Jesu: literarkritische Untersuchungen zur ältesten Jesusüberlieferung*. Darmstadt: Wissenschaftliche Buchgesellschaft, 1969.

Schmithals, Walter. *Jesus Christus in der Verkündigung der Kirche: Aktuelle Beiträge zum notwendigen Streit um Jesus*. Neukirchen-Vluyn: Neukirchener, 1972.

Schürer, Emil. *Geschichte des jüdischen Volkes im Zeitalter Jesu Christi*. Vol. 1. Leipzig: Hinrichs, 1901.

Schweizer, Dorothea. "Das Koreanische Theologische Forschungsinstitut und Prof. Dr. Ahn Byung-Mu." Online: http://www.doam.org/index.php/archiv/personen/772---archiv--person-person-ahn-byungmu/.

Schweizer, Eduard. *Erniedrigung und Erhöhung bei Jesus und seinen Nachfolgern*. Abhandlungen zur Theologie des Alten und Neuen Testaments 28. Zürich: Zwingli, 1955.

Scott, James C. *Domination and the Arts of Resistance: Hidden Transcripts*. New Haven: Yale University Press, 1990.

Shin, Myong-ho. "How and Why Is Korean Society Being Polarized? Its Relation to Globalization and Povertization." *Asian Studies Review* 49/1 (2006) 7–34.

Smith, Mitzi J. "The Problem of the Color Line and the Poverty Line." *Womanist Biblical Scholar Reflections*. Blog. Posted on February 4, 2011. Online: http://www.womanistntprof.blogspot.com/2011/02/problem-of-color-line-and-poverty-line.html

Song, C. S. *Jesus, the Crucified People*. Minneapolis: Fortress, 1996.

Song, Ho-keun. "Structural Change of Organizational System and Hiring System." *Economy and Society* 56. Winter 2002.

St. Clair, Raquel A. *Call and Consequences: A Womanist Reading of Mark*. Minneapolis: Fortress, 2008.

Stauffer, Ethelbert. *Jerusalem und Rom im Zeitalter Jesu Christi*. Dalp-Taschenbucher 331. Bern: Francke, 1957.

———. *Die Botschaft Jesu, damals und heute*. Dalp-Taschenbücher 333. Bern: Francke, 1959.

# Bibliography

Subklew-Jeutner, Marianne. *Der Pankower Friedenskreis: eine Ost-Berliner Gruppe innerhlab der Evangelischen Kirchen in der DDR 1981-1989*. Osnabrück: Der Andere, 2004.

Sugirtharajah, R. S. *The Bible and the Third World: Precolonial, Colonial and Postcolonial*. Cambridge: Cambridge University Press, 2001.

———. *Postcolonial Criticism and Biblical Interpretation*. Oxford: Oxford University Press, 2002.

Suh, Nam Dong. "The Theology of Minjung." *Theological Thought* 24 (Spring 1979) 78-109.

———. "The Task of Minjung Theology as Korean Theology." *Theological Thought* 24 (1979).

———. "Priest of Han." In *Research of Minjung Theology*, 37-44. Seoul: Hangil, 1983.

———. "Embodiment of Han and Its Theological Introspection." In *Research of Minjung Theology*, 83-110. Seoul: Hangil, 1983.

———. "The Hidden Story of Sounds." In *Research of Minjung Theology*, 111-19. Seoul: Hangil, 1983.

———. "The Biblical Authority of Minjung Theology." In *Research of Minjung Theology*. Seoul: Hangil, 1983.

———. *Exploring Minjung Theology*. Seoul: Hangil, 1983.

Suhl, A. *Die Funkition der altestamentliche Zitate and Anspielungen im MK*. Evangelium, 1905. Gutersloh: Mohn, 1965.

Suk, Won Jung, "Guest Workers, They are not 'Latent Criminal Group'—Watch Out 'Xenophobia.'" *Pressian*, February 22, 2008.

Sunlit Center. *Elderly Kijich'on Women's Story-Telling*. Pyongtaek, Gyeong-ghi-do, Korea: Sunlit Center, 2007.

———. *The Story of Yun Sun-Hwa*. Recorded and edited by Sunlit Center. Pyong-Taek, Gyeong-ghi-do: Sunlit Center, n.d.

Tagawa, Kenzo. *Genshi Kirisutokyō shi no ichidanmen: fukuinsho bungaku no seiritsu*. Tokyo : Keiso Shobo, 1968.

Taylor, Vincent. *The Gospel according to St. Mark*. London: Macmillan, 1952.

Terrell, JoAnne. *Power in the Blood?: The Cross in the African American Experience*. Eugene, OR: Wipf & Stock, 2005.

Theissen, Gerd. "Wanderradikalismus: Literatur-soziologische Aspekte der Ueberlieferung von Worten Jesu im Urchristentum." *Zeitschrift für Theologie und Kirche* 70/3 (1973) 245-71.

———. "Die Straken und Schwachen in Korinth: Soziologische Analyse eines theolgogischen Streites." *Evangelische Theologie* (1975/2) 155-72.

———. "Synoptische Wundergeschichten im Lichte unseres Sprachverständnisses." Hermeneutische und didaktische Überlegungen." *Wissenschaft und Praxis in Kirche und Gesellschaft* 65 (1976) 289-308.

———. *Studien zur Soziologie des Urchristentums*. 2nd ed. Wissenschaftliche Untersuch-ungen zum Neuen Testament 19. Tübingen: Mohr/Siebeck, 1983.

———. "The Story of the Syrophoenician Woman and the Border Region between Tyre and Galilee." *Theological Thought* 51 (Winter 1985) 815-47.

Thurman, Howard. *Jesus and the Disinherited*. Boston: Beacon, 1996.

Tödt, Heinz Eduard. *Der Menschensohn in der synoptischen Überlieferung*. Gütersloh: Mohn, 1959.

Ueunten, Wesley Iwao. "Rising Up from a Sea of Discontent: The 1970 Koza Uprising in U.S.-Occupied Okinawa." In *Militarized Currents: Toward a Decolonized Future in Asia and the Pacific*, edited by Setsu Shigematsu and Keith L. Camacho, 91–124. Minneapolis: University of Minnesota Press, 2010.

Uhm, Ki-Ho. *No One Should Care for Other People*. Seoul: Nazeunsan, 2009.

Walker, Alice. "Coming Apart." In *The Womanist Reader*, edited by Layli Phillips, 3–11. New York: Routledge, 2006.

———. *In Search of Our Mothers' Gardens: Womanist Prose*. San Diego: Harcourt Brace Jovanovich, 1983.

Washington, Booker T. "Atlanta Compromise Speech." September 18, 1895.

Wellhausen, J. *Israelitische und jüdische Geschichte*. Berlin: de Gruyter, 1921.

Wieczorek, Ulrike Link. *Reden von Gott in Afrika und Asien. Darstellung und Interpretation afrikanischer Theologie im Vergleich mit der koreanischen Minjung-Theologie*. Forschungen zur systematischen und ökumenischen Theologie 60. Göttingen 1991.

World Council of Churches. *An Ecumenical Call to Just Peace*. Geneva: WCC Publications, 2011. Online: http://www.overcomingviolence.org/fileadmin/dov/files/iepc/resources/ECJustPeace_English.pdf/

———. *Just Peace Companion*. 2nd ed. Geneva: WCC Publications, 2012.

Yi, Yim-Hwa. *Korean War and Gender: Women Stand Up over the War*. Seoul: Seo-hae Mun-jip, 2004.

Yim, Taesoo. *Minjung Theology towards a Second Reformation*. Seoul: Christian Conference of Asia, 2006.

Yoo, Myeong-Gi. "Immigrant Workers: Our Future Still Uncompleted." In *For the Monument of Deserters*, edited by No-Ja Park et al. Seoul: Tree of Thought, 2003.

Yu, Seung-tae and Kyung Dong-hyun. "Subjectification Program of Christianity in Globalized Age and Experience of Community of Youth." *2010 Colloquium: Peace and Publicity—Floating Subjectivity of Youth in Globalized Age and Seeking Publicity*. Oct. 18, 2010.

Yuh, Ji-Yeon. *Beyond the Shadow of Camptown: Korean Military Brides in America*. New York University Press, 2002.

Ziegler, Ignaz. *Die Königsgleichnisse des Midrasch: beleuchtet durch die römische Kaiserzeit*. Breslau: Schottlaender, 1903.

Zimmerli, W. *Grundriss der alttestamentlichen Theologie*. Translated by Kim Jungjoon. Stuttgart: Kohlhammer, 1972.

www.ingramcontent.com/pod-product-compliance
Lightning Source LLC
Chambersburg PA
CBHW050850230426
43667CB00012B/2224